Mathew Carey,   Lang and Ustick

The Spirit of Despotism

Mathew Carey,   Lang and Ustick

The Spirit of Despotism

ISBN/EAN: 9783743365490

Manufactured in Europe, USA, Canada, Australia, Japa

Cover: Foto ©Suzi / pixelio.de

Manufactured and distributed by brebook publishing software (www.brebook.com)

Mathew Carey, Lang and Ustick

The Spirit of Despotism

THE

SPIRIT

OF

POTISM.

MITATUR LUXUS, et LUXUS exit in TYRANNI-
DEM ⸺ attended with Luxury, and Luxury ends in Def-
potif ⸺
ERASMUS.

Ex regum immoderatâ libidine *unjufta* bella temerè plerumquè
fufcipiuntur, fceleratè geruntur, turpitèr deponuntur.——*In confequence of the Spirit of Defpotifm among Kings and Grandees, unjuft wars
are, for the moft part, rafhly undertaken, wickedly conducted, and, after
all, abandoned with defeat and difgrace.* BUCHANAN.

LONDON: PRINTED IN THE YEAR 1795.

PHILADELPHIA:

RE-PRINTED BY LANG AND USTICK, FOR SELVES
AND MATHEW CAREY.

NOV. 28, MDCCXCV.

PREFACE.

THE *heart is deceitful above all things; who can know it?* As far as I know my own, it feels an anxious defire to ferve my fellow-creatures, during the fhort period of my continuance among them, by ftopping the effufion of human blood, by diminifhing or foftening the miferies which man creates for himfelf, by promoting peace and by endeavoring to fecure and extend civil liberty.

I attribute war, and moft of the artificial evils of life, to the *Spirit of Defpotifm*, a rank poifonous weed, which grows and flourifhes even in the foil of liberty, when over-run with corruption. I have attempted to eradicate it, that the falutary and pleafant plants may have room to ftrike root and expand their foliage.

There is one circumftance which induces me to think that, in this inftance, my heart does not deceive me. I am certain, that in attempting to promote the general happinefs of man, without ferving any party, or paying court to any individual, I am not ftudying my own intereft. On the contrary, I am well aware that my very fubject muft give offence to thofe who are poffeffed of power and patronage. I have no perfonal enmities, and therefore am truly concerned that I could not treat the

Spirit of Defpotifm, without advancing
ons that muſt ·difpleaſe the *nominal*
certainly facrifice all view of perſonal a
to what appears to me the public go
flatter ·myſelf that this alone evinces th
of my motive.

Men of feeling and good minds, whoſe
hearts, as the phraſe is, lie in the right place,
will, I think, agree with me in moſt points;
eſpecially when a little time, and the events,
now taking place, ſhall have diffipated the miſt
of paffion and prejudice. Hard-hearted, proud
worldlings, who love themſelves only, and know
no good but money and pageantry, will ſcarcely
agree with me in any. They will be angry;
but, confiftently with their general haughtineſs,
affect contempt to hide their choler.

I pretend not to aſpire at the honor of mar-
tyrdom: yet ſome inconveniences I am ready
to bear patiently, in promoting a cauſe which
deeply concerns the whole of the preſent race,
and ages yet unborn. I am ready to bear patiently the proud man's contumely, the inſult of
rude ignorance, the ſarcaſm of malice, the
hired cenſure of the ſycophantic critic, (whoſe
preferment depends on the proſtitution both
of knowledge and conſcience,) and the virulence of the venal newſpaper. It would be a
diſgrace to an honeſt man not to incur the abuſe
of thoſe who have ſold their integrity and abilities to the enemies of their country and the
human race. *Strike, but hear*, ſaid a noble
ancient. Truth will ultimately prevail, even

though he who uttered it fhould be deftroyed.
Columbus was defpifed, rejeƈed, perfecuted;
but America was difcovered. Men very inconfiderable in the eye of pride, have had the
honor to difcover, divulge, and diffeminate
doƈtrines that have promoted the liberty and
happinefs of the human race. All that was
rich and *great*, in the common acceptation of
that epithet, combined againft Luther; yet
when pontiffs, kings, and lords had difplayed
an impotent rage, and funk into that oblivion
which their perfonal infignificance naturally led
to, Luther prevailed, and his glory is immor-
tal. He broke the chain of fuperftition, and
weakened the bonds of defpotifm.

I have frequently, and from the firft commencement of our prefent unfortunate and difgraceful hoftilities, lifted up my voice—a feeble one indeed—againft war, that great pro-
moter of defpotifm; and while I have liberty
to write, I will write for liberty. I plead
weakly, indeed, but fincerely, the caufe of
mankind; and on them, under GOD, I rely
for proteƈtion againft that mercilefs SPIRIT
which I attempt to explode.

CONTENTS.

Sect.

Spirit of Despotism.

SECTION I.

INTRODUCTORY.

MAN, in a ftate of fimplicity, uncorrupted by the influence of bad education, bad examples, and bad government, poffeffes a tafte for all that is good and beautiful. He is capable of a degree of moral and intellectual improvement, which advances his nature to a participation with the divine. The world, in all its magnificence, appears to him one vaft theatre, richly adorned and illuminated, into which he is freely admitted, to enjoy the glorious fpectacle. Acknowledging no *natural* fuperior but the great architect of the whole fabric, he partakes the delight with confcious dignity, and glows with gratitude. Pleafed with himfelf and all around him, his heart dilates with benevolence, as well as piety; and he finds his joys augmented by communication. His countenance cheerful, his mien erect, he rejoices in exiftence. Life is a con-

B

tinual feaſt to him, highly ſeaſoned by virtue, by liberty, by mutual affection. God formed him to be happy, and he becomes ſo, thus fortunately unmoleſted by falſe policy and oppreſſion. Religion, reaſon, nature, are his guides through the whole of his exiſtence, and the whole is happy. VIRTUOUS INDEPENDENCE, the ſun, which irradiates the morning of his day, and warms its noon, tinges the ſerene evening with every beautiful variety of color, and, on the pillow of religious hope, he ſinks to repoſe in the boſom of Providence.

But where is man to be found, thus noble, thus innocent, thus happy? Not, indeed, in ſo many parts of the terraqueous globe as he ought to be ; but ſtill he is to be found wherever the rights of nature and the virtues of ſimplicity are not violated or baniſhed by the falſe refinements, the baſe artifices of corrupted government.

Unhappily for man, ſociety has been almoſt univerſally corrupted, even by the arts intended for its improvement ; and human nature is gradually depraved in its very progreſs to civilization. Metamorphoſed by the tampering of unſkilful or diſhoneſt politicians, and the craft of intereſted prieſts, co-operating with politicians, MAN at preſent appears, in many countries, a diminutive and diſtorted animal, compared with what he was in his primæval ſtate. He is become the dwarf and the cripple of courts and cities inſtead of the well-formed, beautiful, creature, who once bounded, in the glory of health and ſtrength, over the foreſt and the mountain, glowing with the warmth of virtue, and breathing the ſpirit of independence.

Various are the cauſes which contribute to the factitious depravity of man. Defective and erroneous education corrupts him ; the prevalent examples of a degenerate community corrupt him ; but bad *government* corrupts him more than all other cauſes combined. The grand adverſary of human virtue and happineſs is DESPOTISM. Look over the ſurface of the whole earth, and behold man, the glory and deputed lord of the creation, withering under the influence of deſpotiſm, like the plant of temperate climes ſcorched by the ſun of a torrid zone. The leaf is ſickly, the bloſſom dares not expand its beauty, and no fruit arrives at its juſt ſize and maturity.

Turkey, Italy, Ægypt ! how changed from what ye were when inhabited by antient Greeks, Romans, Ægyptians ! Nature, indeed, ſtill ſmiles upon them with unaltered favor. The blue mantle of the ſkies is ſtill ſpread over them in all its luminous magnificence. There is no reaſon to ſuppoſe the earth leſs fertile. The corn laughs in the vallies. The tree aſpires to Heaven with all its original verdure and majeſty. But MAN decays ; withered, ſhrunk, enervated ; a form without ſpirit, an animal leſs happy than the beaſts of the field, and more ignoble, inaſmuch as degeneracy is

baſer than native, original, created inferiority.
Fallen with the columnar ruins of better times,
over which, in theſe countries, he often tram-
ples, MAN himſelf appears little better than a
ruin, diſplaying all the deformity of the mouldering pile, with ſcarcely any veſtige of its former magnificence. It would equally contradict
philoſophy and experience to attribute this
moral degeneracy to the decay of nature's
vigor. There is no reaſon to conclude that the
natural faculties of men who inhabit countries
once free, but now enſlaved, are produced in a
ſtate of leſs perfection at this hour, than in
the days of their illuſtrious forefathers. Anato-
my diſcovers no defect in the fibres of the
heart or the brain; yet the degeneracy remains unconteſted. In truth, *government* has
counteracted the beneficence of nature. The
MEN are fallen; while the *human figures*, with
their internal and external organization, continue ſimilar, or the ſame. They are inactive
and puſillanimous. They aſpire at no extraordinary excellence or achievements; but
crouch beneath their deſpot, glad of the poor
privilege allowed them by a fellow-creature,
as weak and more wicked than themſelves, to
eat, drink, ſleep and die. Any pre-eminent
degree of merit among them would render the
diſtinguiſhed poſſeſſor of it fatally illuſtrious,
the certain object of a tyrant's vengeance;
and they find their beſt ſecurity in their want of
virtue. By a voluntary ſubmiſſion to con-

tempt, they retain and tranfmit the privilege of breathing, and build the bulwark of their fafety on their perfonal infignificance.

FEAR muft, of neceffity, become the predominant paffion in all countries fubject to the uncontrolled dominion of an individual and his minifters : but fear chills the blood, and freezes the faculties. Under its icy influence there can arife no generous emulation, no daring fpirit of adventure. Enterprize is confidered as dangerous, not merely from the general cafuality of all human affairs, but becaufe it excites notice, and alarms the jealoufy of felfifh power. Under a defpotic government, to fteal through life unobferved, to creep, with timid caution, through the vale of obfcurity, is the firft wifdom ; and to be fuffered to die in old age, without the prifon, the chain, the dagger, or the poifoned bowl, the higheft pitch of human felicity.

IGNORANCE of the groffeft kind, ignorance of man's nature and rights, ignorance of all that tends to make and keep us happy, difgraces and renders wretched more than half the earth, at this moment, in confequence of its fubjugation to defpotic power. Ignorance, robed in imperial purple, with Pride and Cruelty by her fide, fways an iron fcepter over more than one hemifphere. In the fineft and largeft regions of this planet which we inhabit, are no liberal purfuits and profeffions, no contemplative delights, nothing of that pure, intellectual employment which raifes man from the mire of fenfuality and fordid care, to a degree of excellence and dignity, which we conceive to be angelic and celeftial. Without knowledge or the means of obtaining it, without exercife or excitements, the mind falls into a ftate of infantine imbecility and dotage; or acquires a low cunning, intent only on felfifh and mean purfuits, fuch as is vifible in the more ignoble of the irrational creatures, in foxes, apes, and monkies. Among nations fo corrupted, the utmoft effort of genius is a court intrigue or a minifterial cabal.

A degradation of the underftanding, like this, is ufually accompanied with depravity of heart. From an inability to find pleafure and honorable employment in the energies of thought, in noble and virtuous action, in refined converfation, in arts, in commerce in learning, arifes a mifchievous activity in trifles, a perverfion of nature, a wantonnefs of wickednefs, productive of flagitious habits, which render the partaker of reafon the moft defpicable and deteftable animal in the whole circle of exiftence. Thus funk under the preffure of defpotifm, who can recognize, notwithftanding the human fhape they bear, the lineal defcendants of Ægyptian, Grecian, Roman worthies, the glory of their times, the luminaries of their own country and the world, the inftructors and benefactors of human nature? Thus the image of the Deity, ftamped on man at his creation, is defiled or utterly effaced by government, inftituted and exercifed by man over his fellow-man; and his kindred to Heaven is known no more by the divine refemblance. A bad government is therefore the curfe of the earth, the fcourge of man, the grand obftacle to the divine will, the moft copious fource of all moral evil, and for that reafon, of all mifery; but of bad governments, none are comparable, in their mifchievous effects, to the defpotic.

But if defpotifm in its *extreme* produces confequences thus malignant, reafon will infer, and experience will juftify the inference, that all the *fubordinate degrees* of defpotifm are proportionally deftructive. However it may be difguifed by forms, it is ever feeking its own encreafe and aggrandizement, by openly crufhing, or fecretly undermining, the fabric of liberty : it is ever encroaching on the privileges and enjoyments of thofe who are fubjected to it; greedily, though foolifhly, wifhing to engrofs every good of every kind in this fublunary ftate, except the good of virtue.

Power, though *limited* by written laws, in the hands of mortal men, poorly educated, and furrounded by fycophants and flatterers, who wifh, by partaking the power, to partake alfo of its profits and diftinctions, and thus gratify at once their pride and avarice, is always endeavoring to extend itfelf *beyond the limitations ;* and requires to be watched with the moft jealous eye, by all who are fubject to it, and to be reftrained within its bounds,

by the manlieſt efforts, and the moſt determined reſolution of virtue. Every engine of
artifice and terror will be uſed to ſuppreſs ſuch
virtue : but the friend of man and of his
country will defy perſecution, fines, impri-
ſonment, and death, in attempting, by every
lawful and rational means, to puſh back the
gigantic ſtrides of encroaching deſpotiſm, more
deſtructive of happineſs than an earthquake or
a peſtilence. A country deſerves no love, when
it ceaſes to be a country of liberty. Human
beings conſtitute a country, not a ſoil in a
certain latitude ; and an attachment to liberty
is the trueſt loyalty.

It is therefore highly expedient, whenever a
people, free by law and conſtitution, appear
in the *ſmalleſt degree* to remit their attention
to the preſervation of freedom, to urge them,
by the moſt ſerious admonition, to an immediate reſumption of their vigilance. While
they ſlumber and ſleep, lulled by the Circèan
cup of corruption, the enemy is awake, and
buſily making his inſidious approaches to the
citadel. Every inch of ground, they care-
leſsly relinquiſh, is eagerly ſeized by the covetous poſſeſſor of dominion ; the love of
which, like the love of money, increaſes
by acceſſion. Nor are there ever wanting
numbers of artful men who ſtimulate a weak
or a wicked prince in his encroachments ; ſenſible as they are, that their own power and
privileges will be augmented with thoſe of the
prince, whoſe excluſive favor they have gained

by fycophantic arts and by co-operation in the fallacious fervice of enlarging his prerogative. The more the power of the prince is augmented, the greater will be the emoluments, the more brilliant the diftinctions of the courtier. A ftar fhines with higher luftre, a ribband difplays a brighter hue, a title foothes the ear with fweeter mufic, when conferred by a mighty potentate far exalted above vulgar control, and who holds his crown *in contempt of his people.* If kings can be once elevated to the rank of Heaven's vicegerents, how muft admiring plebeians idolize their choice favors and their prime favorites ? There is always, therefore, a fet of men (to whom pomp and vanity are the chief good) who are continually endeavoring to add glory and greatnefs to the orb from which they derive their own luftre. Moons and fatellites would fhine faintly indeed, unlefs the fun of the fyftem glittered with intolerable effulgence. If the fun were fhorn of its beams, their native opaquenefs would pafs without notice.

So many advantages do the profeffors of power enjoy for its extenfion, in all countries where courts have influence, that the people, however great their numbers, are fcarcely a match for its fubtle contrivances, its falfe alarms, its bribes, its fpies, its informers, its conftructive treafons, its military force, its fuperftitious terrors, invented and diffufed by a policy, which often laughs in fecret at the religion which it enforces with folemn hypocrify. A court has an opportunity of gratifying, in a thoufand different ways, both fecretly and openly, the moft prevalent and violent paffions of human nature. When the mafs of the people are artfully feduced to throw their weight into the fame fcale with the court, liberty in the other muft kick the beam. When the ariftocracy of rank and riches unite hand in hand, to feduce the people, the delufion may for a time be fuccefsful, and advantages may be taken, during the temporary delirium, to rifle the caftle of liberty, to weaken its foundations, to break down its battlements, or to lull its watchmen afleep with a powerful opiate.

It has indeed been faid in antient times, and often repeated, that if the *people will be deceived, let them be deceived;* but they have no choice, no chance to efcape deception, unlefs the truth be fairly and publicly exhibited to them, and their minds duly enlightened. When duft is thrown into their eyes, more efpecially gold duft, the political opthalmift muft honeftly endeavor to clear away the obftruction. It becomes every lover of his country, efpecially a country like England, where even the throne itfelf is fixed on liberty as on a corner ftone, to warn his countrymen of the danger, wherever he obferves the fmalleft encroachment on their rights, and the fpirit of the times tending but remotely to defpotifm.

If there be a time, in which the fenate of a free country has declared that the influence of the crown *has increafed, is increafing, and ought to be diminifhed;* and if, inftead of a confequent diminution, there be an evident increafe of that influence; if acts, like the *habeas corpus,* highly favourable to liberty, be fufpended without neceffity; if unconftitutional benevolences be encouraged; if places and penfions be multiplied; if juries be cenfured by great men for honeft verdicts in favor of freedom; if endeavours be made reftrain the prefs by fycophantic affociations; if fpies and informers be kept in pay for the purpofe of profecuting innocent men who efpoufe the caufe of their country; if the prefs be hired to calumniate both liberty and the people; if wars, neither juft nor neceffary, be under-taken to divert the public mind from domeftic reformation; if a party prevail by artifice, who hate the name of liberty, who are conti-nually employed in aggrandizing monarchy, ariftocracy, and in depreciating the people; in fuch a time, and in fuch a conjuncture, it becomes every honeft man, not yet drawn into the whirlpool of political corruption, to warn his fellow-citizens againft an *encroaching fpirit of defpotifm.*

In the following pages, I offer fome fuggef-tions on the fubject. I have indeed few qua-lifications for the tafk befides fincerity, an earneft defire **to** promote public and private happinefs, and an independence of fpirit; but thefe I certainly have, and profefs to maintain. I wifh the rifing generation may be awakened, and learn to place a due value on the liberty handed down to them by their anceftors. I would infpire them with a generofity of mind, which fhould fcorn diffimulation ; which fhould neither practice the arts of corruption, nor become their dupe. I am defirous of difcrediting the whole fyftem of corruption, and of rendering all civil government fair, juft, open, and honorable. All government, founded on infincerity and injuftice, debafes the morals and injures the happinefs, while it infringes on the civil rights of the people. I wifh to revive in the people a due fenfe of their native and conftitutional importance. I endeavour, in this book, to plead the caufe of man ; firmly convinced that the caufe of man is the caufe of GOD.

SECTION II.

Oriental Manners, and the Ideas imbibed in Youth, both in the West and East Indies, favorable to the Spirit of Despotism.

THE foundations of the fair fabric of liberty in Europe were laid in ages when there was but little intercourse, commercial or political, with the remote countries of Asia and America. A hardy race, in ungenial climates, with nerves strung by the northern blast, though little refined by knowledge, felt in an early age, the sentiments of manly virtue, and spurned the baseness of slavery. Luxury had not emasculated their minds; and they threw off, with native elasticity, the burden of unjust dominion. While they submitted with graceful acquiescence, to all lawful authority, established by their own consent, for the general good; they preserved a noble consciousness of native dignity, and maintained a personal grandeur, a proud independence, a greatness unindebted to the morbid tumor of rank and riches.

In later times the facility of navigation and the improvements of science have brought into close connexion the extremes of the habitable globe. The asperity of manners which sometimes disgraced the virtues of our forefathers, has indeed been softened by various and constant intercourse; the manly spirit has ex-

C

changed ferocity for gentlenefs, and rendered the energetic character confiftent with the amiable.   It was a happy change ; for why fhould manly virtue affume a forbidding afpect, and lofe the recommendation of engaging manners, the happinefs of loving and being loved, while it commands, by deferving, cordial reverence ?

.But from the intercourfe of England with the Eaft and Weft Indies, it is to be feared that fomething of a more fervile fpirit has been derived, than was known among thofe who eftablifhed the free conftitutions of Europe, and than would have been adopted, or patiently borne, in ages of virtuous fimplicity.

A very numerous part of our countrymen fpend their moft fufceptible age, in thofe countries, where defpotic manners remarkably prevail.   They are themfelves, when invefted with office, treated by the natives with an idolatrous degree of reverence, which teaches them to expect a .fimilar fubmiffion to their will, on their return to their own country. They have been accuftomed to look up to perfonages greatly their fuperiors in rank and riches, with awe ; and to look down on their inferiors in *property*, with fupreme contempt, as flaves of their will, and minifters of their luxury.   Equal laws, and equal liberty at home, appear to them faucy claims of the poor and vulgar, which tend to diveft riches of one of the greateft charms, overbearing dominion.

We do indeed import gorgeous filks and lufcious fweets from the Indies, but we import, at the fame time, the fpirit of defpotifm, which adds deformity to the purple robe, and bitternefs to the honied beverage.

The vaffals of the feudal times, it is true, were abject flaves; but their flavery was freedom compared to the flavery of the negro. They were not driven by the whip to work in a torrid zone. They were not wanted to adminifter to perfonal luxury; for perfonal luxury did not exift. But the negro is rendered a two-legged beaft of burden; and looks up to the infant fon of his lord, as to a fuperior being, whom he is bound to obey, however vicious, whimfical, or cruel the command. Cradled in defpotifm, the young planter comes to England for education, and brings with him the early impreffions, which a few years refidence in the land of freedom can feldom obliterate. He returns; grows rich by the labor of flaves, over whom, for the fake of perfonal fafety, the moft arbitrary government is exercifed, and then perhaps retires to England to fpend his age and acquirements in the capital, the feat of pleafure, the theatre of commercial fplendor and courtly magnificence. He mixes much in fociety, and inevitably communicates his ideas, which have now taken deep root, on the neceffity of keeping the vulgar in a ftate of depreffion, and ftrengthening the hands of the rich and the powerful. In the virtuous ftruggles of the lower and middle ranks for conftitutional liberty, is it likely that he fhould join the conteft, on the fide of the people? Is it

not moſt probable, that he will throw all his
weight, which, conſidering the *weight of money*,
is often great, in oppoſition to the popular
ſide ? A long ſucceſſion of ſuch men, perſon-
ally reſpectable, but, from peculiar circumſtances, favoring the extenſion of power, and
diſpoſed by habits and principles ſucked in
with the mother's milk, to repel the claims of
their inferiors, muſt contribute greatly to diffuſe,
in a free country, the ſpirit of deſpotiſm.

That *oriental* manners are unfavorable to
liberty, is, I believe, univerſally conceded.
The natives of the Eaſt Indies entertain not
the idea of independence. They treat the
Europeans, who go among them to acquire
their riches, with a reſpect ſimilar to the abject
ſubmiſſion which they pay to their native deſpots. Young men, who in England ſcarcely
poſſeſſed the rank of the gentry, are waited
upon in India, with more attentive ſervility
than is paid or required in many courts of
Europe. Kings of England ſeldom aſſume the
ſtate enjoyed by an Eaſt India governor, or
even by ſubordinate officers.

Enriched at an early age, the adventurer
returns to England. His property admits him
to the higher circles of faſhionable life. He
aims at rivalling or exceeding all the old nobility in the ſplendor of his manſions, the finery
of his carriages, the number of his liveried
train, the profuſion of his table, in every unmanly indulgence, which an empty vanity can
covet, and a full purſe, procure. Such a man,

when he looks from the window of his fuperb manfion, and fees the people pafs, cannot endure the idea, that they are of as much confequence as himfelf, in the eye of the law; and that he dares not infult or opprefs the unfortunate being who rakes his kennel, or fweeps his chimney. He muft wifh to increafe the power of the rich and great, that the faucy vulgar may be kept at a due diftance, that they may know their ftation, and fubmit their necks to the foot of pride.

The property of fuch a man will give him great weight in parliamentary eleótions. He probably purchafes a borough. He fides with the court party on all queftions; and is a great ftickler for the extenfion of prerogative. In his neighbourhood, and as a voter for reprefentatives, he ufes all his intereft in fupporting fuch men as are likely to promote his views of aggrandizing the great, among whom he hopes to be affociated, and in depreffing the little, whom he defpifes and fhuns. Having money fufficient, his prefent objeót is a title. This he knows can only come from the poffeffors of power, to whom, therefore, he pays fuch a fubmiffion as he has feen paid to himfelf in India by oriental flaves. His whole conduót tends to increafe the influence of riches, from which alone, he is confcious, he derives his own importance. What is his eloquence? What his learning? What his beneficence to mankind? Little; perhaps none. But his eftate is large, his houfe large, his park large, his manors many, his equipage, on a birth-day, the moft fplendid in St. James's-ftreet. Long-Acre gives him a paffport to court favor. With a feat in the houfe, and an unrivalled equipage and manfion, he deems himfelf juftly entitled to be made, in due time, a baronet at leaft, if not an hereditary law-giver of his country.

By a conftantly fucceffive influx of fuch men from the eaftern climes, furnifhed with the means of corruption, and inclined to promote arbitrary principles of government, it cannot be doubted, that much is contributed to the fpirit of defpotifm. Who among them would not add to the mafs of that power and fplendor, to poffefs a large fhare of which has been the firft object of a life fpent in unceafing cares, at the rifque of health, and in a torrid zone?

And what is left to oppofe the fpirit of defpotifm thus animated in its progrefs by enormous opulence? Is it the virtue of the honeft country gentleman, who lives on his eftate, poffeffing nothing and hoping nothing from the favor of courts? Is it the independence of the middle and lower ranks, too numerous to be bribed either by gifts or expectations? Both, it is to be feared, will be too flow in their oppofition to the gigantic monfter, if not too feeble. They will not often rifque their repofe in a dangerous conteft with opulence and power. They stand in awe of the sword and the law; which, in bad times, have been equally used as instruments of injustice. Contented with the enjoyment of plenty, or the amusements of rural sports, they sink into a state of indifference to public affairs, and thus leave the field open to those who have no right to occupy it at all, much less exclusively.

Thus the community becomes divided into two descriptions of men; the corruptors and the indifferent; those who seek wealth and honors without virtue, and those who seek only their own ease regardless of the public.

This indifference is scarcely less culpable than corruption. It must be laid aside. The independent country gentleman, seconded by the people, is the character, on whom liberty must rely, as on her firmest supporter, against the incursion of oriental pride. Let him preserve his independence by frugality. Let him beware of emulating either the oriental or occidental upstart, in expences which he cannot equal, without diminishing his patrimony and losing his independence. Let him cultivate every social virtue, reside on his estate, and become popular by exhibiting superior excellence both of heart and understanding. He will then do right to offer himself a candidate in his vicinity for a seat in the senate; because, as a senator, he will gain a power to act with effect against the increasing weight of corrupt influence. The truly WHIG PARTY, the lovers of liberty and the people, is not only the moſt favorable to human happineſs, but certainly moſt congenial to the conſtitution of England, and ought to be ſtrengthened by the junction of all independent men, lovers of peace, liberty, and human nature.

The TORY AND JACOBITE SPIRIT, under other more plauſible names, is ſtill alive, and has encreaſed of late. All who have a juſt idea of the Britiſh conſtitution, and of the value of liberty, will oppoſe it, by cultivating manlineſs of ſpirit, by illuminating the minds of the people, and by inſpiring them with a regard to truth, juſtice, and independence, together with a love of order and of peace, both internal and external.

SECTION III.

Certain Circumstances in Education which promote the Spirit of Despotism.

MANY who have arisen to high elevation of rank or fortune, seem to think that their nature has undergone a real metamorphosis; that they are refined by a kind of chemical process, sublimed by the sunshine of royal favor, and separated from the fæces, the dross and the dregs of ordinary humanity; that humanity, of which the mass of mankind partake, and which, imperfect as it is, God created. They seem to themselves raised to a pinnacle; from which they behold, with sentiments of indifference or contempt, all two-legged and unfeathered beings of inferior order, placed in the vale, as ministers of their pride, and slaves of their luxury, or else burdens of the earth, and *superfluous sharers* of existence.

The great endeavor of their lives, never employed in the essential service of society, is to keep the vulgar at a distance, lest their own purer nature should be contaminated by the foul contagion. Their offspring must be taught, in the first instance, to know and revere, not God, not man, but their own rank in life. The infants are scarcely suffered to breath the common air, to feel the common sun, or to walk upon the common earth. Im-

mured in nurferies till the time for inftruction
arrives, they are then furrounded by a variety
of domeftic tutors. And what is the firft
object in their education? Is it the improvement of their minds, the acquifition of manly
fentiment, ufeful knowledge, expanded ideas,
piety, philanthropy? No; it is the embellifhment of their perfons, an accurate attention to
drefs, to their teeth, to grace in dancing,
attitude in ftanding, uprightnefs, not the uprightnefs of the heart, but the formal and
unnatural perpendicularity of a foldier drilled
on the parade. If a mafter of learned lan-
guages and philofophy be admitted at all, he
feels himfelf in lefs eftimation with the family
than the dancing-mafter; and if poffeffed of
the fpirit, which the nature of his ftudies has
a tendency to infpire, he will foon depart
from a houfe, where he is confidered in the
light of an upper fervant, paid lefs wages,
and fubjected to the caprice of the child,
whom he ought to control with the natural
authority of fuperior wifdom. To affume over
his pupil the rights of that natural fuperiority,
would be to oppofe the favorite ideas of the
family, " *that all real pre-eminence is founded*
" *on birth, fortune, and court favor.*" The
firft object with the pupil, and the laft, the
leffon to be got by heart, and to be repeated
by night and by day, is an adequate concep-
tion of his own native confequence, a difpofition to extend the influence of rank and riches,
and to deprefs and difcourage the natural ten-

dency of perfonal merit to rife to diftinction by its own elaftic force.

If the boy be allowed to go to any fchool at all, which is not always deemed prudent, be-caufe fchools in general have a few plebeians who raife themfelves there, to fome degree of fuperiority, by merit only, it is only to fchools which fafhion recommends, which abound with titled perfons, and where the expences are fo great, as to keep ingenious poverty, or even mediocrity of fortune, at a refpectful dif-tance. Here he is inftructed to form con-nexions with his fuperiors. The principle point is to acquire the haughty air of nobility. Learning and virtue may be added, if perad-venture they come eafily; but the formation of connexions, and the affumption of infolence, is indifpenfable. To promote this purpofe, pocket-money is beftowed on the pupil with a lavifh hand by his parents, and all his coufins who court his favor. He muft fhew his con-fequence, and be outdone by no lord of them all, in the profufion of his expences, in the variety of his pleafures, and, if his great com-panions fhould happen to be vicious, in the enormity of his vice. Infults and injuries may be fhown to poor people who attend the fchool, or live near it, as marks of prefent fpirit and future heroifm. A little money makes a full compenfation, and the glorious actions, on one fide, and the pufillanimous acquiefcence under it, on the other, evinces the great doctrine, that the poor are by nature creatures of other mold, *earth-born perhaps*, and made for the paftime of thofe who have had the good for-tune to be born to opulence or title.   The mafters themfelves are to be kept in due order by the illuftrious pupils, or a rebellion may enfue.   Such an event indeed is fometimes devoutly wifhed, as it affords opportunities for *embryo heroes* to fhew their prowefs and their *noble* pride.   Every ebullition of fpirits, as it is candidly called, difplaying itfelf in infolence or ill-ufage of the inferior ranks, defencelefs old men or women, and the poor in general, is remembered and cherifhed with care, as a flat-tering prognoftic of future eminence in the cabinet, the fenate, at the bar, or in the field. Juftice, generofity, humility, are words indeed in the dictionary, and may adorn a declama-tion ; but infolence, extravagance, and pride, muft mark the conduct of thofe who are fent, rather to fupport the dignity of native gran-deur by the fpirit of arrogance, than to feek wifdom and virtue with the docility of modeft and ingenuous difciples.   Practical oppreffion of inferiors is one of the firft elements of arif-tocratical education ; and the order of *Faggs* (as they are called) contributes much to fami-liarize the exercife of future defpotifm.   Mean fubmiffions prepare the mind, in its turn, to tyrannize.

Let us now fuppofe the ftripling grown too tall for fchool, and entered at an univerfity. The Englifh univerfities are admirably well adapted to flatter the pride of wealth and title.

There is a drefs for the diftinction of the higher orders extremely pleafing to ariftocratical vanity. In the world at large the drefs of all gentlemen is fo fimilar, that nothing is left to point out thofe who think themfelves of a fuperior order; unlefs indeed they ride in their coaches, and exhibit their fplendid liveries behind, and armorial enfigns on the fides; but at Oxford, they never walk the ftreets, on the commoneft occafions, without difplaying their proud pre-eminence by gowns of filk and tufts of gold.

As noblemen, or gentlemen commoners, they not only enjoy the privilege of fplendid veftments, but of neglecting, if they pleafe, both learning and religion. They are not required, like vulgar fcholars, to attend regularly to the inftruction, or to the difcipline of the colleges; and they are allowed a frequent abfence from daily prayer. They are thus taught to believe, that a filken gown and a velvet cap are fubftitutes for knowledge; and that the rank of gentlemen commoners difpenfes with the neceffity of that devotion which others are compelled to profefs in the college chapels. High privileges thefe! and they ufually fill thofe who enjoy them with that attachment to rank, which leads directly to the fpirit of defpotifm. They are flattered in the feats of wifdom, where fcience and liberality are fuppofed to dwell, with an idea of fome inherent virtue in mere rank, independently of merit; and after having learned a leffon fo

D

pleafing to felf-love and idlenefs, they go out into the world with confidence, fully refolved to practice the proud theories they have imbibed, and to demand refpect without endeavoring to deferve it.

Without public or private virtue, and without even the defire of it ; without knowledge, and without even a thirft for it ; many of them, on leaving college, enlift under the banners of the minifter for the time being, or in a felf-interefted oppofition to him, and boldly ftand forth candidates to reprefent boroughs and counties, on the ftrength of ariftocratical influence. Though they appear to afk favors of the people, they pay no refpect to the people, but rely on rank, riches, and powerful connections. Ever inclined to favor and promote the old principles of jacobitifm, toryifm, and unlimited prerogative, they hope to be rewarded by places, penfions, titles ; and then to trample on the *wretches* by whofe venal votes they rofe to eminence.

The ideas acquired and cherifhed at fchool and at the univerfity, are confirmed in the world by affociation with perfons of a fimilar turn, with Oriental adventurers, with penfioners and courtiers, with all who, funk in the frivolity of a diffipated, vain, and ufelefs life, are glad to find a fuccedaneum for every real virtue, in the privileges of titular honor, in fplendid equipage, in luxurious tables, in magnificent houfes, in all that gives diftinction without merit, and notoriety without excellence. Their number and their influence increafe by an union of fimilar views and principles; and a formidable phalanx is formed againft thofe liberties, for which the moft virtuous part of mankind have lived and died. Under the aufpices of multitudes, thus corrupted and united, it is not to be wondered, that the fpirit of defpotifm fhould increafe. Defpotifm is indeed an Afiatic plant; but brought over by thofe who have long lived in Afia, and nurfed in a hot-houfe with indefatigable care, it is found to vegetate, bloom, and bear fruit, even in our cold, ungenial climate.

It might then be worthy a wife legiflator to reform the modes of education, to explode the effeminacy of private and fuperficial nurture, to promote an *equality of rank* in fchools and univerfities, and to fuffer, in the immature age, no other diftinctions than thofe, which may be adjudged by grave and virtuous inftructors, to diftinguifhed improvement, exemplary conduct, goodnefs of heart, and a *regard to the happinefs of inferiors*.

The conftitution of England is founded on liberty, and the people are warmly attached to liberty; then why is it ever in danger, and why is a conftant ftruggle neceffary to preferve it uninfringed? Many caufes combine, and perhaps none is more operative than a corrupt education, in which pride is nourifhed at the tendereft period, and the poffeffion or expectation of wealth and civil honors is tacitly reprefented, even in the fchools of virtue, as fuperfeding the neceffity of perfonal excellence.

SECTION IV.

*Corruption of Manners has a natural Tendency
to promote the Spirit of Despotism.*

WHEN man ceases to venerate
virtue in himself, he soon loses all sense of
moral beauty in the human species. His taste
becomes grofs; and he learns to consider all
that is good and great, as the illusion of simple minds, the unsubstantial phantom of a
young imagination. Extreme selfishness is his
ruling principle, and he is far from scrupulous
in following its dictates. Luxury, vanity,
avarice, are his characteristics. Ambition indeed takes its turn; yet, not that noble ambition, which seeks praise and honors by deserving
them, but the low spirit of intrigue and cunning,
which teaches to secure high appointments,
titular distinctions, or whatever else can flatter
avarice and pride, by petty stratagem, unmanly
compliance, the violation of truth and consiftency, and at last the sacrifice of a country's
interest and safety.

In nations enriched by commerce, and among
families loaded with opulence by the avarice
of their forefarthers, the mere wantonnefs of
unbounded plenty will occasion a corruption of
manners; dangerous to all that renders society
happy, but favorable to the despotic principle.
Pleasure of the meanest kind will be the first

and the laſt purſuit. Splendor, external ſhow, the oſtentation of riches, will be deemed objects of prime conſequence. A COURT will be the place of exhibition; not of great merits, but of fine garments, graceful attitudes, and guady equipages, every frivolous diſtinction, which boldly claims the notice due to virtue, and aſſumes the dignity which public ſervices ought ſolely to appropriate.

The mind of man, ſtill wanting in the midſt of external abundance, an object in futurity; and ſatiated, even to lothing, with the continual banquet of plenty, longs to add titular honors, or official importance, to the poſſeſſion of ſuperfluous property. But theſe, if they mean any thing, are naturally the rewards of virtuous and uſeful exertion; and ſuch exertion is incompatible with the habitual indolence, the ignorance, the diſſipation, the vice of exorbitant wealth, gained only by mean avarice, and expended in enjoyments that degrade, while they enervate. Men, diſtinguiſhed by riches only, poſſeſs not, amidſt all their acquirements, the proper price that ſhould purchaſe civil diſtinctions, if they were diſpoſed of only to *merit*. There they are bankrupts. They have no claims on ſociety; for their purpoſes have been ſelfiſh, and their conduct injurious: yet the diſtinctions muſt be obtained, or they ſicken in the midſt of health, and ſtarve, though ſurrounded with plenty. How then ſhall they be obtained? They muſt be bought with money; but how bought? Not directly, not in the market-place, not at public fale. But is there a borough hitherto anti-minifterial, and to convert which from the error of its ways, a very expenfive election muft be engaged in? The ambitious afpirant at honors is ready with his purfe. By money he triumphs over oppofition, and adds the weight of his wealth to minifterial preponderance. He affifts others in the fame noble and generous fervices of his country. Though covetous, he perfeveres, regardlefs of expence, and at laft richly merits, from his patron, the glittering bauble which hung on high, and led him patiently through thofe dark and dirty paths which terminate in the temple of proftituted honor. His brilliant fuccefs excites others to tread in his fteps with eager emulation; and though many fail of the glorious prize, yet all contribute, in the felfifh purfuit, to increafe and to diffufe the fpirit of defpotifm.

Men deftitute of perfonal merit, and unrecommended by the plea of public fervices, can never obtain illuftrious honors, where the people poffefs a due fhare of power, where liberty flourifhes, unblighted by corruption; and therefore fuch men will ever be oppofed to the people, and determined enemies to liberty. The atmofphere of liberty is too pure and defecated for their lungs to inhale. Gentles and other vermin can exift only in filth and putrefaction. Such animals, if they poffeffed reafon, would therefore endeavor to contaminate every healthy climate, to deftroy the vital falubrity of the liberal air, and diffuse corruption with fyftematic induftry. Are there not political phænomena, which would almoft juftify a belief in the exiftence of fuch animals in the human form; and is not mankind interefted, as they value their health, in impeding the progrefs of infectious pollution?

Corruption does not operate, in the increafe of the defpotic fpirit, on the higheft orders only, and the afpirants at political diftinction and confequence, but alfo on the crouded ranks of commercial life. In a great and rich nation, an immenfe quantity and variety of articles is ever wanted to fupply the army and the navy. No cuftomers are fo valuable as the public. The pay is fure and liberal, the demand enormous, and a very fcrupulous vigilance againft fraud and extortion feldom maintained with rigid uniformity. Happy the mercantile men who can procure a contract! The hope of it will caufe an obfequious acquiefcence in the meafures of the ruling minifter. But it happens that fuch acquiefcence, in fuch men, is peculiarly dangerous, in a commercial country, to the caufe of freedom. The mercantile orders conftitute corporate bodies, rich, powerful, influential; they therefore have great weight in elections. Juries are chiefly chofen from mercantile life. In ftate trials, minifters are anxious to obtain verdicts favorable to their retention of emolument and place. If the hope of contracts and other douceurs fhould ever overcome the fanctity of oaths, in an age when religion has loft much of its influence, then will the firmeſt pillar of freedom be undermined, and courts of juſtice become mere regiſters of miniſterial edicts. Thus both ſenatorial and judicial proceedings will be vitiated by the ſame means : and LIBERTY left to deplore a declining cauſe, while CORRUPTION laughs from a Lord Mayor's coach, as ſhe rides in triumph to Court, to preſent, on her knees, the addreſs of ſycophancy.

When the public mind is ſo debauched as to conſider titles and money as the chief good of man, weighed with which honeſty and conſcience are but as duſt in the balance, can it be ſuppoſed that a due reverence will be paid to the obſolete parchments of a *magna charta*, to bills of rights, or to revolutions which baniſhed the principles of the Stuarts, together with their families, which broke their deſpotiſm in pieces together with their ſceptres, and trampled their pride under foot with their crowns and robes of purple ? The prevalence of corruption can call back to life the race of *jacobites* and *tories*, and place on the throne of liberty, an imaginary Stuart. It was not the perſon, but the principles which rendered the old family deteſtable to a people who deſerved liberty, becauſe they dared to claim it. The revival of thoſe principles might render a *ſucceſſor*, though *crowned* by Liberty herſelf, equally deteſtable.

To avoid ſuch principles, the corruption that infallibly leads to them muſt be repelled.

The people fhould be tinctured with philofophy and religion ; and learn, under their
divine inftruction, not to confider titular diftinction and enormous riches as the chief good,
and indifpenfably requifite to the happinefs of
life. A noble fpirit of perfonal virtue fhould
be encouraged in the rifing race. They
fhould be taught to feek and find refources in
themfelves, in an honeft independence, in the
poffeffion of knowledge, in confcious integrity,
in manlinefs of fentiment, in contemplation
and ftudy, in every thing which adds vigor to
the nerves of the mind, and teaches it to deem
all honors difgraceful, and all profits vile,
which accrue, as the reward of bafe compliance, and of a daftardly defertion from the
upright ftandard of truth, the unfpotted banner of juftice.

SECTION V.

*An Abhorrence of Despotism and an ardent
Love of Liberty perfectly consistent with Order
and Tranquillity; and the natural Consequence
of well-informed Understandings and benevolent Dispositions.*

THOSE who are possessed of exorbitant power, who pant for its extension, and
tremble at the apprehension of losing it, are
always sufficiently artful to dwell with emphasis,
on the evils of licentiousness; under which
opprobrious name, they wish to stigmatize
liberty. They describe the horrors of anarchy
and confusion, in the blackest colors; and
boldly affirm, that they are the necessary consequences of *entrusting* the people with power.
Indeed, they hardly condescend to recognize
the idea of a PEOPLE; but whenever they
speak of the mass of the community, denominate them the mob, the rabble, or the swinish
multitude. Language is at a loss for appella-
tives, significant of their contempt for those,
who are undistinguished by wealth or titles,
and is obliged to content itself with such words
as reptiles, scum, dregs, or the many-headed
monster.

Man, that noble animal, formed with powers
capable of the sublimest virtues, possessed of

reafon, and tremulously alive to every finer feeling, is degraded by his fellow man, when dreft in a little brief authority, to a rank below that of the beafts of the field; for the beafts of the field are not treated with epithets of contumely, but regarded with a degree of efteem. The proud grandee views the horfes in his ftable and the dogs in his kennel with affection, pampers them with food, lodges them in habitations, not only commodious, but luxurious; and, at the fame time, defpifes his fellow-creatures, fcarcely fed, wretchedly cloathed, and barely fheltered in the neighboring cottage. And if this fellow-creature dares to remonftrate, his complaint is contumacy and fedition, and his endeavor to meliorate his own ftate and that of his peers, by the moft lawful means, downright treafon and rebellion.

Villainous oppreffion on one hand, and on the other, contemptible fubmiffion! If fuch acquiefcence, under the moft iniquitous inequality; fuch wretchednefs, without the privilege of complaint, is the peace, the order, and the tranquillity of defpotifm; then peace, order, and tranquillity change their nature, and become the curfe and bane of human nature. Welcome, in comparifon, all the feuds, animofities, and revolutions attributed to a ftate of freedom; for they are fymptoms of life and robuft health, while the repofe of defpotifm is the deadnefs of a palfy. Life, active, enterprifing life, with all its tumult, difafter, and difappointment, is to be preferred to the filence of death, the ftillnefs of defolation.

But I deny that a love of liberty, or a ftate of liberty, is of neceffity productive of injurious or fatal diforder. I prefuppofe that the minds of the people, even the loweft of the people, are duly enlightened ; that the favagenefs of grofs ignorance is mitigated by culture ; by that culture, which all well-regulated ftates are folicitous to beftow on every partaker of the rational faculty.

In a ftate of liberty, every man learns to value himfelf as man ; to confider himfelf as of importance in the fyftem which himfelf has approved and contributed to eftablifh ; and therefore refolves to regulate his own behaviour confiftently with its fafety and prefervation. He feels as a proprietor, not as a tenant. He loves the ftate becaufe he participates in it. His obedience is not the cold reluctant refult of terror ; but the lively, cheerful, and fpontaneous effect of love. The violation of laws, formed on the pure principle of general beneficence, and to which he has given his full affent, by a juft and perfect reprefentation, he confiders as a crime of the deepeft die. He will think freely, and fpeak freely, of the conftitution. He will inceffantly endeavor to improve it ; and enter ferioufly into all political debate. In the collifion of agitated minds, fparks will fometimes be emitted ; but they will only give a favorable light and a genial warmth. They will never produce an injurious conflagration.

What employment, in the busy scene in which man engages from the cradle to the tomb, is more worthy of him than political discussion? It affords a field for intellectual energy, and all the finest feelings of benevolence. It exercises and strengthens every faculty. It calls forth latent virtues, which else had slept in the bosom, like the diamond in the mine. And is this employment, thus useful and honorable, to be confined to a few among the race of mortals? Is there to be a monopoly of political action and speculation? Why then did Heaven bestow reason and speech, powers of activity, and a spirit of enterprize, in as great perfection on the lowest among the people, as on those who, by no merit of their own, inherit wealth and high station? Heaven has declared its will by its acts. Man contravenes it; but time, and the progressive improvement of the understanding, will reduce the anomaly to its natural rectitude. And if a few irregularities should sometimes arise in the process, they are of no importance when weighed with the happy result; the return of distorted systems to truth, to reason, and the will of God. Occasional ferments, with all their inconveniences, are infinitely preferable to the putrescence of stagnation. They are symptoms of health and vigor; and though they may be attended with transient pain, yet while they continue to appear at

E

intervals, there is no danger of mortification. Good hearts, accompanied with good under-ftandings, feldom produce, even where mif-taken, lafting evil. They repair and compen-fate.

But I repeat that the people fhould be en-lightened, in every rank, the higheft as well as the loweft, to render them capable of perfect liberty, without danger of thofe evils which its enemies are always afferting to be its una-voidable confequences. The vulgar muft be inftructed not merely in the arts which tend to the acquifition, increafe and prefervation of money, but in a generous philofophy. They muft be liberalized. They muft early learn to view human life and fociety in their juft light; to confider themfelves as effential parts of a whole, the integrity of which is defirable to every component member. Their tafte will improve with their underftanding; and they will fee the beauty of order, while they are convinced of its utility. Thus principled by virtue, and illuminated with knowledge, they will eagerly return, after every deviation, which even a warmth of virtue may caufe, to regular obedience, and to all the functions of citizens; valuing the public peace and prof-perity, becaufe they underftand clearly that the public happinefs is intimately combined with their own. They may infringe laws, from the imperfection of their nature; but they will return to their obedience without force; having been convinced that no laws are made, but such as are neceſſary to their well-being in ſociety. They will conſider laws, not as chains and fetters, but as helmets and ſhields for their protection. The light of the underſtanding will correct the eccentricities of the heart; and all deviations, however rapid at their commencement, will be ſhort in extent and tranſitory in duration.

Such would be the effect of enlightening the people with political knowledge, and enlarging their minds by pure philoſophy. But what ſay the deſpots? Like the tyrannical ſon of Philip, when he reprimanded Ariſtotle for publiſhing his Diſcoveries, they whiſper to their myrmidons, " Let us diffuſe darkneſs round the land*. Let the people be kept in a brutal ſtate. Let their conduct, when aſſembled, be riotous and irrational as ignorance and *our* SPIES can make it, that they may be brought into diſcredit, and deemed unfit for the management of their own affairs. Let power be rendered dangerous in their hands, that it may continue unmoleſted in our own. Let them not taſte the fruit of the tree of knowledge, left they become as we are, and learn to know good and evil."

That ſuch are the ſentiments of the men who wiſh for the extenſion of royaliſm and the depreſſion of the people, is evident from the uneaſineſs they have ſhewn at all benevolent attempts to diffuſe knowledge among the poor.

* Σκοτισον, σκοτισον, *darken your doctrines,* ſaid the deſpot Alexander, to the great philoſopher.

They have exprefled, in terms of anger and
mortification, their diflike of Sunday fchools.
The very newfpapers which they have engaged
in the fervice of falfehood and toryifm, have
endeavored to difcountenance, by malignant
paragraphs, the progrefs of thofe patriotic inftitutions. Scribblers of books and pamphlets,
in the fame vile caufe, have intimated their
apprehenfions that the poor may learn to read
political books in learning to read their Bible ;
and that the reading of political books muft
unavoidably produce difcontent. A wretched
compliment to the caufe which they mean to
defend! It is impoffible not to infer from
their apprehenfions, that as men increafe in
underftanding and knowledge, they muft fee
reafon to difapprove the fyftems eftablifhed.
Thefe men breathe the very fpirit of defpotifm,
and wifh to communicate it. But their conduct, in this inftance, is an argument againft
the fpirit which they endeavor to diffufe.
Their conduct feems to fay, The fpirit of defpotifm is fo unreafonable, that it can never be
approved by the mafs of the people, when
their reafon is fuffered to receive its proper
cultivation. Their conduct feems to fay, Let
there be light, and the deformity of defpotifm
will create abhorrence.

Be the confequence what it may, let the
light of knowledge be diffufed among all who
partake of reafon ; and let us remember that
it was THE LORD GOD ALMIGHTY who firft
faid : LET THERE BE LIGHT.

SECTION VI.

On the Venality of the Press under the Influence of the despotic Spirit, and its Effects in diffusing that Spirit.

THE most succesful, as well as the most insidious mode of abolishing an institution which favors liberty, and, for that reason, alarms the jealousy of encroaching power, is to leave the form untouched, and gradually to annihilate the essence. The voracious worm eats out the kernel completely, while the husk continues fair to the eye, and apparently entire. The gardener would crush the insect, if it commenced the attack on the external tegument; but it carries on the work of destruction with efficacy and safety, while it corrodes the unseen fruit, and spares the outside shell.

The liberty of the press in England is not openly infringed. It is our happiness and our glory. No man or set of men, whatever be their power or their wishes, dares to violate this sacred privilege. But in the heathen mythology we learn, that when Jupiter himself could not force certain obstacles by his thunder-bolt he found an easy admission, in the shape of a golden shower.

In times when the jacobitical, tory, selfish, and despotic principles rear their heads, and think opportunities favor their efforts for re-

vival, the prefs is bought up as a powerful
engine of oppreffion. The people muft be deceived, or the defpots have no chance to prevail
in the diffemination of doctrines, unnatural,
nonfenfical, and injurious to the rights human
nature. The only channel, through wnich the
knowledge of what it moft imports them to
know, next to morality and religion, devolves
upon the mafs of the community, is a newfpaper. This channel muft therefore be fecured.
The people's money muft be employed to pol-
lute the waters of truth, to divert their courfe,
and, if occafion requires, to ftop them with
dams, locks, and floodgates. The prefs, that
grand battery, erected by the people to defend
the citadel of liberty, muft be turned againft
it. Pamphlets are tranfient, and confined in
their operation. Nothing will fatisfy the zeal
of the affailant, but the *diurnal* papers of
intelligence. They keep up a daily attack,
and reach every part of the affaulted edifice.

Newfpapers, thus bought with the people's
money, for the purpofe of deceiving the people, are, in the next place, circulated with all
the induftry of zealous partizans, and all the
fuccefs, that muft attend the full exertion of
minifterial influence. Public houfes in great
towns, are frequently the property of overgrown
traders, who fupply them with the commodities
they vend ; and who dictate the choice of the
papers, which they fhall purchafe for the perufal
of their cuftomers. Whoever frequents fuch
houfes, ruled as they are by petty defpots, muft

swallow the false politics, together with the adulterated beverage, of the lordly manufacturer. A distress for rent, or an arrest for debt, might follow the rash choice of a paper favorable to truth, justice, and humanity. If any conversation should arise among the customers, friendly to liberty, in consequence of perusing an interdicted print of this kind, the licence of the house might be in danger, and an honest tradesman with his family turned out of doors to starve. Spies are sent to his house to mix with the guests, that in the moment of convivial exhilaration, when prudence sleeps, some incautious comment on the newspaper may be seized and carried to the agent of despotism, who, like the tiger, thirsting for human blood, lies watching for his prey in the covert of obscurity. The host, therefore, for the sake of safety, gladly rejects all papers of intelligence, which are free to speak the truth, and becomes a useful instrument, in the hands of selfish placemen, in the dissemination of doctrines subversive of liberty, and therefore of the constitution which is founded upon it as a corner stone.

So far as such venal papers are diffused, under influence thus arbitrary, the liberty of the press is, in effect, destroyed. It is made to serve the purposes of slavery, by propagating principles unfavorable to the people's rights, by palliating public abuses, varnishing ministerial misconduct, and concealing facts in which the people are most deeply interested. Perhaps there is nothing which contributes so much to diffuse the spirit of despotism as venal newspapers, hired by the poffeffors of power, for the purpofe of defending and prolonging their pof-feffion. The more ignorant claffes have a won-derful propenfity to be credulous in all that they fee in print, and will obftinately continue to believe, a newfpaper, to which they have been, accuftomed, even when notorious facts give it the lie. They know little of hiftory, nothing of philofophy, and adopt their political ideas from the daily lectures of a paper efta-blifhed folely to gain their favor to one party, the party poffeffed of prefent power; zealous for its extenfion and prolongation, and natu-rally defirous of preventing all fcrupulous en-quiry into its abufe. Such means, fo ufed, certainly ferve the caufe of perfons in office, and gratify avarice and pride; but it is a fer-vice which, while it promotes the fordid views of a few individuals, militates againft the fpirit of conftitutional freedom. It is a vile caufe, which cannot be maintained to the fecurity and fatisfaction of thofe who wifh to maintain it, without recourfe to daily falfehood, and the cowardly concealment of confcious malverfation. Honeft purpofes love the light of truth, and court fcrutiny; becaufe the more they are known, the more they muft be honored. The friends of liberty and man are juftly alarmed, whenever they fee the prefs pre-occupied by power, and every artifice ufed to poifon the fources of public intelligence.

In every free country, the people, who pay all expences, claim a right to know the true ftate of public affairs. The only means of acquiring that knowledge, within reach of the multitude, is the prefs; and it ought to supply them with all important information, which may be divulged without betraying intended meafures, the accomplifhment of which would be fruftrated by communication to a public enemy. The very papers themfelves, which communicate intelligence, pay a tax above the intrinfic value of the work and materials, to the fupport of the government : and the ftamp, which vouches for the payment, ought, at the fame time, if any regard were paid to juftice and honor, to be an authentic teftimony that government ufes no arts of deception in the intelligence afforded.

But let any one review, if it be not too naufeous an employment, the prints which of late years have been notorioufly in the pay of minifterial agency. There he will fee the groffeft attempts to impofe on the public credulity. He will fee the exiftence of known facts, when they militate againft the credit of a miniftry, doubted or denied; doubtful victories extolled beyond all refemblance to truth ; and defeats, in the higheft degree difgraceful and injurious, artfully extenuated. All who have had apportunities of receiving true intelligence, after fome great and unfortunate action, have been aftonifhed at the effrontery which has diminifhed the number of lives loft to a fum fo fmall, as contradicts the evident conclufions of common fenfe, and betrays the features of falfehood at the firft appearance. All who have been able to judge of the privileges of Englifh-men, and the rights of human nature, have feen with abhorrence, doctrines boldly broached and fophiftically defended, which ftrike at once at the Englifh conftitution, and the happinefs of man in fociety. They have feen this done by thofe who pretended an almoft exclufive regard to law, order, and religion; themfelves grofsly violating all of them, while they are reviling others for the fuppofed violation, in the bittereft language which rancour, ftimulated by pride and avarice, can utter.

When great minifters, poffeffed of a thoufand means of patronizing and rewarding obfequious inftruments of their ambition, are willing to corrupt, there will never be wanting needy, unprincipled, and afpiring perfons to receive the infection. But can men be really great, really honorable—can they be patriots and philanthropifts—can they be zealous and fincere friends to law, order, and religion, who thus hefitate not to break down all the fences of honor, truth, and integrity; and render their adminiftration of affairs more fimilar to the juggling tricks of confederate fharpers, than to the grave, ingenuous conduct of ftatefmen, renowned for their wifdom and revered for their virtue? Do men thus exalted, whofe conduct is a model, and whofe opinion is oracular, mean to teach a great nation that confcience is but a name, and honor a phantom? No books of thofe innovators, whom they perfecute, contribute to difcredit the fyftem, which thefe men fupport, fo much as their own finifter meafures of felf-defence.

There is little hope of preventing the corruption of the diurnal papers by any remonftrance addreffed to men, who, entrenched behind wealth and power, fcorn to yield at the fummons of reafon. There may be more hope in appealing to the readers and encouragers of fuch papers. Do they wifh to be deceived? Is it pleafant to be mifled by partial, mutilated, and diftorted narratives? Is it manly to become voluntary dupes? Or is it honorable, is it honeft, to co-operate with any men, for any purpofes, in duping others? No; let the prefs, however it may be perverted by private perfons, to the injury of fociety, be preferved by the public, by men high in office, the guardians of every valuable inftitution, as an inftrument of good to the community, as the fupport of truth, as the lamp of knowledge.

Though the liberty of the prefs fhould be preferved, yet let it be remembered, that the corruption of the prefs, by high and overbearing influence, will be almoft as pernicious to a free country as its deftruction. An *imprimatur* on the prefs would fpread an alarm which would immediately remove the reftraint; but the corruption of the prefs may infinuate itfelf unperceived, till the fpirit of defpotifm, promoted by it, fhall at laft connive at, or even confent to, its total abolition.

SECTION VII.

The fashionable Invectives against Philosophy and Reason, a Proof of the Spirit of Despotism.

PERSONS who owe all their pre-eminence to the merit of their forefathers, or casual events, which constitute good fortune, are usually desirous of fixing a standard of dignity, very different, from real worth, and spare no pains to depreciate personal excellence ; all such excellence as is, in fact, the most honorable, because it cannot exist without talents or virtues. Birth and riches, fashion and rank, are in their estimation infinitely more honorable and valauble, than all the penetrating sagacity and wonderful science of a Newton. Such persons value Newton more as a knight than as a philosopher ; more for the title bestowed upon him by Queen Anne, than the endowment given him by God, and improved by his own meritorious exertion.

Upon this principle, many men in our times, who wish to extend and aggrandize that POWER, from whose arbitrary bounty they derive all the honor they are capable of acquiring, endeavor to throw contempt on PHILOSOPHY. It may indeed be doubted whether they all know the meaning of the word ; but they know it implies a merit not derived from princes, and therefore they wish to degrade it. Their fountain of honor, they conceive, has no resemblance, in its nature or efficacy, to the famed fountains of Parnaffus: it conveys no infpiration, except that which difplays itfelf in the tumor of pride.

The prefent age has heard upftart noblemen give to philofophers (whofe genius and difcoveries entitle them to rank, in Reafon's table of precedency, above every nobleman in the red book) the opprobrious appellation of wretches and mifcreants. Philofophy and philofophers have been mentioned by men, whofe attainments would only qualify them for diftinction in a ball-room, with expreffions of hatred and contempt due only to thieves, murderers, the very outcafts and refufe of human nature.

The mind is naturally led to inveftigate the caufe of fuch virulence, and to afk how has Philofophy merited this ufage from the tongue of factitious grandeur. The refentment expreffed againft Philofophy is expreffed with a peevifhnefs and acrimony that proves it to proceed from the fenfe of a fore place. How has pride been fo feverely hurt by philofophy? It has been expofed, laid open to the eye of mankind in all its nakednefs. Philofophy has held the fcales, and rejected the coin that wanted weight. Philofophy has applied the touchftone, and thrown away the counterfeit. Hence the fpirit of defpotifm is incenfed againft Philofophy; and if proclamations or cannonballs could deftroy her, her perdition would be inevitable and eternal. Folly exclaims aloud, "Let there be no light to detect my paint and tinfel." But happily, the command of Folly, however imperial her tone, is not the fiat of Omnipotence. Philofophy therefore will furvive the anathema; and, ftanding on the rock of truth, laugh at the artillery of confederated defpots.

When fhe deferts truth, fhe no longer deferves to be called Philofophy : and it muft be owned, that when fhe has attacked religion, fhe has juftly loft her reputation. But here it is well worthy of remark, that thofe who now moft bitterly revile her, gave themfelves little concern about her, till fhe defcended to *politics*. She might have continued to argue againft *religion*; and many of her prefent oppofers would have joined in her cry with alacrity : but the moment fhe entered on the holy ground of politics, the ignorant grandees fhuddered at the profanation, and ' Avaunt, Philofophy,' was the word of alarm.

Philofophy, fo far from deferving contempt, is the glory of human nature. Man approaches by contemplation to what we conceive of celeftial purity and excellence. Without the aid of philofophy, the mafs of mankind, all over the terraqueous globe, would have funk in flavery and fuperftition, the natural confequences of grofs ignorance. Men at the very bottom of fociety, have been enabled by the natural talents they poffeffed, feconded by favorable opportunities, to reach the higheft improvements in philofophy ; and have thus lifted up a torch in the valley, which has expofed the weaknefs and deformity of the caftle on the mountain, from which the oppreffors fallied, in the night of darknefs, and fpread defolation with impunity. Defpots, the meaneft, the bafeft, the moft brutal and ignorant of the human race, would have trampled on the rights and the happinefs of men unrefifted, if philofophy had not opened the eyes of the fufferers, fhewn them their own power and dignity, and taught them to defpife thofe giants of power, as they appeared through the mifts of ignorance, who ruled a vaffal world with a mace of iron. Liberty is the daughter of Philofophy; and they who deteft the offspring, do all that they can to vilify and difcountenance the mother.

But let us calmly confider what is the object of this philofophy, fo formidable in the eyes of thofe who are bigotted to antient abufes, who hate every improvement, and who wifh to fubject the many to the control of an arbitrary few. Philofophy is ever employed in finding out whatever is GOOD, and whatever TRUE. She darts her eagle eye over all the bufy world, detects error and mifchief, and points out modes of improvement. In the multiform ftate of human affairs, ever obnoxious to decay and abufe, it is her's to meditate on the means of melioration. She

wifhes to demolifh nothing but what is a nuifance.   To build, to repair, to ftrengthen,
and to polifh, thefe are the works which fhe
delights to plan ; and, in concerting the beft
methods of directing their accomplifhment,
fhe confumes the midnight oil.   How can
fhe difturb human affairs, fince fhe dwells in
contemplation, and defcends not to action ?
neither does fhe impel others to action by the
arts of delufive eloquence.   She applies to
reafon alone ; and if reafon is not convinced,
all that fhe has done, is fwept away, like the
web of Arachne.

But it is modern philofophy, and *French*
philofophy, which gives fuch umbrage to the
lovers of old errors, and the favorers of abfolute power ; juft as if philofophy were mu-
table by time or place.   Philofophy, by which
I mean the inveftigation of the good and true,
on all fubjects, is the fame, like the fun, whether it fhines in China or Peru.   Truth and
good are eternal and immutable ; and therefore
philofophy, which is folely attached to thefe,
is ftill one and the fame, whether antient or
modern, in England or in France.

It is *fophiftry*, and not philofophy, which is
juftly reprobated ; and there has at all times
been more fophiftry difplayed by the fycophant
defenders of defpotifm, than by the friends
to liberty.   England has ever abounded with
fophifts, when the high prerogative notions,
Toryifm, and Jacobitifm, and the fervile prin-

ciples which flow from them, have required the support of eloquence ; either written or oral. Besides our modern *Filmers*, we have had an army of ten thousand mercenary speakers and writers, whose names are as little remembered as their venal productions. Such men, contending against the light of nature, and common sense, have been obliged to seek succour of sophistry. Theirs is the philosophy, falsely so called, which deserves reprobation. They have had recourse to VERBOSITY, to puzzle and perplex the plainest points ; they have seduced the reader from the direct road of common sense, to delude his imagination in the fairy land of metaphor ; they have fine-spun their arguments to a degree of tenuity neither tangible nor visible, that they might excite the awe which is always felt for the *incomprehen-sible* by the ignorant ; and, at the same time, elude the refutation of the learned and the wise : they have acquired a lubricity, which, like the eel, enables them to slip from the grasp of the captor, whom they could not have escaped, by the fair exertion of muscular vigor. Animated with the hope of reward from that POWER which they labor to extend, they have, like good servants to their masters, bestowed art and labor in proportion to the weakness of their cause : they have assumed an air of wisdom to impose on the multitude, and uttered the language of knavery and folly with the grave confidence of an oracle. It is not necessary to cross the Channel in order to find

Sophiftry, decking herfelf, like the afs in the fkin of the lion, with the venerable name of Philofophy.

As we value a free prefs, or wifh to preferve a due efteem for genius and fcience, let us ever be on our guard, when we hear GREAT MEN, poffeffing neither genius nor fcience, rail againft philofophy. Let us remember, that it was a Roman tyrant, in the decline of all human excellence, (when Providence permitted fuch monfters to fhew the world the deformity of defpotifm), who wifhed to extinguifh the light of learning by abolifhing the fineft productions of genius. There are men, in recent times, who difplay all the propenfities of a Caligula; be it the PEOPLE's care, that they never poffefs his power.

SECTION VIII.

Of Loyalty, and certain miſtaken Ideas of it.

THE maſs of the community, on whom the arts of deluſion are chiefly practiſed by politicians, are ſeldom accurate in the uſe of words : and among others which they miſunderſtand, and are led, by the ſatellites of deſpotiſm, to miſapply, is the term, Loyalty.

Loyalty means, in its true ſenſe, a firm and faithful adherence to the law and conſtitution, of the community of which we are members. If monarchy be a part of that conſtitution, it certainly means a firm and faithful attachment to the perſon of the monarch, as well as to the monarchical form, and all the other branches of the ſyſtem. It is nearly ſynonymous with fidelity; but as fidelity may be actuated ſolely by principles of duty, loyalty ſeems, in its common acceptation, to include in it alſo a ſentiment of affection. It is the obedience of love, and anticipates compulſion. It is a ſentiment, which all good men will feel, when they live under a good government honeſtly adminiſtered.

But mark the diſingenuity of men impelled by high-church, high tory, or jacobitical principles. They would limit this liberal comprehenſive principle, which takes in the whole of the conftitution, and therefore tends to the confervation of it all, in its full integrity; they would limit it to the *perfon of the monarch*, to that part of the whole, which favors, in their opinion, their own purpofes, and the extenfion of power and prerogative, the largeffes of which they hope to fhare in reward for their fycophantic zeal, their flavifh, felfifh, perfidious adulation.

They reprefent this confined loyalty as a religious duty, partaking the nature of divine worfhip. They fet up an idol, and command all men, upon their duty, to adore it. The people are not entitled even to attention by the propagators of this inhuman, anti-chriftian idolatry.

- Let us confider a moment the mifchief this artifice has in former times occafioned to our country. It attached great numbers to the family of the Stuarts, after they had forfeited all right to the crown; to the *perfons* of the Stuarts, and for a long period, haraffed the lawful king and the people of this nation with wars, alarms, feditions, and treafons. Tory zealots fhed their blood freely, on the impulfe of this unreafonable loyalty, which difregarded the ruling powers of their country eftablifhed by law; and, in promoting the intereft of a difpoffeffed individual, confidered a whole people, either as a non-entity, or as worthy to be facrificed for ONE MAN. Such men, acting in confiftency with their principles of falfe loyalty, would have drenched their country in blood to

reftore an exiled Nero, of the *true-bred*, royal
family.

Narrow loyalty, like this, which is but another name for bigotry, muft ever be inimical to a monarch limited by laws, wifhing to
govern by them, and owing his feat on his
throne to a revolution, to the expulfion of
a pre-occupant, and the refufal of a pretender's claim. It muft ever keep alive a
doubt of his title. If it affumes the appearance of affection for him, it may be fufpected as
the kifs of Judas. If it fhould feduce him to
extend his power beyond the conftitutional
limits, it would lead him to deftruction ; and
involve a people in all the mifery of revolu-
tionary diforder. Is then fuch loyalty a public
virtue ? In cunning men it is but mean fervility endeavoring to ingratiate itfelf with the
prince, for honors and emoluments. In the
fimple ones, it is filly fuperftition. In both,
it is injurious to the king of a free country
and to the conftitution. It confines that attention to one branch, which ought duly to be
diftributed among ALL, and to comprehend, in
its attachment, that *main root and ftock*, from
which all the branches grow, the PEOPLE AT
LARGE.

Neverthelefs, fuch is the fubtle policy of
thofe who are actuated by the principles of
Tories, Jacobites, royalifts, defpots, (call
them by which name you pleafe,) that they
continue to reprefent every fpirited effort in
favor of the people's rights, as originating in

disloyalty. The best friends to the constitution in its purity, and therefore the best friends to the limited monarch, are held out, both to public and to royal detestation, as disaffected to the person of the prince. Every stratagem is used to delude the common and unthinking part of the people into a belief, that their only way of displaying loyalty is, to display a most servile obsequiousness to the throne, and to oppose every popular measure. The procurers of addresses, couch them in the most unmanly language of submission, and approach with a degree of prostration of sentiment, worthier to be received by the great mogul or the Chinese emperor, than the chief magistrate of a free people. The composers and presenters of such testimonies of loyalty, hoping for knighthood at least, if not some more splendid or substantial effect of royal gratitude, exhaust the language of all its synonymous terms, to express their abject servility. Yet, after all, of such a nature is their loyalty, that, if a Stuart or a Robespierre were the possessor of power, their mean and hollow professions of attachment would be equally ardent and importunate. *The powers that be* are the powers which they worship. The proffer of their lives and fortunes is the common sacrifice. But to distinguish their loyalty, they would go farther than the addressers of the foolish and unfortunate James, and present their souls to be disposed of by their earthly Deity; knowing it to be a *safe* oblation.

As great refpect is due to the office of the
fupreme magiftrate, fo alfo is great affection
due to his perfon, while he conducts himfelf
with propriety, and confults the happinefs of
the people. The moft decorous language
fhould be ufed to him, the moft refpectful
behaviour preferved towards him ; every mode
adopted of fhewing him proofs of love and
honor, *on this fide idolatry.* Arduous is his
tafk, though honorable. It fhould be fweet-
ened by every mode which true and fincere
loyalty can devife. I would rather exceed,
than fall fhort of the deference due to the office
and the man. But I will not pay a limited
monarch, at the head of a free people, fo ill a
compliment, as to treat him as if he were a
defpot, ruling over a land of flaves. I cannot
adopt the fpirit of defpotifm in a land of
liberty ; and I muft reprobate that falfe, felfifh,
adulatory loyalty, which, feeking nothing but
its own bafe ends of avarice or ambition, and
feeling no real attachment either to the perfon
or the office of the king, contributes neverthelefs to diffufe by its example, a fervile, abject
temper, highly promotive of the defpotic fpirit.

But the *minifters* of ftate have fometimes
prefumed fo far on prefent poffeffion of power,
as to attempt to make the people believe, that a
loyalty is due to *them* ; that an oppofition to
their will is a proof of defective loyalty ; a
remonftrance againft *their* meafures, a mark
of difaffection. They have not been unfuc-
cefsful. The fervile herds who come forward

into public life, folely *to be bought up*, when marketable, are, for the moft part, more inclined to worfhip the minifter than the monarch. While it is the *prieft* who divides among the facrificers the flefh of the victim, many attend with devotion at the facrifice; who are more defirous of propitiating the prieft than the Deity. There are many who, if they had it in their power, would make it conftructive treafon to cenfure any minifter, whofe continuance in place is neceffary to realize their profpects of riches and titular diftinction. Such men wander up and down fociety as fpies, and mark thofe who blame the *minifter*, as perfons to be fufpected of difloyalty. They ufually fix on them fome nickname, in order to depreciate their characters in the eyes of the people, and prevent them from ever rifing to fuch a degree of public efteem, as might render them competitors for minifterial douceurs. Affociations are formed by fuch men, under pretence of patriotifm and loyalty, but with no other real defign, than that of keeping the minifter in place, whom they hope to find a bountiful pay-mafter of their fervices, at the public expence.

True loyalty has no connection with all this meannefs and felfifhnefs. True loyalty is manly, while obedient, and refpects itfelf, while it pays a voluntary and cheerful deference to authority and the perfons invefted with it. It throws fordid confiderations afide, and having nothing in view but the general good, bears an affection, and shews that affection, to the whole of a system established for the preservation of order and liberty. It is not misguided by pompous names, nor blinded by the glitter of external parade; but values offices and officers in the state, for the good they actually promote, for the important functions they perform, for the efficient place they fill, in the finely constituted machine of a well-regulated community.

Such loyalty, I believe, does abound in England, notwithstanding the calumnies of interested men, who would misrepresent and cry down all real patriotism, that their own counterfeit may obtain currency. Men who possess such loyalty, will be found the best friends to kings; if ever those times should return, which are said to afford the truest test of friendship, the times of adversity.

May those times never come! but yet let us cherish the true loyalty and explode the false; because the true is the best security to limited monarchy and constitutional liberty: while the false, by diffusing a spirit of despotism, equally inimical to the constitution and to human happiness, is destroying the legal limitations, undermining the established systems, and introducing manners and principles at once degrading to human nature, and pregnant with misery to nations.

G.

SECTION IX.

On taking Advantage of popular Commotions, accidental Exceffes, and foreign Revolutions, to extend Prerogative and Power, and encroach on the Liberties of the People.

THE riots in London, which, to the difgrace of magiftracy, and the boafted vigilance of minifters, (richly paid as they are, to guard the public fafety), arrived from contemptible beginnings to a formidable magnitude in the year 1780, have been confidered by courtiers, and thofe who are continually laboring to exalt prerogative at the expence of liberty, as extremely favorable to their purpofe. They caufed an univerfal panic. The cowardice, folly, and perhaps wickednefs of certain public functionaries, were the true caufe of the extenfive mifchief; but the exceffes of a few moft wretched rioters, who fcarcely knew what they were doing; children, women, and drunken perfons, were attributed to the PEOPLE. Arguments were drawn from the event againft popular characters, popular books, popular affemblies, and in favor of military coercion. Military affociations in the capital were encouraged, and the bank of England became a barrack. Liberty has few votaries in comparifon with Property. The alarm was artfully increafed, and the fpirit of defpotifm

grew under its operation. The Tory and Jacobite party exulted over the ruins, and would
have rejoiced in building a Baftille with the
dilapidations. " See," faid they, as they
triumphed over the fcene, " the effects of *power*
in the hands of the PEOPLE!"

But the truth is, the *people*, the grand mafs
of the community, were not at all concerned
in effecting the mifchief; for I cannot call a
fortuitous affemblage of boys, beggars, women,
and drunkards, the people. The firft irregularities might have been fuppreffed by the
flighteft exertions of manly fpirit. But thofe
who were poffeffed of efficient places and their
emoluments, enjoying the fweets of office without fuffering a fenfe of its duties to embitter
them, difplayed no fpirit, and left it to be fairly
inferred that they had it not. The people at
large were not to be blamed for thefe unfortunate events; the whole of the culpability be-
longed to the appointed minifters of the law,
in whom the people trufted and were deceived.
The blame, however, was laid on the people;
and thofe who, from their arbitrary principles,
wifhed to difcredit all popular interference in
government, rejoiced at the calamity, as an
aufpicious event, confirming all their theories,
and juftifying their practice.

The artful encroachers on liberty were not
deceived in calculating the effects refulting
from this total dereliction of duty on the part
of the civil magiftrate. Almoft immediately a
a damp was caft on the generous ardor, which,

under a Wyvil, a Richmond, a Portland, and a Pitt, was feeking the falvation of the country, in a well-timed and deliberate reform of the houfe of commons. A few, indeed, remained equally zealous in the virtuous caufe; but the minds of the many were palfied by the panic, and feemed ready to acquiefce under every corruption attended with tranquillity, rather than rifk a reform, which, they were taught to believe, could not be effected without popular commotion. Toryifm faw the change with delight, and employed all its influence in augmenting and continuing the political torpor.

In a few years the public mind feemed to have relinquifhed its intentions of effecting a fpeedy reform. It feemed to adopt the phyfician's maxim, *Malum bene* pofitum ne moveto;* and hefitated to undertake the removal of a local pain, left it fhould throw the morbid matter over the whole habit. The fear of exciting a general inflammation prevented men from probing and cleaning the inveterate ulcer. In the mean time, the fore is growing worfe, and if not ftopped in its progrefs, muft terminate in a mortification.

Thus important and extenfive were the confequences of a popular tumult, dangerous indeed and terrible in itfelf, but artfully exaggerated and abufed by interefted courtiers, for the prevention of parliamentary reform, and the difcredit of all popular proceedings.

---

* Though this evil is *malum* male *pofitum.*

When any appeal to the people was in agitation, on any bufinefs whatever, it was fufficient to fay, " Remember the riots," and the intended meafure was immediately relinquifhed. A glorious opportunity for the growth of defpotic opinions! The high-church, and high-government bigots rejoiced as if they had gained a complete victory. They already fang Te Deum.

But in the midft of their triumphs, as human affairs are feldom long ftationary, the French revolution commenced. Every honeft and enlightened mind exulted at it; but the news was like a death-bell to the ears of the fycophants. So large, fo powerful a part of Europe emancipated from the fangs of defpotifm, blafted all the budding hopes of thofe who are rather meditating the eftablifhment than the demolition of abfolute rule. Ariftocratical pride was mortified. Every fullen fentiment, every angry paffion, rofe in the difappointed bofom of that ambition, which feeks its own elevation on the depreffion of the people. But liberty and humanity fympathized in the joy of millions, reftored to the rights which God and Nature gave them; and which had been gradually ftolen from them by the fpirit of defpotifm, acting, for mutual aid, in alliance with fuperftition.

But the morning which rofe fo beautifully in the political horizon of France was foon overclouded. The paffions of leaders, jealous of each other, menaced from within and from

without, hunted by furrounding enemies till
they were driven to phrenzy, burft forth in
tremendous fury. Cruelties, which even defpots
might fhudder to perpetrate, were the effects of
a fituation rendered dangerous in the extreme,
and almoft defperate, by the general attack of
all neighboring nations. The friends of liberty
and humanity wept ; but the factors of defpotifm triumphed once more. " Here," faid
they, " we have another inftance of the unfitnefs of the people for the poffeffion of power,
and the mifchievous effects of exceffive liberty."
Every art which ingenuity can practife, and
influence affift in its operation, was exerted to
abufe and villify the French revolution. Affociations were formed to diffeminate childifh
books, favoring the fpirit of defpotifm, addreffed to the meaneft of the people, who yet
had too much fenfe to be feduced by fentiments, doctrines, and language calculated only
for the meridian of the nurfery. Profecutions
and perfecutions abounded ; and it become *fedition* to hint the propriety of parliamentary
reformation. The alarmifts, as they were
called, were fo fuccefsful in propagating the
old tory tenets, under the favorable influence
of the panic of real danger, and the deteſta-
tion which French executions had juſtly occaſioned, that fome of the ftauncheft friends of
the people, men brought into the country at
the revolution, owing all their honours and
emoluments to it, and hitherto profeffed and
zealous whigs, deferted the ftandard of liberty,

and took diftinguifhed pofts under the banners of the enemy.

The fpirit of defpotifm now went forth with greater confidence than it had ever affumed fince the expulfion of the Stuarts. Its advocates no longer fculked ; no longer walked in mafquerade. They boafted of their principles, and pretended that they alone were friends to law, order, and religion They talked of the laws of England not being fevere enough for the punifhment of fedition, and boldly expreffed a wifh that the laws of Scotland might be adopted in their place. Active promoters of parliamentary reform were now accufed of treafonable intentions by the very perfons who were onee loudeft in their invectives againft the corruption of the houfe of commons. Newfpapers were hired to calumniate the beft friends of freedom. Writers appeared in various modes, commending the old government of France ; and pouring the moft virulent abufe on all who promoted or defended its abolition. Priefts who panted for preferment preached defpotifm in their pulpits, and garretteers who hungered after places or penfions, racked their invention to propagate its fpirit by their pamphlets. Fear in the well-meaning, felf-intereft in the knavifh, and fyftematic fubtilty in the great party of tories, caufed a general uproar in favor of principles and practices hoftile to conftitutional liberty.

It is, however, the nature of all violent paroxyfms to be of tranfient duration. The friends of man may therefore hope that panic fears, fervile fycophantifm, and artful bigotry, will not long prevail over cool reafon and liberal philanthropy. The drunken delirium will pafs off; and fober fenfe will foon fee and acknowledge, that the accidental evils which have arifen in a neighboring nation, during a fingular ftruggle for liberty, can be no arguments in favor of defpotifm, which is a *conftant evil* of the moft deftructive nature. The body in high and robuft health is moft fubject to the heat of an inflammatory fever ; but no man in his fenfes will therefore ceafe to wifh for high and robuft health.

Senfible men, and true friends to the conftitution, and therefore to the king, who forms fo confiderable a part of it, will be on their guard againft falfe alarms excited by courtiers ; left in the fear of fome future evil, from popular commotion, they lay afide that everwaking vigilance which is neceffary to guard the good in poffeffion, their conftitutional liberty, from the fecret depredation of the artful fpoiler, who is always on the watch to encroach on popular rights and privileges.

Riots, tumults, and popular commotions, are indeed truly dreadful, and to be avoided with the utmoft care by the lovers of liberty. Peace, good order, and fecurity to all ranks, are the natural fruits of a free conftitution. True patriots will be careful to difcourage every thing which tends to deftroy them ; not only becaufe whatever tends to deftroy them

tends to deſtroy all human happineſs, but alſo
becauſe even an accidental outrage in popular
aſſemblies and proceedings, is uſed by the
artful to diſcredit the cauſe of liberty. By the
utmoſt attention to preſerving the public peace,
true patriots will defeat the malicious deſigns
of ſervile courtiers; but, whatever may happen, they will not deſert the cauſe of human
nature. Through a dread of licentiouſneſs,
they will not forſake the ſtandard of liberty.
It is the part of fools to fall upon Scylla in
ſtriving to avoid Charybdis. Who but a fool
would wiſh to reſtore the perpetual deſpotiſm
of the old French government, through a
dread of the tranſient outrages of a Pariſian
tumult? Both are deſpotic while they laſt.
But the former is a torrent that flows for ever;
the latter only a land flood, that covers the
meadows to-day, and diſappears on the mor-
row.

Dr. Price has a paſſage ſo applicable to the
preſent ſubject, that I ſhall beg leave to cloſe
this ſection by the citation of it: and on the
mention of his name, I muſt pay a trifling tri-
bute to his memory, which is the more neceſſary, as his character has been ſcandalouſly
aſperſed by thoſe who are ever buſy in diſ-
crediting the people and their friends, and who,
pretending a love of goodneſs and religion,
blacken with their fouleſt calumny thoſe who
are ſingularly remarkable for both, for no other
reaſon than that, under the influence of goodneſs and religion, ſuch perſons eſpouſe the

caufe of freedom, and prefer the happinefs of millions to the pomp and pride of a few afpirants at unlimited dominion. Meek, gentle, and humane; acute, eloquent, and profoundly fkilled in politics and philofophy; take him for all and all, the qualities of his heart, with the abilities of his head, and you may rank PRICE among the firft ornaments of his age. Let his enemies produce from all their boafted defpots and defpotical Satraps, any one of his contemporaries whom, in the manner of Plutarch, they may place by his fide as a parallel. Pofterity will do him the juftice of which the proud have robbed him, and fnatch him from the calumniators, to place him in the temple of perfonal honor, high among the benefactors to the human race.

But I return from the digreffion, into which I was led by an honeft indignation againft the vileft of calumnies againft the beft of men. Thefe are the words of Dr. Price:

' Licentioufnefs and defpotifm are more near-
' ly allied than is commonly imagined. They
' are both alike inconfiftent with liberty, and
' the true end of government; nor is there any
' other difference between them, than that one
' is the *licentioufnefs* of GREAT MEN, and the
' other the licentioufnefs of *little* men; or that
' by one, the perfons and property of a people
' are fubject to outrage and invafion from a
' king, or a lawlefs body of grandees; and that
' by the other, they are fubject to the like out-
' rage from a lawlefs mob. *In avoiding one of*

‘ *thefe evils, mankind have often run into the*
‘ *other.* But all well-conftituted governments
‘ guard equally againft both. Indeed, of the
‘ two, the laft is, on feveral accounts, the leaft
‘ to be dreaded, and has done the leaft mifchief.
‘ It may truly be faid, if licentioufnefs has def-
‘ troyed its thoufands, defpotifm has deftroyed
‘ its millions. The former having little power,
‘ AND NO SYSTEM TO SUPPORT IT, neceffa-
‘ rily finds its own remedy; and a people foon
‘ get out of the tumult and anarchy attending
‘ it. But a defpotifm, wearing a form of go-
‘ vernment, and being armed with its force, is
‘ an evil not to be conquered without dreadful
‘ ftruggles. It goes on from age to age, debaf-
‘ ing the human faculties, levelling all diftinc-
‘ tions, and preying on the rights and bleffings
‘ of fociety. It deferves to be added, that in
‘ a ftate difturbed by licentioufnefs, there is an
‘ ANIMATION which is favourable to the hu-
‘ man mind, and puts it upon exerting its pow-
‘ ers; but in a ftate habituated to defpotifm,
‘ all is ftill and torpid. A dark and favage
‘ tyranny ftifles every effort of genius, and the
‘ mind lofes all its fpirit and dignity.’

Heaven grant, that in guarding againft a
fever, we fall not into a palfy!

SECTION X.

When Human Life is held cheap, it is a Symptom of a prevailing Spirit of Despotism.

THERE is nothing which I can so relactantly pardon in the GREAT ONES of this world, as the little value they entertain for the life of a man. Property, if seized or lost, may be restored; and, without property, man may enjoy a thousand delightful pleasures of existence. The sun shines as warmly on the poor as on the rich; and the gale of health breathes its balsam into the cottage casement on the heath, no less sweetly and salubriously than into the portals of the palace. But can the lords of this world, who are so lavish of the lives of their inferiors, with all their boasted power, give the cold heart to beat again, or relume the light of the eye once dimmed by the shades of death? Accursed despots, shew me your authority for taking away that which ye never gave, and cannot give; for undoing the work of God, and extinguishing the lamp of life which was illuminated with a ray from heaven. Where is your charter to privilege murder? You do the work of Satan, who was a destroyer; and your right, if you possess any, must have originated from the father of mischief and misery.

There is nothing ſo precious as the life of a man. A philoſopher of antiquity, who poſ-ſeſſed not the religion of philanthropy, who knew not that man came from heaven, and is to return thither; who never heard the doc-trine authenticated, that man is favored with a communication of the divine nature by the Holy Spirit of God; yet, under all theſe diſ-advantages, maintained that HOMO EST RES SACRA, that every HUMAN CREATURE is CONSECRATED to God, and therefore invio-lable by his fellow man, without profanation. All the gold of Ophir, all the gems of Gol-conda, cannot buy a ſingle life, nor pay for its loſs. It is above all price.

Yet take a view of the world, and you will immediately be led to conclude, that ſcarcely any thing is viler than human life. Crimes which have very little moral evil, if any, and which therefore cannot incur the vengeance of a juſt and merciful Deity, are puniſhed with death at a human tribunal. I mean ſtate crimes; ſuch actions, conduct, ſpeeches, as are made crimes by deſpots, but are not recogniſed as ſuch in the decalogue; ſuch as may proceed from the pureſt and moſt virtuous principle, from the moſt enlarged benevolence, from wiſdom and unaffected patriotiſm; ſuch as may proceed from mere warmth of temper, neither intending nor accompliſhing any miſchief; the mere effects of error, as innocent too in its conſequences as its origin. But the deſpot is offended or frightened; for guilt trembles at

H

the leaft alarm, and nothing but the blood of the accufed can expiate the offence.

Yet numerous as are the innocent victims of the tribunal, where to offend the ftate is the greateft abomination that man can commit, they are loft and difappear when compared to the myriads facrificed to the demon of war. Defpotifm delights in war. It is its element. As the bull knows, by inftinct, that his ftrength is in his horns, and the eagle trufts in his talons; fo the defpot feels his puiffance moft, when furrounded by his foldiery arrayed for battle. With the fword in his hand, and his artillery around him, he rejoices in his might, and glories in his greatnefs. Blood muft mark his path; and his triumph is incomplete, till death and deftruction ftalk over the land, the harbingers of his triumphant cavalcade.

We hear much of neceffary wars; but it is certainly true, that a real, abfolute, unavoidable neceffity for war, fuch as alone can render it juft, has feldom occurred in the hiftory of man. The pride, the wanton cruelty of abfolute princes, caring nothing for human life, have in all ages, without the leaft neceffity, involved the world in war; and therefore it is the common caufe of all mankind to abolifh abfolute power; and to difcourage, by every lawful means, the fpirit that leads to any degree of it. No individual, however good, is fit to be trufted with fo dangerous a depofit. His goodnefs may be corrupted by the magnitude of the truft; and it is the nature of power, uncontrolled by fear or law, to vitiate the beſt diſpoſitions. He who would have ſhuddered to ſpill a drop of blood, in a hoſtile conteſt, as a private man, ſhall deluge whole provinces, as an abſolute prince, and laugh over the ſubjugated plains which he has fertilized with human gore.

What are the chief conſiderations with ſuch men, previouſly to going to war, and at its concluſion ? Evidently the expence of MONEY. Little is ſaid or thought of the lives loſt, or devoted to be loſt, except as matters of *pecuniary* value. Humanity, indeed, weeps in ſilence and ſolitude, in the ſequeſtered ſhade of private life ; but is a ſingle tear ſhed in courts, and camps, and cabinets ? When men high in command, men of fortune and family, fall, their deeds are blazoned, and they figure in hiſtory ; but who, ſave the poor widow and the orphan, enquire after the very names of the rank and file ? There they lie, a maſs of human fleſh, not ſo much regretted by the deſpots as the horſes they rode, or the arms they bore. While ſhips often go down to the bottom, ſtruck by the iron thunderbolts of war, and not a life is ſaved ; the national loſs is eſtimated by the deſpot, according to the weight of metal waſted, and the magnitude and expence of the wooden caſtle.

Ploratur lachrymis amiſſa pecunia veris !

God, we read, made man in his own image ; and our Saviour taught us that he was the heir of immortality. God made no diftinction of perfons; but behold a being, born to a fceptre, though a poor, puny, fhivering mortal like the reft, prefumes to fell, and let out for hire, thefe images of God, to do the work of butchers, in any caufe, and for any paymafter, on any number of unoffending fellow-creatures, who are ftanding up in defence of their hearths, their altars, their wives, their children, and their liberty. Great numbers of men, trained to the trade of human butchery, are conftantly ready to be let to hire, to carry on the work of defpotifm, and to fupport, by the money they earn in this hellifh employment, the luxurious vices of the wretch who calls them his property. Can that ftate of human affairs be right and proper, which permits a mifcreant, fcarcely worthy the name of a man, funk in effeminacy, the flave of vice, often the moft abominable kind of vice, ignorant and illiterate, debilitated with difeafe, weak in body as in mind, to have fuch dominion of hundreds of thoufands, his fuperiors by nature, as to let them out for pay, to murder the innocent ftranger in cold blood?

Though, in free countries and limited monarchies, fuch attrocious villainy is never permitted, yet it becomes the friends of liberty and humanity to be on their guard againft the prevalence of any opinions and practices which depreciate man, as man, and vilify human life. None can tell to what enormous depravity fmall conceffions may lead; when the horror of crimes is gradually foftened by the wicked arts of proud intriguers, idolizing grandeur and trampling on poverty.

What fhall we think of the practice of what is called CRIMPING? Is it to be allowed in a free country? Are not men bought, inveigled, or forced by it, as if they were cattle, beafts of the field or the foreft, and capable of becoming the *property* of the purchafer or the captor? If a nation fhould behold with patience fuch a practice increafing and encouraged by the great, would there not be reafon to fufpect, that it had loft the fpirit of freedom, and was preparing to fubmit its neck to the yoke of defpotifm? Is not an impreffed failor or a kidnapped foldier one of the images of God? Is he not entitled to all the rights of nature, and the fociety of which he is a member? Does poverty disfranchize a man, rob him of his rights, and render his *life* a commodity to be bought and fold, or thrown away, at the will of a rich man, who is enabled to take advantage of his want, and add to the misfortune of indigence the curfe of flavery? Are a few pieces of filver to be allowed, by connivance, if not by legal permiffion, as the price of blood, when poverty, but not the will, confents to the fale?

Even if BOXING were ever to become a fpectacle patronized by princes, and encouraged by a people, there would be reafon to fear left MAN, AS MAN, had loft his value; left life were eftimated of little price: and left the ſpirit of deſpotiſm were gradually inſinuating itſelf into the community. There would be reaſon to fear leſt times, like thoſe of the latter Roman emperors, were returning, and that men might be kept like wild beaſts, to be brought on the ſtage and fight for public diverſion, and to be murdered for the evening's amuſement of faſhionable lords and ladies, at an opera-houſe.

The dignity of human nature, in deſpotical countries, is treated as a burleſque. A man is leſs dignified than a pampered horſe, and his life infinitely leſs valued. But in a land of liberty, like ours, every man ſhould learn to venerate himſelf and his neighbor, as a noble creature, dependent only on God, on reaſon, on law. Life, under ſuch circumſtances, is a pearl of great price. Every human being, under ſuch circumſtances, is of equal value in the fight of God. They, therefore, who, in conſequence of civil elevation, hold any man's life cheap and vile, unleſs he has forfeited his rights by enormous crimes, are guilty of rebellion againſt God, and ought to be hunted out of ſociety; as the wolf, once the native of England's foreſts, was exterminated from the iſland.

SECTION XI.

Indifference of the middle and lower Claſſes of the People to public Affairs, highly favorable to the encroachments of the Tory Principle, and therefore to the Spirit of Deſpotiſm.

THE opinion, that the majority of the PEOPLE have no concern in political diſquiſitions, is at once inſulting and injurious. They who maintain it, evidently mean to make a ſeparation in the minds of men, between the government and the nation. It is inſulting to the nation, as it inſinuates that they are either incapable or unworthy of interfering; and it is injurious to the government and the whole community, as it renders that power, which ought to be an object of love, an object of terror and jealouſy.

Such an opinion is fit only for a country ſubject to abſolute power, and in which the people, conſidered only as conquered ſlaves, hold their lives and all their enjoyments at the will of the conqueror. As it originates in deſpotic principles, ſo it tends to produce and diffuſe them.

As to the intellectual abilities of the people, it is certain that ſome of the ableſt ſtateſmen, law-givers, and men of buſineſs, have originated from that order which is called plebeian. There is a ſingular vigor of mind, as well as of body, in men who have been placed out of the reach of luxury and corruption by their poor or obſcure condition ; and when this vigor of mind has been improved by a competent education, and ſubſequent opportunities of experience and obſervation, it has led to very high degrees of mental excellence. Plebeians have arrived at the very firſt rank in all arts and ſciences ; and there is nothing in politics ſo peculiarly abſtruſe or recondite, as to be incomprehenſible by intellects that have penetrated into the profoundeſt depths of philoſophy.

As to the right of the people to think, let him who denies it, deny, at the ſame time, their right to breathe. They can no more avoid thinking than breathing. God formed them to do both ; and though ſtateſmen often act as if they wiſhed to oppoſe the will of the Deity, yet happily they want the power. And ſince men muſt think, is it poſſible to prevent them from thinking of the *government* ? upon the right conduct of which depend their liberty, their property, and their lives. It is their duty to watch over the poſſeſſors of power, leſt they ſhould be prevented, by the encroaching nature of power, from leaving to their poſterity that freedom which they inherited ; a natural right, preſerved from the oppreſſor's infringement by the blood of their virtuous anceſtors.

But ſuch is the effect of political artifice, under the management of court ſycophants, that the middle ranks of people are taught to

believe, that they ought not to trouble themfelves with affairs of ftate. They are taught
to think that a certain fet of men come into
the world like demigods, poffeffed of right,
power, and intellectual abilities, to rule the
earth, as God rules the univerfe, without
control. They are taught to believe, that free
inquiry and manly remonftrance are the fin of
fedition. They are taught to believe, that
they are to labor by the fweat of their brow to
get money for the taxes ; and when they have
paid them, to go to work again for more, to
pay the next demand without a murmur. Their
children may ftarve : they may be obliged to
fhut out the light of heaven, and the common
air which the beafts on the wafte enjoy ; they
may be difabled from procuring a draught of
wholefome and refrefhing beverege after the
day's labor which has raifed the money to pay
the tax ; they may not be able to buy the materials for cleanlinefs of their perfons, when
defiled by the fame labor ; yet they muft acquiefce in total filence. They muft read no
obnoxious papers or pamphlets, and they muft
not utter a complaint, at the houfe where they
are compelled to go for refrefhment, which
the tax prevents them from enjoying at home
with their little ones. Yet they have nothing
to do with public affairs ; and if they fhew the
leaft tendency to inquiry or oppofition, they
fuffer a double punifhment, firft, from their
lordly landlord and employer, and fecondly,
from profecution for turbulence and fedition.

The legal punifhments attending the expreffion of difcontent, by any overt-act, are fo
fevere, and the ill-grounded terrors of them fo
artfully diffeminated, that rather than incur
the leaft danger, they fubmit in filence to the
hardeft oppreffion.

Even the middle ranks are terrified into a
tame and filent acquiefcence. They learn to
confider politics as a dangerous fubject, not to
be touched without hazard of liberty or life.
They fhrink therefore from the fubject. They
will neither read nor converfe upon it. They
pay their contribution to a war, and take a
minifter's word that it is juft and neceffary.
Better part with a little money patiently, fince
part with it we muft, fay they, than by daring
to inveftigate the caufes or conduct of public
meafures, rifk a prifon or a gibbet.

Great and opulent landholders often exercife
a defpotifm in their petty dominions, which
ftifles the voice of truth, and blinds the eye of
inquiry. If tenants utter a fentiment in public, adverfe to the courtly opinions of the great
man, who is looking up to a minifter for a
douceur for himfelf, his fons, his natural fons,
or his nephews, or coufins, the beneficial leafe
will not be renewed at its expiration. What
has fuch a fellow to do with politics? Fine
times, indeed, when ruftics dare to have an
opinion on the poffibility of avoiding a war,
which a minifter has declared unavoidable! A
thoufand modes of harraffing and embarraffing
the fubordinate neighbor, who dares think

for himſelf, are practiſed by the ſlaviſh rich
man, who, poſſeſſing enough to maintain a
thouſand poor families, is yet greedily graſp-
ing at a place or a penſion ; or, if he be too
opulent to think of ſuch addition, which is
ſeldom the caſe, ſtill views with eager eye and
panting heart, at leaſt a baronetage, and perhaps a coronet, glittering on high with irre-
ſiſtible brilliancy.

Groſs ignorance, unmanly fear of puniſh-
ment, and obſequiouſneſs to overgrown ariſto-
crats, at once ſervile and tyrannic, operate in
conjunction to prevent the middle and lower
ranks from attending to the concerns of the
community, of which they are very important
members ; contributing to its ſupport by their
perſonal exertions, their conſumption of taxed
commodities, and the payment of impoſts.

There is alſo an habitual indolence which
prevents many from concerning themſelves
with any thing but that which immediately
affects their pecuniary intereſt. Such perſons
would be content to live under the Grand
Seignor, ſo long as they might eat, drink, and
ſleep in peace. But ſuch muſt never be the
prevailing ſentiment of a people, whoſe anceftors have left them the inheritance of liberty,
as an eſtate unalienable, and of more value
than the mines of Peru. Such indolence is
treachery to poſterity ; it is a baſe and cowardly dereliction of a truſt, which they who
confided it are prevented by death from guarding or withdrawing.

The middle and lower ranks, too numerous to be bribed by a minister, and almost out of the reach of court corruption, constitute the best bulwarks of liberty. They are a natural and most efficacious check on the strides of power. They ought therefore to know their consequence, and to preserve it with unwinking vigilance. They have a stake, as it is called, a most important stake, in the country. Let not the overgrown rich only pretend to have a stake in the country, and claim from it an exclusive privilege to regard its concerns. The middle ranks have their native *freedom* to preserve; their birth-right to protect from the dangerous attacks of enormous and overbearing affluence. Inasmuch as liberty and security are more conducive to happiness than excessive riches, it must be allowed, that the poor man's stake in the country is as great as the rich man's. If he should lose this stake, his poverty, which was consoled by the consciousness of his liberty and security, becomes an evil infinitely aggravated. He has nothing left to defend him from the oppressor's wrong and the proud man's contumely. He may soon degenerate to a beast of burden; for the mind sinks with the slavery of the condition. But while a man feels that he is free, and fills a respectable rank, as a freeman, in the community, he walks with upright port, conscious, even in rags, of comparative dignity.

While the middle and lower ranks acquaint themselves with their rights, they should also imprefs on their minds a fenfe of their duties, and return obedience and allegiance for protection.

To perform the part of good members of the community, their underftandings muft be duly enlightened, and they muft be encouraged, rather than forbidden, to give a clofe attention to all public tranfactions. Difagreements in private life are often juftly called mifunderftandings. It is through want of clear conceptions that feuds and animofities frequently happen in public. The *many* are not fo mad as they are reprefented. They act honeftly and zealoufly according to their knowledge. Give them fair and full information, and they will do the thing that is right, in confequence of it. But nothing more generally and juftly offends them, than an attempt to conceal or diftort facts which concern them; an attempt to render them the dupes of interefted ambition, planning its own elevation on the ruins of their independence.

I wifh, as a friend to peace, and an enemy to all tumultuary and riotous proceedings, that the mafs of the people fhould underftand the conftitution, and know, that redrefs of grievances is to be fought and obtained by appeals to the law; by appeals to reafon; without appealing, except in cafes of the very laft neceffity, which feldom occur, to the arm of violence. I advife them patiently to bear, while there is but a hope of melioration, even flagrant

I

abufes, if no other mode of redrefs appears, for the prefent, but convulfion. I would exhort them, not to fly from the defpotifm of an adminiftration, to the defpotifm of an enraged populace. I would have them value the life, the tranquillity, the property, of the rich and great, as well as thofe of the poor and obfcure. I would wifh them to labor at promoting human happinefs in all ranks, and be affured, that happinefs, like health, is not to be enjoyed in a fever.

To accomplifh thefe ends, I think too much pains cannot be beftowed in teaching them to underftand the true nature of civil liberty ; and in demonftrating to them, that it is injured by all exceffes, whether the exceffes originate in courts or cottages.

And furely thofe men are neither friends to their country nor to human nature, who, for the fake of keeping down the lower orders, would object to teaching the people the value of a pure reprefentation, free fuffrage, a free prefs, and trial by jury. Thefe are the things that are moft likely to endear the conftitution to them, to render them truly loyal, chearfully obedient, and zealoufly peaceable.

It is not the delufive publications of interefted and fycophantic affociators which can produce this valuable purpofe. Writings fo evidently partial, perfuade none but thofe that are already perfuaded ; and deceive none but thofe that are willing to be deceived. Truth only, will have weight with the great body of the people, who have nothing to hope from minifterial favor, or to fear, while the conftitution is unimpaired, from minifterial difpleafure.

Let the people, then, be at liberty, uninterrupted by perfons actuated by tory and high prerogative principles, to ftudy politics, to read pamphlets, and to debate, if they choofe it, in focieties. The more they know of a good conftitution and a good adminiftration, the better they will behave. Miniftry need not hire newfpapers, or employ fpies. Let them build their confidence in truth and juftice, and the enlightened people will conftitute its firmeft buttrefs. Let it never be faid, that the people have nothing to do with politics, left it fhould be inferred, that fuch politics have no regard to the people.

SECTION XII.

The despotic Spirit is inclined to discourage Commerce, as unfavorable to its Purposes.

IS man a reasonable creature? Is he then most perfect and happy, when his conduct is regulated by reason? If so, then the boasted age of CHIVALRY was an age of folly, madness, and misery. It was an age in which a romantic imagination triumphed by force over the plainest and strongest decisions of common sense. It was an age in which pride and wanton insolence trampled on the rights and happiness of human nature. To express my idea of it in a word, it was an age of QUIXOTISM, in which Europe appeared as one vast country of bedlamites. Yet, wonderful to relate, men have lately arisen, pretending to extraordinary degrees of the distinctive faculty of man, professing the most unbounded philanthropy, but at the same time regretting that the age of chivalry is no more.

The truth is, the spirit of chivalry was highly favorable to the spirit of despotism. Every feudal baron was a petty tyrant, little differing from the chieftain of a banditti. They were absolute sovereigns over their vassals. Their castles were fortified palaces, from which they issued, regardless of government or law, like lions or tigers from their dens, to deform the land with blood and devaftation. What was the fituation of the PEOPLE, the million, in thofe days of mifchievous folly? It was fcarcely better than that of the negroes in the iflands of America. And are thefe times to be regretted in the prefent day? Yes, certainly, by thofe who pine at feeing the condition of the multitude meliorated, and who confider the unfortunate part of their fellow-creatures as a herd of fwine.

At this period of Englifh hiftory, flaves, natives of England, were bought and fold on Englifh ground, juft in the fame manner as the negroes in Africa. One of the chief articles of export from England, in the time of the Anglo-Saxons, was the SLAVE. Slaves were always appendant to manors, like the ftock of cattle on a farm. They were attached to the foil, and were conveyed or defcended with the eftate, under the name of *villains regardant*, *gleba adfcriptitii*. They were never confider-ed as *citizens*; they had no vote, no rights; and were in every refpect, in the eye of the great men who poffeffed them, like goods, chattels, and beafts of burden.

As honeft labor was confidered as SLAVISH, fo alfo was every kind of TRADE. The only clafs efteemed, was that which we fhould now call GENTLEMEN or ESQUIRES. And what was their employment? *Deftruction of their fellow creatures*. They neither *toiled nor fpun*; but they wielded the fword, and fhed blood under the banners of their chief, whenever

he thought proper to wage war with an unoffending neighbor. They were, however,
honorable men ; *all, all honorable* men. But
honor will not fill the belly, nor cloathe the
back ; and pride was obliged to ftoop for food,
raiment, dwellings, and all the comforts and
accommodations of life, to the villain and vaffal ; who were exactly in the rank occupied by
modern tradefmen, mechanics, and artifans.
The *gentleman* of thofe days availed himfelf of
their labor and ingenuity, and then defpifed them.
The GENTLEMEN of modern days, who admire the age of chivalry, and who adopt tory
and arbitrary principles, would be glad to confider this ufeful and ingenious clafs of citizens
in the fame light. ' *Perifh our commerce, live*
' *cur conftitution*. Perifh the loom, the plough,
' the hammer, the axe ; but flourifh the fword.
' Sink the merchant fhip, but let the man of
' war ride on the waves in all her glory."

Such fentiments refemble thofe of the feudal
barons, the moft defpotic GENTLEMEN that
ever difgraced human nature. The old feudal
barons, however, could not always find employment for the fword at home ; and Peter
the monk told them they would be rewarded in
heaven by waging war on Paleftine. They
embarked with the bleffings of the pope on
their banners. It was a fortunate event for the
defpifed vaffals who were left at home. Both
commerce and liberty are greatly indebted to
the crufades for their fubfequent flourifhing
flate. In the abfence of the tyrants, the tradef-

men and artifans exercifed their art and induftry on their own account, and gradually acquired a degree of independence. Many of the barons never returned to opprefs them. Many returned, greatly injured in ftrength, fpirit, and property. Confequently they loft their power. Charters were now fold or granted, and Commerce lifted up her front in defiance of Pride, that, looking down from her caftle on the fhip and manufacturer, defpifed her lowly occupation, while fhe envied her opulence. The country was enriched by arts which the nobles deemed vile. The mafs of the people acquired property, and with it, power and independence. The tyranny of the feudal fyftem, and the nonfenfe of chivalry, which endeavored to create a fantaftic merit, independent of virtue and utility, foon vanifhed when the human mind was at liberty to think for itfelf; and men were emboldened to act freely by a confcioufnefs of poffeffing fkill and property.

But while the human heart is fubject to pride, and fond of power, the fpirit of tyranny, which actuated the old barons in feudal times, will manifeft itfelf, in fome mode or degree, whenever opportunities occur. Commerce was defpifed under the late monarchy in France; and commerce, we have reafon to think, is looked upon with a jealous eye in England, by thofe who are violently attached to fenfelefs grandeur.

Men of this defcription are averfe to commerce, not only from pride, but from policy. They fee commerce enriching and exalting plebeians to a rank in fociety equal to their own; and often furnifhing the means of luxurious enjoyment and fplendor, which they themfelves, with all the pride of birth and the prefumption of office, cannot fupport. Though a war may injure trade, and ruin manufacturing towns, yet it is eagerly engaged in, if it gratifies the revenge of courts, and the pride of nobles. Its ill effects on commerce may be a recommendation of it to thofe who exclaim, " *Perifh commerce, live our conftitution.*" It reduces that afpiring greatnefs of the merchant, which treads on the heels of the grandee, and overtops him. It bleeds the body which appears in the eyes of the great to fhew fymptoms of plethora. It clips the wings which feem ready to emulate the flight of the eagle. It lops the tree which gives umbrage by its fhadow. The favorers of abfolute power would have a nation of gentlemen foldiers, of courtiers, and of titled noblemen; and they view with pain, a nation of gentlemen merchants, of men independent both in fpirit and fortune, enlightened by education, improved by experience, enriched by virtues and ufeful exertion, poffeffing principles of honor founded on honefty, and therefore quite as fcrupulous and nice as if they had been bred in idlenefs, bloated with the pride of anceftry, tyrannically imperious over the active claffes, and at the fame time abject flaves to courtly fafhion.

But, as in a commercial nation, it is impoffible to prevent men of this defcription from fometimes acquiring princely fortunes, it be-

comes a very defirable object, among the politicians attached to arbitrary power, to corrupt
the principal commercial houfes, by raifing in
them the fpirit of vanity and ambition. They
have already acquired money more than fufficient for all the purpofes of aggrandizement.
The next object is honor; that is, a title. A
baronetage is a charming lure to the whole
family. Any favor indeed from the court is
a feather. A title is now and then judicioufly
beftowed. This operates on the rifing race,
and teaches them to undervalue their independence in competition with the fmile of a minifter. The minifter, indeed, has means of
gratifying the avarice as well as the vanity of
the commercial order. Contracts are delicious
douceurs to the afpiring trader : they not only
enrich, but lead to a connection with the
powers that be, and pave with gold the road
of ambition.

But the fun of tory favor which irradiates
the tops of the mountain, feldom reaches the
vale. The millions of humbler adventurers in
commerce and manufacture, who are enriching
their country, and accommodating human life,
in ten thoufand modes that require both virtue
and fkill, are viewed by the promoters of arbitrary power with fovereign contempt. The
truth is, that moft of thefe, notwithftanding
the difdain with which they are treated, are
fome of the moft independent members of the
community. They conftitute a very large portion of the middle rank. They are a firm
phalanx, and commonly enlifted on the fide of

liberty. They can scarcely be otherwise; for they have little to hope or fear from those who call themselves their superiors. They perform a work, or vend a commodity, equivalent to the compensation they receive; and owe no obligation beyond that which civility or benevolence, towards those with whom they negociate, imposes. The customer applies to them for his own convenience. If they be fair traders, they vend their wares at the market price; and if one will not accede to it, they wait patiently for another offer. They do not think themselves bound to make any unmanly submissions to those who deal with them for their own advantage.

A numerous body of men like these, possessing, in the aggregate, a vast property, and consequently, if they could act in concert, a vast power also, cannot but be an object of uneasiness to the co-partners in a proud aristocracy, wishing to engross to themselves the whole world, with all its pleasures, honors, emoluments, and rights. As they cannot destroy this body, their next endeavor is to vilify it, to render it insignificant, to discourage its attention to public affairs, to lessen its profits, and to embarrass its operations by taxes on its most vendible productions. They would gladly render a tradesman as contemptible in England, as it was in France before the revolution. In France, we all know, under its despotic kings, no virtue, no merit, no services to the public or mankind, could wipe off the filthy stain fixed on the character by merchandize. The poorest, most villainous and vicious idiot, who partook of nobleffe, would have been efteemed, in that unhappy period, infinitely fuperior to a Grefham, a Barnard, or a Skinner.

My purpofe in thefe remarks is to exhort the mercantile order to preferve their independence, by preferving a juft fenfe of their own dignity. I fee with pain and alarm the firft men in a great city, the metropolis of the world, whofe *merchants are princes,* crouding with flavifh fubmiffion to the minifter of the day, feconding all his artful purpofes in a corporation, calling out the military on the flighteft occafion, at once to overawe the multitude, and at the fame time to annihilate their own civil and conftitutional authority. If they would but preferve their independence, and retain a due attachment to the people, and the rights of their fellow-citizens, their power and confequence would be infinitely augmented, and the very minifter who buys or cajoles them, would hold them in high eftimation. Ultimately, perhaps, their prefent fordid views might be accomplifhed with greater fuccefs; as they certainly would be, if accomplifhed at all, with more honor and fatisfaction.

Inftead of feparating their interefts, I would fay, let our commerce and our conftitution ever flourifh together. Certain I am, that a flourifhing commerce, by giving power and confequence to the middle and lower ranks of the people, tends more than all the military affociations to preferve the genuine fpirit of the conftitution.

SECTION XII.

The Spirit of Despotism displaying itself in private Life, and proceeding thence to avail itself of the Church and the Military.

MANY who enjoy the great advantages of distinguished rank and enormous wealth, either hereditary or acquired, not contented with those advantages, seem, by their behaviour, to envy the less fortunate of their species the little happiness they retain in their humble sphere. Unsatisfied with the elevation which their birth or fortune has given them, they wish to trample on their inferiors, and to force them still lower in society. Base pride! sordid greediness of wretches, who, notwithstanding they are gratified with all external splendor, and pampered even to loathing with plenty of all good things, yet insult those who minister to their luxuries, and who (however deserving by virtue all that the others possess by chance) sit down with a bare competence, and often in want of real necessaries, food, raiment, and habitation.

The insolence of many among the great, who possess neither knowledge nor virtue, nor any quality useful to mankind, and the contempt with which they look down upon men, whom, though both virtuous and useful, they call their inferiors, excites the honest indignation of all who can think and feel, and who are remote from the fphere of corrupting influ-ence. The natural fenfations of an honeft heart revolt againft it. It is not only moft highly culpable in a moral view, but extremely dangerous in a political. It arifes from the genuine fpirit of defpotifm, and if not checked by the people, muft lead to its univerfal pre-valence. Such a fpirit would allow no rights to the poor, but thofe which cannot be taken away, fuch as the fwine poffefs; the rights of mere animal nature. Such a fpirit hates the people, and would gladly annihilate all of them, but thofe who adminifter to pride and luxury, either as menial fervants, dependent tradefmen or me-chanics, or common foldiers, ready to fhed their own and others blood for a morfel of bread.

Even the beafts are held in higher honor by many *ariftocrats,* than the poor people in their vicinage. Dogs and horfes are fed, lodged, nay, the horfes fometimes clothed fumptuoufly; while the poor laborers in the cot on the fide of the common, are ftarved, fcarcely fheltered by their roofs, and almoft naked. As you ride by the fplendid palace and extenfive park of fome inheritor of overgrown opulence, fome fortunate adventurer, fome favored contractor, penfioner, or placeman, you behold ftables and dog-kennels erected in a ftile of magnificence; externally grand and internally commodious. The dogs and horfes are waited on by MEN appointed for the purpofe, and more amply paid than the laborer, who rifes early, and late takes reft

K

in the work of agriculture or manufacture. After viewing the magnificent ftables, proceed a little farther, and you fee, on the road-fide, and in the village, wretched houfes, without glafs in the windows; the poor laborer, his wife, and children in rags; fcarcely able to procure the fmalleft fire in the coldeft weather, threatened with profecution if they pick up fticks in the park ; and, if they refufe to *endure* extreme cold and hunger, in danger of being hanged, and certain of imprifonment. The great man, who fpends much of his time in the ftable and kennel, and who careffes the horfes and dogs, condefcends not to enter the cottages. He receives the lowly obeifance of the inhabitants without returning it. Look at yonder corner of his park, and you fee a board with an infcription, threatening all who enter with MAN traps and fpring guns. If, tempted by hunger, the poor man fhould venture to catch a hare or patridge, the horfe-whip is threatened, and perhaps inflicted in the firft inftance : and on a repetition of the atrocious crime, he and his whole family are turned out of their cottage ; happy if himfelf be not imprifoned, though the bread of the helplefs depends on his liberty and labor.

This petty tyrant of a village domain fhall neverthelefs think himfelf entitled to reprefent the next borough in Parliament. What can be expected from fuch a wretch, but that he fhould be as fervilely mean and obfequious to a minifter, as he is cruel and unfeeling in his

behaviour to the poor of his vicinity? He has
fhewn already the difpofitions of a Nero and
Domitian in miniature; and if he could obtain
a throne, his fceptre would be a rod of iron.
He would be inclined to confider all the *people*
as a tribe of POACHERS.

If no confiderable diftrict of a country be
without fuch overbearing defpots; if they are
viewed without abhorrence, and confidered as
affuming only the common privileges of country gentlemen; if fuch men, availing themfelves of a corrupt ftate of reprefentation, often
procure a fhare in the legiflature; is not that
country, if there be fuch an one, in danger of
being over-run with the fpirit of defpotifm? Are
not the YEOMANRY, who are ufually tenants of
thefe lordly Nimrods, likely to be influenced
by them, through fear of lofing their farms, in
their votes, and in all their fentiments and conduct? And will not Liberty lofe fome of her
ableft, as they were probably among her fin-
cereft and manlieft, defenders, when the yeomanry defert her banners?

Among all that defcription of perfons who
have been lately called ARISTOCRATS, proud
and felfifh in their nature, Tories and Jacobites
in their political principles, it is obvious to remark the moft haughty, overbearing manners
in the tranfactions of common life, in their domeftic arrangements, in their pleafurable ex-
curfions, their vifits, their converfation, and
general intercourfe. In all thefe, their grand
object is to keep the *vulgar*, under which appel-

lation they comprehend many truly, though not nominally, NOBLE, at a diftance. They form a little world of their own, and entitle it, the *circles of fafhion*. Folly and vanity govern this little world with defpotic rule; and virtue, learning, ufefulnefs have no claim to admiffion into it. Pride, fervility to courts, and a mutual, though tacit, agreement to treat the PEOPLE with contempt, are among the principal recommendations to it. The grand fecret of its conftitution is to claim dignity, diftinction, power, and place, exclufively, without the painful labor of deferving either by perfonal merit, or by fervices to the commonwealth.

Thefe people pufh themfelves forward to notice at all public places. Though they contribute no more than others to the fupport of fuch places, (for they are *fordidly parfimonious*) yet they claim a right to dictate every regulation. Countenanced by each other, they affume at theatres a bold behaviour, fuch as argues a fovereign contempt of the *canaille*. They talk loud, they laugh loud, they applaud each other's wit, they ftrut with airs of perfect felf-complacency; but would not be fuppofed to caft an eye at the inferior crowd, whofe admiration they are at the fame time courting, by every filly effort of pragmatical vanity. They cannot live long at home. No; they muft have the eyes of the very people whom they affect to defpife, conftantly upon their perfons, their coaches, their livery fervants; or elfe wealth lofes its power to gratify, and grandeur is no better than infignificance.

Nothing flatters fuch perfons more, than to have a number of their fellow-creatures engaged as fervants about their *perfons*, with nothing to do, or with fuch employments as MAN, properly fo called, could not endure to have done by another. It adds greatly to their happinefs, if they can clothe thefe fuperfluous menials in very fine and coftly drefs, far exceeding any thing which the middle, yet independent, ranks of the people can either afford or would choofe to difplay. They alfo choofe that their footmen fhould be handfome in their perfons, as well as fumptuoufly clad; the intention being to lead the fpectator to exclaim, when even the fervants are fuch refpectable perfonages, "how ftupenduoufly great muft be the lordly mafter!"

A court, with all its forms and finery, is the very element of fuch perfons. They flutter about it like butterflies in the funfhine; and happy he, who, in his way to it, excites the moft admiration of his gaudy coach and coat in the crowd of St. James's-ftreet; that crowd, which neverthelefs they *fcorn*, through fear of pollution, to look at, with eyes deftined in a few minutes to enjoy the beatific vifion of royalty. But as a court is their delight, no wonder that their fentiments on political matters are perfectly courtier-like. They are for extending the powers and prerogatives of royalty, from a felfifh idea that they can recom-

K 2

mend themfelves to the notice and patronage of courts by fervile compliance, by riches and pomp; whereas the *people* would require *perfonal merit* as the paffport to their favor. They think the people have little to beftow but bare efteem, or fuch offices as are honorable only in proportion as they are well or ill difcharged; fuch as require virtues and abilities: whereas, a court can beftow on its favorites, without requiring painful virtues, ribbands, garters, ftars, and titles, all which gratify fuperficial minds by their external finery and diftinction, independently of any idea that they are, or fhould be, the public rewards of long and faithful fervices, in promoting the welfare of the community, and the happinefs of the human race.

To form an adequate idea of the proud and frivolous minds of thofe who are intent on nothing but aggrandizing themfelves by augmenting the power of courts and minifters, whofe favor they feek with the moft defpicable meannefs, it will be neceffary to entertain right notions of the court of France, and the manners of the nobleffe, previoufly to the revolution. ' The two great aims' (fays an obferving French writer) ' of the modern courtiers of ' France, like fome of another nation, where ' *diffipation* and the *means of repairing* the rui- ' nous confequences of that diffipation to their ' private fortunes. To obtain the former end, ' they purfued her through all the fantaftical ' labyrinth of verfatile folly; and to accom-

' plifh the latter, they ftartled at no depravity
' or corruption which prefented itfelf.' Thus,
the greateft perfonages in the nation were moft
diftinguifhable for vice and meannefs; the fole
objeƈt was to indulge in every vain and every
fenfual gratification, and then to procure places
and appointments, the profits of which were
to pay the expences of pride and debauchery.
The financier robbed the people. The great
(as they are abufively called) received the ftolen
goods; and the people, in return for their
property thus extorted from them, were at
once oppreffed, plundered and defpifed. If a
nobleman, impoverifhed by his enormous vices
and filly vanity, married into a rich but plebeian family, they called this degrading conduƈt, the taking DUNG to fertilize their eftates.
At the fame time, *pollution* as it was to *marry*
the honeft daughter of an honeft merchant,
they prided themfelves in choofing for *miftreffes*
not only the loweft, but the moft vicious perfons, opera-dancers, and aƈtreffes, notorious for
proftitution. Such were many of the courtiers,
the nobleffe, and fticklers for arbitrary power,
in France; and have there not appeared in
other nations, inftances of fimilar conduƈt in
perfons of fimilar rank, and fimilar political
principles ?

In France, bifhoprics were ufually confidered
as genteel provifions for the fons of noble
families. Religious confiderations had little
influence in the appointment of them. Learning was not a fufficient recommendation.

BLOOD was the prime requifite. If by chance a man, with every kind of merit proper for that ftation, rofe to a bifhopric, without the reccommendation of blood, he was defpifed by the fraternity, and called a BISHOP OF FORTUNE. I have heard in England fuch men as Dr. Watfon, and Dr. Porteus, and Dr. Secker, with all their learning, fpoken of as men that muft not think themfelves of any political confequence ; as men who fhould be fatsfied with their *good fortune*, and not pretend to vie with the NORTHS, and Cornwallifes, and Kepples. How would fuch men have defpifed JESUS CHRIST and the poor fifhermen ! yet they love bifhoprics, fo far as they contribute to fecular pomp and parade.

A fimilar fpirit muft produce fimilar conduct. Therefore thofe who would not wifh the manners of the French, as they exifted before the revolution, to prevail in their own country, will check the fpirit that gives rife to fuch manners, by every rational means of oppofition to it. That fpirit and thofe manners at once fupported the French monarchy, and caufed its abolition.

Indeed, the overbearing manners of the TORIES, or friends of arbitrary power, are fo difgufting in private life to every man of fenfe and independence, that they muft be exploded, wherever fenfe and independence can prevail over the arts of fycophantifm. They are no lefs offenfive to humanity, and injurious to all the fweet equality of focial in-

tercourfe, than they are to public liberty.
Obferve one of thefe perfons, who fwells to an
unnatural fize of felf-confequence, from the
emptinefs of his head and the pride of his
heart, entering a coffee-houfe or public room
at a watering place. To fhew his contempt of
all around him, he begins *whiftling*, or beating
a tune with his fingers or with a ftick on the
table. He ftands with his back to the fire,
holding up the fkirts of his coat, protruding
his lips, picking his teeth, adjufting his cravat,
furveying his buckles, and turning out his
knees or toes; fhewing, by every fign he can
think of, his own opinion of his own importance, and his fovereign contempt for the company. Prefently he calls the waiter with a
loud voice and imperious tone. " Damn you,
" Sir, why don't you bring me a paper?"
Then after ftrutting up and down two or three
times, viewing himfelf in the glafs, bowing
through the window to a coach with coronets
on the fides, he haftily rufhes out, fhutting the
door with a found that difturbs the whole
room. He fteps back a moment, and having
hallooed to the waiter—" Has Sir John been
here?" fhuts the door ftill louder, and departs
to the other rooms, to difplay the fame airs of
felf-importance.

Liften to him while he gives orders to his
fervants or workmen. His tone is fo imperious,
you might imagine them negroes, and himfelf
a negro-driver. And happy, he thinks, would

he be, if the laws of this country would allow him to ufe the whip at once, inftead of wearing out his precious lungs on fuch low-born wretches. But as he *dares not* ufe the whip, (and indeed, he is generally a coward as well as bully), he makes up for it as well as he can, by *threatening* to ufe it on all occafions, whenever his will is not minutely and inftantaneoufly executed. He urges the propriety of keeping thefe people at a diftance, making them know their ftation, and preferving his own dignity. Porters, hackney-coachmen, chairmen, whoever is fo unfortunate as to be obliged, through poverty and a low ftation, to minifter to his luxury, are fure, at the fame time to be infulted by his infolence. *He pays no more than others;* often lefs; but he fwears and calls names. In truth, he confiders this order of ufeful people, certainly refpectable when honeft, fober, and induftrious, as not of the fame flefh and blood with himfelf, but to be ranked with the afs and the fwine.

    —— Animos fervorum et corpora noftrâ
Materiâ conftare putat, paribufque elementis?
" O Demens! ita *fervus* HOMO eft* ?   Juv.

This proud pretender to fuperiority, this fneaking flave of courts, and tyrant of his houfehold, would monopolize not only all the luxuries of habitation, food, raiment, vehicles,

* Have fervants fouls?—and are their bodies then
  Of the fame flefh and blood as gentlemen?
  Have fervants RIGHTS OF MEN to plead?   O fure
  'Tis madnefs thus to patronize the poor.

attendants, but all notice, all refpeÆt, all confideration. The world was made for him, and
fuch as he, to take their paftime in it. His
family, his children, his houfe muft all be kept
from plebeian contamination. It is worth while
to obferve the fences of his premifes, his high
rails, gates, the walls before his houfe, the
grim porter at his door, and the furly maftiff,
taught to hunt down the poor man and the
ftranger that fojourns near the magnificent
palace of felfifh grandeur. The well-barred
portals, however, fly open at the approach of
lords and dukes; and he himfelf would lick
the fhoes of a king or prime minifter, if fuch
fhould, for the fake of fecuring the influence
of his wealth in parliament, condefcend to enter
his manfion.

The ariftocratical infolence is vifible where
one would leaft expeÆt it; where all the par-
takers of this frail and mortal ftate fhould
appear in a ftate of equality; even at church,
in the immediate prefence of Him who made
high and low, rich and poor; and where the
gilded and painted ornaments on the walls
feem to mock the folly of all human pride.
The pew of the great man is raifed above the
others, though its elevation is an obftacle both
to the eyes and ears of thofe who are placed
in its vicinity. It is furnifhed with curtains,
adorned with linings, and accommodated with
cufhions. Servants walk in his train, open
the door of his luxurious feat, and carry the
burden of the prayer-book. The firft rever-

ence is paid to perfons of condition around. Thofe who do not bow at the name of Jefus Chrift, bend with all lowlinefs to the lord in the gallery. The whole behaviour leads a thinking man to conclude, that the felf-important being would fcarcely deign to enter Heaven, any more than he does the church, if he muft be reduced to an equality with the ruftic vulgar.

Such perfons, confiftently, with their arbitrary principles, are always high-churchmen. Though they may be indifferent to religion, they are zealous for the church. They confider the church as ufeful, not only in providing genteelly for relations and dependents, but as an engine to keep down the people. Upon the head of their defpot, they would but a triple covering, the crown, the mitre, and the helmet. The Devil offered our Saviour all the kingdoms of this world and their glory, if he would fall down and worfhip him; and there is reafon to fear, that fuch idolaters of the kingdoms of this world and their glory, would apoftatize from him who faid *his kingdom was not of this world*, if the fame evil being were to make them the fame offer. The temporalities and fplendors of the church triumphant endear it to them; but, if it continued in its primitive ftate, or in the condition in which it was when poor fifhermen were its bifhops, they would foon fide, in religious matters, with the *mifcreant philofophers* of France. But while mitres and ftalls may be

made highly fubfervient to the views of a minifter, and the promoters of arbitrary power
and principles, they honor the church, though
they know nothing of Chrift; they ftickle for
the bench, though they abandon the creed.
An ally, like the *church*, poffeffed of great
power, muft be cherifhed; though the very
perfons who wifh to avail themfelves of that
power, would be the firft, if that power were
in real danger, to queftion its rights, and to
accelerate its fubverfion.

There is one circumftance in the conduct of
the *Tory* friends to *abfolute fway* truly alarming
to the champions of liberty. They are always
inclined, on the fmalleft tumult, to call in the
military. They would depreciate the civil
powers, and break the conftable's ftaff to introduce the bayonet. In their opinion, the beft
executive powers of government are a party of
dragoons. They are therefore conftantly founding alarms, and aggravating every petty dif-
turbance into a riot or rebellion. They are
not for parleying with the many-headed monfter; they fcorn lenient meafures; and while
their own perfons are in perfect fafety, boldly
command the military to fire. What is the life
or the limb of a poor man, in their opinion?
Not fo much as the life or limb of a favorite
pointer or race-horfe. They are always eager to
augment the army. They would build barracks
in every part of the country, and be glad to fee
a free country over-run, like fome of the enfla-
ved nations of the continent, from eaft to weft,

L

from north to south, with men armed to over-awe the saucy advocates of charters, privileges, rights, and reformations.

Against principles so dangerous in public life, and odious in private, every friend to his king and country, every lover of his fellow creatures, every competent judge of those *manners*, which sweeten the intercourse of man with man, will shew a determined opposition. But how shall he shew it with effect? By RIDICULE. Nothing lowers the pride from which such principles proceed, so much as general contempt and derision. The insolence of petty despots in private life should be laughed at by an Aristophanes, while it is rebuked by a Cato.

SECTION XIV.

The despotic Spirit inclined to avail itself of Spies, Informers, false Witnesses, pretended Conspiracies, and self-interested Associations affecting Patriotism*.

IT is not unfair to infer the existence of similar principles from similarity of conduct. In that black page of history which disgraces human nature; I mean the records of the Roman emperors, in the decline of Roman virtue; we read, that spies and informers were considered as necessary functionaries of government; that they became favorites at court, and were encouraged by rewards due only to exemplary patriotism and public service. There have been periods also in the history of England, when spies, informers, false witnesses, and pretended plots, were deemed lawful and useful expedients by the rulers of the state. In testimony of this assertion, we need only call to mind the pretended Popish plot, with all its

---

* ‘ *Sub Tiberio Cæsare fuit accusandi frequens et pæne* ‘ *publica rabies, quæ omni civili bello gravius togatam civi-* ‘ *tatem confecit. Excipiebatur* EBRIORUM *sermo, simplicitas* ‘ JOCANTIUM.’ SENECA de Benef.

‘ *Under Tiberius Cæsar, the rage of* accusing *or* inform-‘ ing *was so common, as to harass the peaceful citizens more* ‘ *than a civil war. The words of* drunken men *and the* ‘ *unguarded joke of the thoughtless, were taken down, and* ‘ *handed to the Emperor.’*

villainous circumſtances, in the reign of Charles
the Second; a reign in many parts of it reſem-
bling the times of the Roman Tiberius. But
at whatever period ſpies, informers, falſe witneſſes, and pretended plots are adopted by men
in power, to ſtrengthen themſelves in office,
and deſtroy virtuous oppoſition, there is reaſon
to fear, in ſpite of all profeſſions of the contrary, that the tyrannic ſpirit of the degenerate
Cæſars waits but for opportunities to diſplay
itſelf in acts of Neronian atrocity. Power is
deficient; but inclination is equally hoſtile to
the maſs of mankind, denominated the People,
whom ſome politicians ſcarcely condeſcend to
acknowledge as poſſeſſed of any political exiſtence.

The employment of ſpies and informers is
a virtual declaration of hoſtilities againſt the
people. It argues a want of confidence in
them. It argues a fear and jealouſy of them.
It argues a deſire to deſtroy them by ambuſ-
cade. It is, in civil government, what ſtrata-
gems are in a ſtate of war. It tends alſo to
excite retaliation.

A miniſtry muſt be ſadly corrupt, and unworthy the confidence either of king or people,
which can ſo far degrade itſelf as to require the
aſſiſtance of the vileſt of the human race. Such
are the whole race of ſpies, *ſycophants*, (I uſe
the word in its *proper* ſenſe), informers, and
falſe witneſſes. So great is the unfortunate
corruption of human nature, that men have
been always found to execute the moſt

infamous offices, when a government has thought proper to feek their co-operation. Extreme poverty, united with extreme profligacy of conduct, and a total deftitution of moral and religious principle, prepare men for the moft nefarious deeds which tyrants can meditate. For tyrants only, the robbers and murderers of men, be fuch mifcreants referved. Tacitus has called them INSTRUMENTA REGNI, *the implements of government*, when government falls into hands which are fkilled in the ufe of no better; into the hands of Neros and Caligulas. May the minifter of a free country, who has recourfe to fuch tools, be himfelf the firft to feel their deftroying edge!

Seneca, in the quotation at the head of this fection, has handed down a circumftance, in the reign of Tiberius, which muft caufe every man, who has a juft regard for the comforts of free intercourfe and converfation, to fhudder at the profpect of being governed by a fyftem fupported by fpies and informers. He tells us, that the convivial merriment of friends affembled over a glafs, the innocent raillery and banter of jocular converfation, were, through the encouragement given to informers by the government, made the grounds of a ferious charge of fedition and treafon. *The words of the drunken*, and *the unguarded opennefs of the joker*, were taken hold of by perfons who mixed with the guefts, in order to recommend themfelves to government, by reporting the free language that might efcape in the hour of unreferved confidence ; when the heart is opened by friendfhip, and the tongue loofened by wine.

He who dippeth with me in the difh, the fame fhall betray me, faid our Saviour. But be it remembered, that the fame perfons who hired and paid Judas Ifcariot, crucified J E S U S C H R I S T.

But what fhall we fay ? Have there been no Judas Ifcariots in modern days ? Have our coffee-houfes, taverns, and places of public amufement, been quite free from hired wretches, who, while they *dipped in the fame difh* with us, were feeking to betray us, if poffible, to prifons and to death ? Did they this wickednefs of themfelves, or were they hired and paid by perfons influenced by tory principles or high in office ? Have not certain fpies confeffed, at a folemn trial, that they were hired and paid by men in office ? Have not the fame fpies led to thofe extravagant fpeeches, or thofe offenfive meafures, which they after-wards informed againft for hire ; hoping to deprive the perfons they betrayed either of liberty or life ? If fuch things have been, is it not time to be alarmed, to guard againft fpies, informers, and falfe witneffes ? And is it not right to exprefs, and increafe, if poffible, the public indignation againft both them and their employers ?

When men high in office, of reputed abili-ties, and certainly poffeffing extenfive know-ledge, patronize fuch mifcreants as fpies and informers, they certainly corrupt the public morals, by leading the people, over whom their examples muſt always have great influence, to believe, that treachery, perjury, and murder are crimes of a venial nature. They teach men to carry the profligacy of public characters and conduct into the ſequeſtered walks of private life. They teach one of the moſt corrupting maxims ; for they teach, " That when " ends eagerly deſired by knaves in power are " to be accompliſhed, the means muſt be purſued, however baſe and diſhoneſt." They deſtroy at once the confidential comforts and the moſt valuable virtues of private life.

But ſtate-neceſſity is urged in defence of that policy which employs ſpies and informers. I deny the exiſtence of ſuch neceſſity. There are excellent laws, and there are magiſtrates and officers diſperſed all over the kingdom, who are bound to take cognizance of any illegal and injurious practices, and to prevent them by a timely interference. If ſuch magiſtrates and officers neglect their duty, it is incumbent on thoſe who appointed them, and who are amply paid for their vigilance, to inſtitute proſecutions, to puniſh and to remove them. The law knows nothing of ſpies and informers. The only watchmen it recognizes are magiſtrates, regularly appointed. The whole body of a people, well governed, and conſequently contented with their governors, are the natural and voluntary guardians againſt ſeditions, treaſons, and conſpiracies to ſubvert the ſtate.

When fpies and informers are called in, it argues a diftruft of the magiftrates, and of the whole body of the people. It argues an endeavor to govern in a manner unauthorized by that conftitution which the employers of fpies and informers pretend to protect, by inftruments fo dangerous and unjuftifiable.

- I have a better opinion of men in power, in our times, corrupting as the poffeffion of power is allowed to be, than to believe that any of them would hire a falfe witnefs. But let them be affured, that a hired fpy and informer will, by an eafy tranfition, become a falfe witnefs, even in trials where liberty and life are at ftake. In trials of lefs confequence, there is no doubt but that his confcience will ftretch with the occafion. His object is not truth or juftice; but filthy lucre; and when he afpires at great rewards, great muft be his venture. Having once broken down, as a treacherous fpy, the fences of honor and confcience, nothing but fear will reftrain him, as a witnefs, from overleaping the bounds of truth, juftice, and mercy. He will rob and murder under the forms of law; and add to the atrocity of blood-guiltinefs, the crime of perjury. No man is fafe, where fuch men are countenanced by officers of ftate. They themfelves may perifh by his falfe tongue; fuffering the vengeance due to their bafe encouragement of a traitor to the public, by falling unpitied victims to his difappointed treachery. The peftilential breath of fpies and informers is not to be endured in the pure healthy atmofphere of a free ftate. It brings with it the fickly defpotifm of oriental climes.

But how ominous to liberty, if large affociations of rich men, either poffeffing or expecting places, penfions, and titles for themfelves or their relations, fhould ever take upon them the office of fpying and informing! by their *numbers* braving the fhame, and evading the perfonal refponfibility, that would fall on an individual or unconnected fpy or informer! Such an affociation would be a moft dangerous confpiracy of fycophants againft a free conftitution. If the public fhould ever behold the venal tribe thus undermining the fair fabric of liberty, and behold them without indignation, would it not give reafon to fufpect, that the Tory and Jacobite principles, or the fpirit of defpotifm, had pervaded the body of the people?

The honeft, independent, and thinking part of the community will be juftly alarmed, when they fee either individuals or bodies of men encouraged by minifterial favors, in calumniating the people, and falfely accufing the advocates of conftitutional freedom. They will think it time to ftem the torrent of corruption, which, rolling down its foul but impetuous tide from the hills, threatens devaftation to the cottages in the valley. But how fhall they ftop an evil, promoted and encouraged, for private and felfifh motives, by the whole influence of grandeur and opulence acting in combination? By bearing their teftimony in favor of truth and juftice; by giving their fuffrages to honeft men; by rejecting the fervile adulator of courts, and the mean fycophant of minifters: and by fhunning as peftilences *every defcription of fpies and informers, whether poor or rich, mercenary or volunteer* *. If they fail, they will feel the comfort of having difcharged their duty.

---

* I fubjoin a curious paffage from the 14th book of Ammianus Marcellinus, on the manner in which fpies executed their office, under the imperial authority of Conftantius Gallus.

'*Excogitatum eft fuper his, ut homines quidam ignoti,* ' VILITATE IPSA *parùm cavendi, ad colligendos rumores* ' *per Antiochiæ latera cuncta deftinarentur, relaturi que audi-* ' *rent. Hi peragranter et diffimulanter honoratorum circulis* ' *affiftendo, pervadendoque divitum domus egentium habitu,* ' *quicquid nofcere poterant vel audire, latenter intromiffi per* ' POSTICAS *in regiam, nuntiabant: id obfervantes confpira-* ' *tione concordi, ut fingerent quædam, et cognita duplicarent* ' *in pejus:* LAUDES VERO SUPPRIMERENT CÆSARIS, quos ' INVITIS QUAMPLURIMIS, *formido malorum impendentium* ' *exprimebat.*'

' *Another expedient was, to place at every corner of the* ' *city certain obfcure perfons, not likely to excite fufpicion or* ' *caution, becaufe of their apparent infignificancy, who were* ' *to repeat whatever they heard. Thefe perfons, by ftanding* ' *near gentlemen, or getting entrance into the houfes of the* ' *rich, in the difguife of poverty, reported whatever they* ' *faw or heard, at court, being privately admitted into the* ' *palace by the* BACK STAIRS: *having concerted it between* ' *themfelves to add a great deal, from their own invention,* ' *to whatever they really faw or heard, and to make the* ' *matter ten times worfe. They agreed alfo to fupprefs the* ' *mention of thofe* LOYAL SONGS OR TOASTS, or) *fpeeches,* ' *in favor of the emperor, which the dread of impending evil* ' *fqueezed out of many againft their will and better judgment.*'

The decline of the Roman empire was diftinguifhed by fpies and informers: it is to be hoped that the ufe of fpies and informers does not portend the decline of the Britifh empire.

SECTION XV.

The Manners of Tory Courtiers, and of those who ape them, as People of Fashion, inconsistent with Manliness, Truth, and Honesty; and their Prevalence injurious to a free Constitution, and the Happiness of Human Nature.

AMONG a thousand anecdotes of the frivolity of the governing part of a despotic country, I select the following, merely as a slight specimen of the trifling disposition of those who, as they pretend, claim their elevated situations for the GOOD OF MANKIND.

' In the summer of the year 1775, the queen
' of France, being dressed in a light-brown
' silk, the king good-naturedly observed, it was
' *couleur de puce*, the color of fleas; and in-
' stantly every lady in the land was uneasy till
' she had dressed herself in a silk gown of a flea
' color. The rage was caught by the men;
' and the dyers worked night and day, without
' being able to supply the demand for flea-color.
' They nicely distinguished between an old
' and a young flea, and subdivided even the
' shades of its body. The belly, the back, the
' thigh, the head, were all marked by varying
' tints. This prevailing color promised to be
' the fashion of the winter. The silk-mercers
' found it would hurt their trade. They there-

' fore prefented her majefty with patterns of new
' fattins ; who having chofen one, Monsieur
' exclaimed, it was the color of her *majefty's*
' hair !

' Immediately the *fleas* ceafed to be favorites
' at court, and all were eager to be dreffed in
' the color of her majefty's hair. Servants
' were fent off at the moment from Fontain-
' bleu to Paris, to purchafe velvets, ratteens,
' and cloths of this color. The current price
' of an ell in the morning had been forty livres,
' and it rofe in the evening to eighty and ninety.
' The demand was fo great, and the anxiety
' fo eager, that fome of her majefty's hair was
' actually obtained by bribery, and fent to the
' Gobelins, to Lyons, and other manufactories,
' that the exact fhade might be caught and re-
' ligioufly preferved."

Such was the little, mean, adulatory fpirit
of the court of France, and of the people who
at that time imitated the court with more than
apifh mimicry. To fhew how little there is of
truth and honefty in fuch fervility, be it remembered, that the nation fo eager to catch the
very color of the queen's hair, foon afterwards
cut off the head on which it grew. Nothing
filly, nothing overftrained, can be lafting, becaufe it wants a folid foundation. Let kings
be careful how they confide in court compli-
ments and the addreffes of corruption. Maftiffs
guard their mafter and his houfe better than
fpaniels.

While fuch a fpirit prevails among the great, it is impoffible that the happinefs of man can be duly regarded by thofe who claim a right to govern him. Where frivolity and meannefs are general, it is impoffible that the people can be wife or happy. Gaiety founded on levity or affectation, is not happinefs. It laughs and talks, while the heart is either unmoved or dejected. Happinefs is ferious. The noife of folly is intended to diffipate thought; but no man would wifh his thoughts to be dif-fipated, who finds any thing within him to think of with complacency.

Princes have always fomething important to think of, which, it might be fuppofed, would preclude the neceffity of trifling amufements to kill time. Yet courts have always been re-markable for frivolity. This frivolity is not only contemptible in itfelf, unworthy of rational beings, efpecially when executing a moft mo-mentous truft, but productive of meannefs, weaknefs, and corruption. Long experience has affociated with the idea of a courtier in defpotic courts, duplicity, infincerity, violation of promifes, adulation, all the bafe and mean qualities, rendered ftill bafer and meaner, by affuming, on public occafions, the varnifh of hypocrify.

Erafmus gives directions to a young man, in the manner of Swift, how to conduct himfelf at court. I believe they never have been prefented to the Englifh reader, and therefore

M

I fhall take the liberty of tranflating them, not only for the fake of affording amufement, but that it may be duly confidered, whether or not perfons who form their manners and principles after fuch models, are likely to be the friends of man, the affertors of the guardians of liberty : whether the flaves of *fafhion*, who feem to feparate themfelves from others, as if they were a chofen tribe among the fons of men ; as if they were made of fuch clay as forms the porcelain, while others are merely earthen ware ; whether, I fay, the flaves of *fafhion*, which always apes a court in all its extravagancies, are likely to confult the happinefs of the majority of mankind, the middle, loweft, and moft ufeful claffes, whom they defpife, as an inferior fpecies of beings ; as the whites in the Weft Indies formerly looked down upon the negroes with difdain.

" As you are now going to live at court," fays Erafmus, " I advife you, in the firft place, never to repofe the fmalleft degree of confidence in any man there who profeffes himfelf your friend, though he may fmile upon you, and embrace you, and promife you ; aye, and confirm his promife with an oath. Believe no man there a fincere friend to you ; and do you take care to be a fincere friend to no man—Neverthelefs, you muft pretend to love all you fee, and fhew the utmoft fuavity of manners and attentions to every individual. Thefe attentions coft you not a farthing ; therefore you may be as lavifh of them as you pleafe. Pay your falutations with the fofteft fmiles on your countenance, fhake hands with the appearance of moft ardent cordiality, bow and give way to all, ftand cap in hand, addrefs every body by their titles of honor, praife without bounds, and promife moft liberally.

" I would have you every morning, before you go to the levee, practife in making up your face for the day at your looking-glafs at home, that it may be ready to affume any part in the farce, and that no glimpfe of your real thoughts and feelings may appear. You muft ftudy your geftures carefully at home, that in the acting of the day your countenance, perfon, and converfation may all correfpond, and affift each other in keeping up your character at the court mafquerade.

" Thefe are the elements of the courtier's philofophy, in learning which, no man can be an apt fcholar, unlefs he firft of all divefts himfelf of all fenfe of fhame; and leaving his natural face at home, puts on a vizor, and wears it conftantly too. In the next place, get fcent of the various cabals and parties of the court; but be not in a hurry to attach yourfelf to any of them, till you have duly reconnoitred. When you have found out who is the king's favorite, you have your cue; mind to keep on the fafe fide of the veffel. If the king's favorite be a downright fool, you muft not fcruple to flatter him, fo long as he is in favor with the god of your idolatry.

" The god himſelf, to be ſure, will require the main efforts of your ſkill. As often as you happen to be IN THE PRESENCE, you muſt exhibit a face of apparently honeſt delight, as if you were tranſported with the privilege of being ſo near the *royal perſon*. When once you have obſerved what he likes and diſlikes, your buſineſs is done."

He proceeds to adviſe his pupil to purſue his own intereſt, regardleſs of all honor and ho-neſty, whenever they may be violated without detection. He tells him, in conſulting his in-tereſt, to pay more court to *enemies* than friends, that he may turn their hearts, and bring them over to his ſide. I cannot, in this place, give the whole of the letter; but the curious reader may find it under number fifty-ſeven, in the twenty-eighth book of the London edition.

Eraſmus drew from the life. Though a moſt profound ſcholar, yet he was not merely a ſcholar. He read the book of the world with as much accuracy as the volumes of his library. I have brought forward this letter, becauſe I find it exemplified in the Precepts of Lord Cheſ-terfield, and the Diary of Lord Melcombe. It appears, under the teſtimony of their own hands, that theſe men actually were the cha-racters which Eraſmus, in a vein of irony and ſarcaſm, adviſes his court-pupil to become. It appears from them, that many of the perſons, with whom they acted, were ſimilar. It fol-lows that, if ſuch men were great, wiſe, and good men, truth, honor, fincerity, friendfhip, and patriotifm are but empty names, devifed by politicians to amufe and delude a fubject and an abject people.

But the people (I mean not a venal mob, employed by a minifter or by a faction) are not fo corrupted. They value truth, honor, fincerity, and patriotifm; and in their conduct often difplay them in their utmoft purity. Shall courtiers, then, be liftened to, when they reprefent the people as the fwinifh multitude, or as venal wretches? Shall courtiers, fuch as Lord Melcombe, claim an exclufive right to direct human affairs? influencing fenates to make and unmake laws at pleafure, and to cry havoc, when they pleafe, and let flip the dogs of war on the *poor*, either at home or abroad? Shall a whole nation be proud to mimic a court, not only in drefs, amufements, and all the vanity of fafhion, but in fentiments, in morals, in politics, in religion, in no religion, in hypocrify, in CRUELTY?

Lord Melcombe and Lord Chefterfield were leading men, able men, eloquent men, confidered in their day as ornaments of the court and of the nation. But if even they exhibit both precepts and examples of extreme felfifhnefs, of deceit, and of a total difregard to human happinefs, what may we think of their numerous dependents, under-agents, perfons attached to them by places, penfions, ribbands, titles, expecting favors for themfelves, or their natural children, or their coufins? Can we suppose these men to retain any regard for the PUBLIC? Would they make any sacrifice to the general happiness of human nature? Would they assert liberty, or undergo trouble, loss, persecution, in defence of a constitution? They themselves would laugh at you, if you should suppose it possible. They can be considered in no other light than as vermin, sucking the blood of the people whom they despise.

Yet these, and such as these, are the men who are indefatigable in declaiming against the people, talking of the mischiefs of popular government, and the danger of admitting the rights of man. These, and such as these, are the strenuous opposers of all reform in the representation. These, and such as these, call all attempts at innovations, though evidently improvements, seditious. These are the alarmists, who cry out, the church or the state is in danger, in order to persecute honest men, or to introduce the military. The military is their delight, their fortress; and to compass their own base ends, they will not hesitate to bathe their arms in human blood, even up to their very shoulders. Their whole object is to aggrandize a POWER, of which they pant to participate, and from which alone, destitute as they are of merit and goodness, they can hope for lucre and the distinctions of vanity.

" Where the ruling mischief," says the author of the Estimate, " prevails among the great, then even the palliative remedies cannot easily be applied. The reason is manifest: a coercive power is wanting. They who fhould cure the evil, are the very delinquents ; and moral and political phyfic no diftempered mind will ever adminifter to itfelf.

" Neceffity therefore, and neceffity alone, muft in fuch a cafe be the parent of reformation. So long as degenerate and unprincipled manners can fupport themfelves, they will be deaf to reafon, blind to confequences, and obftinate in the long-eftablifhed purfuit of GAIN and PLEASURE. IN SUCH MINDS, THE IDEA OF A PUBLIC HAS NO PLACE. Nor can fuch minds be ever awakened from their fatal dream, till either the VOICE of an ABUSED people roufe them INTO FEAR, or the ftate itfelf totter, through the general incapacity, cowardice, and difunion of thofe who fupport it.

" Whenever, this compelling power, Neceffity, fhall appear, then, and not till then, may we hope that our deliverance is at hand. Effeminacy, rapacity, and faction, will then be ready to *refign* the reins they would now ufurp. One common danger, would create one common intereft. Virtue may rife on the ruins of corruption.

" One kind of NECESSITY, and which I call an internal NECESSITY, would arife, when the voice of an abufed people fhould roufe the GREAT into FEAR.

" I am not ignorant, that it hath been a point of debate, whether, in POLITICAL MATTERS, THE GENERAL VOICE OF A PEOPLE

OUGHT to be held worth much regard ? Right forry I am to obferve, that this doubt is the growth of *later times;* of times, too, which boaft their love of freedom; but ought, furely, to blufh, when they look back on the generous fentiments of ancient days, which days we ftigmatize with the name of *flavifh.*

"Thus runs the writ of fummons to the parliament of the 23d of Edward the Firft :— *The King, to the venerable father in Chrift* R. *Archbifhop of Canterbury, greeting : As the moft juft law, eftablifhed by the provident wif- dom of princes, doth appoint, that what* con- cerns ALL, *fhould be* approved *by* ALL *; fo it evidently implies, that dangers common to all, fhould be obviated by remedies provided by all.* Ut quod OMNES *tangit,* ab OMNIBUS appro- betur ;—fic et innuit evidenter, *ut* COMMUNI- BUS *periculis per remedia provifa* COMMUNITER *obvietur.* A noble acknowledgement from an Englifh king, which ought never, fure, to be forgotten, or trodden under foot, by Englifh fubjects.

"There are two manifeft reafons why, in a *degenerate ftate,* and a *declining* period, the united voice of a people is, in general, the fureft teft of truth in all effential matters on which their own welfare depends, fo far as the ends of political meafures are concerned.

"*Firft,* Becaufe in fuch a period, and fuch a ftate, the body of a people are naturally the leaft corrupt part of fuch a people: for all general corruptions, of whatever kind, begin among the leaders, and defcend from thefe to the lower ranks. Take fuch a ftate, therefore, in what period of degeneracy you pleafe, the *higher ranks* will, in the natural courfe of things, be farther gone in the ruling evils than the lower; and therefore THE LESS TO BE RELIED ON.

" *Secondly,* A ftill more cogent reafon is, that the general body of the people have not fuch a *bias* hung upon their judgment by the prevalence of *perfonal* and *particular* intereft, as the GREAT, in all things which relate to ftate matters. It is of no *particulr* and *perfonal* confequence to the *general body* of a people, what men are employed, provided the general welfare be accomplifhed; becaufe nothing but the general welfare can be an objeft of defire to the *general body*. But it is of much particular and perfonal confequence to the GREAT, what *men* are *employed*; becaufe, through their conneftions and alliances, they muft generally find either their *friends* or *enemies* in *power*. Their own private interefts, therefore, naturally throw a bias on their judgments, and deftroy that *impartiality* which the general body of an uncorrupt people doth naturally poflefs.

" Hence, then, it appears, that the united voice of an uncorrupt PEOPLE is, in general, the fafeft teft of POLITICAL GOOD AND EVIL."

Is it not then time to be alarmed for the public good, when great pains are taken to depreciate the people; when the names of Ja-

cobin, democrat, leveller, traitor, and mover
of fedition, are artfully thrown, by courtiers
and their adherents, on every man who has
fenfe and virtue enough to maintain the caufe
of liberty; that caufe, which eftablifhed the
revolution on the ruins of defpotifm, and placed the prefent family on the throne, as the
guardians of a free conftitution? I cannot
think fuch courtiers, however they may fawn,
for their own interest, on the perfon of the
monarch, friends, in their hearts, to a limited
monarchy. If they could and dared, they
would reftore a Stuart. But as that is imprac-
ticable, they would transfufe the principles of
the Stuarts into the bofom of a Brunfwick. To
expofe their felfifh meannefs, and fruftrate their
bafe defign, is equally the duty and interest of
the king and the people.

SECTION XVI.

The Spirit of Truth, Liberty, and Virtue, public as well as private, chiefly to be found in the middle ranks of the people.

Nemo altero nobilior, nisi cui rectius ingenium et artibus bonis aptius. Qui imagines in atrio exponunt et nomina familiæ suæ..... Noti magis quam *nobiles* sunt .... Dicenda hæc fuerunt ad contundendam *insolentiam* hominum ex fortunâ pendentium.* SENECA *de Benef.*

THE people of this land are usually divided into nobility, gentry, and *commonalty.* The nobility and gentry seem to be estimated as officers in an army; the commonalty, or the whole body of the people, as the rank and file.

There might be no original impropriety in these appellations; but that of *commonalty* has been often used, by aristocratical upstarts, with insolence. The commonalty comprize the grand mass of the nation; form the great fabric of the political building; while the GENTRY, after all, are but the carving and gilding, or the

* " *No man is* nobler born *than another, unless he is* born *with better abilities and a more amiable disposition.* They *who make such a parade with their* family pictures *and* pedigrees, *are, properly speaking, rather to be called* NOTED *or* NOTORIOUS *than* NOBLE *persons.* I thought it right to say *thus much, in order to repel the* insolence *of men who depend entirely upon* chance *and* accidental *circumstances for distinction, and not at all on public services and personal merit.*

capitals of the pillars, that add to the fupport of the roof, but conftitute neither the walls nor the foundation. The commonalty, therefore, being the main fabric, are worthy, in the eye of reafon, of the higheft efteem, and the firft degree of a patriot's folicitude. There can be no rational end in our government but the happinefs of the whole PEOPLE, King, Lords, and COMMONS.

The commonalty are, beyond all comparifon, the moft numerous order : and as every individual of them is entitled to comfort and fecurity in a well regulated nation, the whole together muft demand the greateft attention of the philofopher, the divine, the philanthropift, of every man of fenfe, goodnefs of heart, and liberality. The pomp and parade, the fuperfluous luxury, the vain diftinctions of the FEW, fink to nothing, compared, in the mind of reafonable and humane men, with the happinefs of the *million*.

It is certainly true, that the greateft inftances of virtue and excellence of every kind have originated in the middle order. ' Give me neither poverty nor riches,' was a prayer founded on a knowledge of human nature, and fully juftified by experience. The middle ftation affords the beft opportunities for improvement of mind, is the leaft expofed to temptation, and the moft capable of happinefs and virtue.

This opinion has long been received and acknowledged. I could cite, from the fermons of our best divines on *Agúr's Prayer*, many passages in confirmation of it. I dwell upon it now, for no other reason, but because it has *lately* been the fashion, among those who are alarmed for their privileges by the French revolution, to run down the people, and to cry up that silly spirit of chivalry which established the systems of false honor, claiming rank and respect from society, without rendering it any service, without possessing any just claim to esteem, much less to public honor, exclusive privileges, and titular distinction. The terms *sans culottes, canaille, bourgeoise,* scum of the earth, *venal wretches,* and the never to be forgotten *swinish multitude,* have been reserved for the people, especially those among them who have had sense and spirit enough personally to oppose the progress of despotic principles and practices. Every thing that malice, urged by the fear of losing the ribands, the titles, and the solid pence which a corrupt and corrupting minister can bestow, has been thrown out, in newspapers hired by the people's money for the purpose of vilifying the people.

It is time, therefore, that the people should vindicate their honor. What are these insolent courtiers, what these placemen and pensioners, who live on the public bounty, that they should thus insult those whose bread they eat? For the most part, they are persons who, if they were stripped of the false splendor of great mansions, numerous retinues, painted carriages, would appear among the meanest and most des-

picable members of fociety. They
to be pitied and borne with, while
from infulting the people ; but whe
pride prefumes to trample on the i
community, they become deferving (
as well as commiferation.

Thefe are the perfons whom a pa
defcribes " as giving themfelves up
fuit of honors and dignities, as LC
SPLENDOR OF A COURT, and atta(
felves to the caufe of monarchy, (n(
conviction that monarchy is the mo
to human happinefs, not even fr(
attachment to the monarch,) but b(
fee in the *increafed power* of the n
fource of additional weight and SP
thofe (that is, themfelves) who ft
throne, and an increafe of value t(
which the fovereign can confer ; ft
garters, ribands, and titles."

But is a paffion, childifh from
and diabolical in its unfeeling greed
borne with any longer, when, i
with engroffing the profits of offi
pageantry of ftate, it dares to fpeak
dle and lower claffes, as beings fcar
ing notice, as mere *nuifances* when
ed in the fervile office of adminifterii
cratic pride.

Virtue is nobility. Perfonal m(
generous, benevolent exertion, the
able diftinction. The trappings v
taylor can make to clothe a poor p(

add no real dignity. In ages of ignorance, they might ftrike with awe. Thofe ages are no more. Nor will they ever return, notwith-ftanding the efforts of petty defpots, (fearing the lofs of thofe diftinctions which they know they never earned), to keep the people in the groffeft ignorance.

God Almighty, who gives his fun to fhine with as much warmth and radiance on the cot-tage as on the palace, has difpenfed the glorious privilege of genius and virtue to the poor and middle claffes, with a bounty perhaps feldom experienced in any of the proud pretenders to hereditary or official grandeur. Let us call to mind a few among the worthies who have adorned the ages that have elapfed: Socrates; was he *noble* in the fenfe of a king at arms? Would he have condefcended to be bedizened with ribands, and ftars, and garters? Cicero; was he not a *novus homo?* a man unconnected with patricians, and deriving his glory from the pureft fountain of honor, his own genius and virtue? Demofthenes would have fcorned to owe his eftimation to a pedigree.

Who were the great reformers, to whom we of England and all Europe are indebted for emancipation from the chains of fuperftition? ERASMUS and LUTHER; Erafmus, as the monks of his day objected to him, laid the egg, and Luther hatched it. But was it Archbifhop Erafmus? Lord Luther, Marquis Luther, Sir Martin Luther? Did they, either of them, feek the favor of courts? Were they not among the *fwinifh multitude*?

Thomas Paine contributed much, by his *Common Senfe*, to the happy revolution in America. I need not obferve, that he had nothing of the luftre of courts or nobility to recommend him. The virulent malice of courtiers and venal fcribblers has blackened him as they once blackened Luther, when they afferted of him, that he was actually a *devil incarnate*, difguifed in the fhape of a monk with a cowl. I do not advert to any of his fubfequent publications. I only fay, if they are fo *contemptible* as they are faid by courtiers and ariftocrats to be, why not undertake the *eafy* tafk of refuting him? Bloody wars and profecutions are no refutation.

"Who is this *Luther?*" (faid Margaret, governefs of the Netherlands.) The courtiers around her replied, "He is an ILLITERATE MONK." "Is he fo? (faid fhe.) I am glad to hear it. Then do you, gentlemen, who are not illiterate, who are both learned and numerous, do you, I charge you, write againft this *illiterate monk*. That is all you have to do. The bufinefs is eafy; for the world will furely pay more regard to a great many *fcholars*, and great men, as you are, than to one poor *illiterate monk*."

Many did write againft him, and poured forth the virulence of a malice unchecked by truth, and encouraged by crowned heads.

prevailed, and we Englifhmen have
celebrate the victory of truth and
corrupt influence and cruel per-

ateft fcholars, poets, orators, phi-
warriors, ftatefmen, inventors and
f the arts, arofe from the loweft of
If we had waited till courtiers
d the art of printing, clock-making,
and a thoufand others, we fhould
ave continued in darknefs to this
y had fomething elfe to do, than to
comforts and conveniencies of or-
They had to worfhip an idol,
ncenfe of flattery, who was often
ftupid than themfelves, and who
had no more care or knowledge of
under him, or their wants, than he
or literature.
cation of the middle claffes is infi-
r than the education of thofe who
great people. Their time is lefs
y that vanity and diffipation which
e mind, while it precludes oppor-
ading and reflection. They ufually
rd to *character*, which contributes
ie prefervation of virtue. Their
integrity are valued by them, as
eat price. Thefe are their ftars,
heir coronets. They are for the
tached to their religion. They are
frugal, and induftrious. In one
and that one adds a value above all

that *courts* can give, they greatly excel the GREAT, and that particular is SINCERITY. They are in earneſt in their words and deeds. They have little occaſion for ſimulation and diſſimulation. Courtiers are too often varniſhed, factitious perſons, whom God and nature never made; while the people preſerve the image uneffaced, which the Supreme Being impreſſed when he cerated MAN.

SECTION XVII.

*On debauching the Minds of the rising Genera-
tion and a whole People, by giving them
Military Notions in a free and commercial
Country.*

IN proportion as great men refuse to
submit to reason, they are inclined to govern
by violence. They who have the sword in their
hands, are unwilling to wait for the slow operation of argument. The sword cuts away all
opposition. No troublesome contradiction, no
unwelcome truth, will impede the progress of
him who uses the *ratio ultima regum*, and mows
down all obstacles with the scythed car.

Hence the abettors of high prerogative, of
absolute monarchy, and aristocratical pride,
always delight in war. Not satisfied with at-
tacking foreign nations, and keeping up a standing army even in time of peace, they wish, after
they have once corrupted the mass of the people by universal influence, to render a whole
nation military. The aggregate of military
force, however great, being under their entire
direction, they feel their power infinitely augmented, and bid defiance to the unarmed philosopher and politician, who brings into the
field truth without a spear, and argument un-
backed with artillery.

But fuch a fyftem tends to gothicize a nation, to extinguifh the light of learning and philofophy, and once more to raife thick fogs from the putrid pools of ignorance and fuperftition, the bane of all happinefs, but the very element of defpotifm.

The diffufion of a military tafte among all ranks, even the loweft of the people, tends to a general corruption of morals, by teaching habits of idlenefs, or trifling activity, and the vanity of guady drefs and empty parade.

The ftrict difcipline which is found neceffary to render an army a machine in the hands of its directors, requiring, under the feverest penalties, the moft implicit fubmiffion to abfolute command, has a direct tendency to familiarize the mind to civil defpotifm. Men, rational, thinking animals, equal to their commanders by nature, and often fuperior, are bound to obey the impulfe of a conftituted authority, and to perform their functions as mechanically as the trigger which they pull to difcharge their mufkets. They cannot, indeed help having a will of their own: but they muft fupprefs it, or die. They muft confider their official fuperiors as fuperiors in wifdom and in virtue, even though they know them to be weak and vicious. They muft fee, if they fee at all, with the eyes of others; their duty is not to have an opinion of their own, but to follow blindly the beheft of him who has had intereft enough to obtain the appointment of a leader.

They become living automatons, and felf-acting tools of defpotifm.

While a few only are in this condition, the danger may not be great to conftitutional liberty; but when a majority of the people are made foldiers, it is evident that the fame obfequioufnefs will become habitual to the majority of the people. Their minds will be broken down to the yoke, the energy of independence weakened, the manly fpirit tamed; like animals that once ranged in the foreft, delighting in their liberty, and fearlefs of man, caught in fnares, confined in cages, and taught to ftand upon their hind legs, and play tricks for the entertainment of the idle. They obey the word of command given by the keeper of the *menagerie*, becaufe they have been taught obedience by hunger, by the lafh of the whip, by every mode of difcipline confiftent with their lives, which are *faleable property.* But they are degenerate, contemptible animals. Compare a bird or a beaft, thus broken down, with one of the fame fpecies flying in clear expanfe of air, or roaming in the foreft. Their very looks fpeak their degradation. The difcipline of Mr. Aftley caufes the fiery fteed to bend his knees in apparent fupplication. But how are the mighty fallen! when the animal has broken from his obedience to nature, to fall down proftrate before Mr. Aftley.

Suppofe a whole nation, thus *tamed,* and taught fubmiffion to the command of one of their own fpecies. Be it remembered, the horſe, in learning unnatural tricks, ſubmits to one of another ſpecies, who is naturally his ſuperior. But ſuppoſe a whole nation, or at leaſt the maſs of the *common people* thus *broken in* by a ſkilful rider. Will they not loſe all energy? Will they dare, I do not ſay to ſpeak, but to think of liberty? No; they will ſink to the rank of *German mercenaries* let out for hire, claiming no rights, enjoying no privileges above the SWINE; a ſtate of degradation at which the ſpirit of *man*, unſpoiled by deſpotic government, revolts; and rather than fall into which, every true Engliſhman, from the palace to the hovel of the itinerant beggar, will be ready to exclaim, in the language of the ſcriptures, " Why died I not from the womb?"

Is it not time, then, for the virtuous guardians of Heaven's beſt gift, LIBERTY, to be alarmed, when they ſee a propenſity in miniſters, who have gained enormous power and corrupt influence, to render a whole people *military?* The gold chain of corruption is thus let down and ramified, in a million of directions, among thoſe who never thought of courts or courtiers; but enjoying a noble independence, the independence of honeſt induſtry, chaunted their carols at the plough and the loom, glorying in the name of Engliſhmen, becauſe England is free; and delighting in peace, becauſe peace is the parent of plenty.

But, under the auſpices of ſuch a miniſtry, many an emulous eſquire, hoping to be diſtinguiſhed and rewarded, in ſome mode or other,

by *court* favors, fond of the drefs and name of
a CAPTAIN, and the privilege of *commanding*
with abfolute fway, bribes volunteers from
behind the counter and the plough. He clothes
them in the fineft frippery that his own or his
lady's imagination can invent. He himfelf
parades at their head; a very pretty fight on a
fummer's day. And now HE is diftinguifhed
as a SOLDIER, who before only figured as a
hunter of hares or foxes, and a profecutor of
poachers. Ambition, as well as vanity, begins
to fire his foul. The raifing of fo many men
in his neighborhood muft pleafe the minifter;
efpecially if the efquire ufes the influence he
gains over the vicinity, in a *proper* manner,
at a *general election*. If the efquire wants not
money, he may want *honor*. Then let the
minifter make him a baronet. If he has no
fons of his own in the army, navy, law, or
church, he may have nephews or coufins. If
not thefe, he muft have *nominal* friends, to
direct on whom the favors of minifters, though
it proceed not from benevolence, muft flatter
pride, and add to rural confequence.

The whole of the military fyftem is much
indebted for its fupport, to that prevailing
paffion of human nature, Pride. Politicians
know it, and flatter pride even in the loweft of
the people. Hence recruiting-officers invite
gentlemen only, who are above *fervile* labor.
" The vanity of the poor men (fays a fagacious
author) is to be worked upon at the cheapeft
rate poffible. Things we are accuftomed to

we do not mind, or elſe what mortal, that never had ſeen a ſoldier, could look, without laughing, upon a man accoutred with ſo much paltry gaudineſs and affected finery? The coarſeſt manufacture that can be made of wool, dyed of a brick-duſt color, goes down with him, becauſe it is in imitation of ſcarlet or crimſon cloth ; and to make him think himſelf as like his officer as it is poſſible, with little or no coſt, inſtead of ſilver or gold lace, his hat is trimmed with white or yellow worſted, which in others would deſerve bedlam ; yet theſe fine allurements, and the noiſe made upon a calf-ſkin, have drawn in and been the *deſtruction* of more men in reality, than all the killing eyes and bewitching voices of women ever ſlew in jeſt.   To-day the *ſwineherd* puts on his red coat, and believes every body in earneſt that calls him *gentleman ;* and two days after, *Ser-jeant Kite gives him a ſwinging rap with his cain,* for holding his muſket an inch higher than he ſhould do. . . . When a man reflects on all this, and the uſage they generally receive—their pay—and the *care that is taken of them when they are not wanted,* muſt he not wonder how wretches can be ſo ſilly, as to be proud of being called *gentlemen ſoldiers?* Yet if they were not ſo called, no art, diſcipline, or money, would be capable of making them ſo brave as thouſands of them are.''

When all the baſe arts which cuſtom is ſaid to have rendered *neceſſary,* are practiſed only to raiſe and ſupport a regular army, perhaps they might, however reluctantly, be connived at by the watchful friend of freedom. But when the major part of the laboring poor, and all the yeomanry, are made *gentlemen* foldiers, merely to fupport a MINISTER, it is time for every virtuous and independent mind to ex-prefs, as well as feel, ALARM.

It appears from the above-cited paffage of an author who had anatomized human nature, to find out its moft latent energies, that the *fpirit of pride* is rendered, by artful ftatefmen, the chief means of fupplying an army. But the fpirit of pride is in fact the fpirit of defpotifm ; efpecially when it is that fort of pride which plumes itfelf on COMMAND, on external deco-ration, and the idle vanity of military parade.

When this pride takes place univerfally in a nation, there will remain little induftry, and lefs independence. The grand object will be to rife above our neighbors in fhow and autho-rity. All will bow to the man in power, in the hope of diftinction. Men will no longer rely on their *own* laborious exertions ; but the poor man will court, by the moft obfequious fubmif-fion, the favor of the efquire ; the efquire cringe to the next baronet, lord, or duke, efpecially if he be a lord-lieutenant of the county ; and the baronet, lord, or duke, or lieutenant of the county, will fall proftrate before the firft lord of the treafury ; and the firft lord of the trea-fury will idolize PREROGATIVE. Thus the military rage will trample on liberty ; and DES-POTISM *triumphant* march through the land, with *drums beating and colors flying.*

O

SECTION XVIII.

Levity, Effeminacy, Ignorance, and Want of Principle in private Life, inimical to all public Virtue, and favorable to the Spirit of Despotism.

" THE conftitution of the Britifh government (fays Bolingbroke) fuppofes our KINGS may abufe their power, and our REPRÉ-SENTATIVES betray their truft, and provides againft both thefe contingencies. Here let us obferve, that the fame conftitution is very far from fuppofing the PEOPLE will ever betray *themfelves;* and yet this cafe is poffible.

" A wife and brave PEOPLE will neither be cozened nor bullied out of their liberty ; but a wife and brave people may ceafe to be fuch ; they may degenerate ; they may fink into floth and luxury ; they may refign themfelves to a treacherous conduct ; or ABET THE ENEMIES OF THE CONSTITUTION, under a notion of fupporting the FRIENDS OF GOVERNMENT ; they may want the fenfe to difcern their danger in time, or *the courage to refift when it ftares them in the face.*

" The Tarquins were expelled, and Rome refumed her liberty ; Cæfar was murdered, and all his race extinct ; but Rome remained in bondage. Whence this difference ? In the days of Tarquin, the *people* of Rome were not yet corrupted; in the days of Cæsar, they were moſt corrupt.

" A free people may be ſometimes betrayed; but no people will betray themſelves, and ſacrifice their liberty, unleſs they fall into a ſtate of UNNIVERSAL CORRUPTION.

" As all government began, ſo all government muſt END by the people; tyrannical government, by their virtue and courage; and even free governments, by their VICE and BASENESS. Our conſtitution indeed makes it impoſſible to deſtroy liberty by any ſudden blaſt of popular fury, or by the TREACHERY OF THE FEW; but if the MANY will concur with the FEW; if they will adviſedly and deliberately ſuffer their liberty to be *taken away*, by thoſe on whom they DELEGATE POWER TO PRESERVE IT, this no conſtitution can prevent. God would not ſupport his own theocracy againſt the concurrent deſire of the children of Iſrael; but *gave them a king in his anger*.

" How then ſhould our human conſtitution of government ſupport itſelf againſt ſo univerſal a CHANGE, as we here ſuppoſe, in the TEMPER and CHARACTER of the PEOPLE. It cannot be. We may give ourſelves a tyrant, if we pleaſe. But this can never happen, till the whole nation falls into a ſtate of political reprobation. Then, and not till then, political damnation will be our lot."

So far a political writer, who ſtrenuouſly ſupports the cauſe of liberty, and who has been, for that reaſon, lately depreciated. The words juſt now cited are worthy the ſerious conſideration of every man who wiſhes to leave the inheritance of liberty, which he received from his forefathers, unimpaired to his poſterity. We are jealous of charters, privileges, and laws, but not ſufficiently aware of the danger which liberty incurs from degencracy of manners. But what avail laws preventing *conſtructive* treaſon, and bills of rights, aſcertaining our liberties, without virtuous diſpoſitions in the people?

———— Quid leges ſine moribus
Vanæ proficient? Hor.

A charter, as an advocate at the Engliſh bar expreſſed it, it is but a piece of parchment with a bit of wax dangling to it, if men have loſt that energy of mind which is neceſſary to preſerve the rights it was intended to confer or ſecure. The trial by jury, the bulwark of liberty, as we have lately experienced it in very remarkable inſtances, will be but a tottering wall, when oaths have loſt their ſanctity, and when truth and juſtice are conſidered only as phantoms. What will avail a conſtitution, when every one is immerſed in private concerns, private pleaſures, and private intereſt, acknowledging no PUBLIC CARE, no *general* concern, nothing out of the ſphere of domeſtic or perſonal affairs, worthy of anxious regard?

I lately heard a ſenſible man affirm, in a tone of apparent deſpondency, that in England there was, at the time he ſpoke, NO PUBLIC.

I thought the expreſſion ſtrong, and pauſed to conſider it. I hope it was the ebullition of ſudden vexation at circumſtances, which, when it was ſpoken, ſeemed to argue a general inſenſibility in the PEOPLE to the bleſſings of a free country. It was uttered at a time when a zeal, real or pretended, for the *miniſters* of government, ſeemed totally to overlook, in its miſtaken ardor, the PUBLIC WARFARE.

"There is NO PUBLIC," ſaid the ſagacious obſerver. I underſtood him to mean, that from an ambitious attachment to party, in ſome of the higher ranks; to ſelf-intereſt, in ſome of the lower; to general diſſipation, in all, the number of independent, liberally minded, and well-informed men who zealouſly wiſhed and ſought the *public good* and the *happineſs of man*, was too inconſiderable to effect any great and important purpoſe. Public virtue muſt ariſe from private. Great pretenſions to it may be made by the profligate, but they will be found to originate in ſelfiſhneſs, in rancour, in envy, or ſome corrupt principle inconſiſtent with a virtuous character and benevolent conduct.

If there be ſuch a defection from private and public virtue, what is to preſerve a regard for the conſtitution, whenever miniſterial influence ſhall ſo far prevail as to render it the perſonal intereſt of great majorities of POWERFUL, becauſe RICH, men, to neglect it, or even to connive at infringements upon it? If the people fall into univerſal corruption, the words *liberty* and *conftitution* will be confidered by them as fit only to adorn a fchool-boy's declamation. In fuch a ftate there will be no more fecurity for the tenant of a throne than of a cottage. A junto, that has no regard for either, and is folely actuated by the love of power, its diftinctions and emoluments may, by diftributing diftinctions and emoluments on *many*, and by raifing the hopes and expectations of *more*, make the mafs of the people themfelves (thus corrupted at the very fountain-head) become the inftruments of annihilating the beft part of the conftitution. A limited monarch, whofe throne is founded on the bafis of a people's affection, and a judicious preference both of his perfon and form of government, will be as reafonably anxious as any among the people can be, to guard againft the prevalence of fuch corruption, and the fuccefs of fuch corruptors. It is the caufe of *courts*, if they mean to confult their ftability, as much as it is of popular conventions, to preferve public virtue, and prevent the people from lofing all *fenfibility* to the value of a free conftitution, the liberty of the prefent age, and of ages to come.

I firmly maintain, that the prevention of this popular degeneracy is to be effected, not by political artifices, not by profecutions, not by fycophantic affociations of placemen, penfioners, and expectants of titles and emoluments, but by reforming the manners of the people. Principles of religion, honor, and public fpirit muft be cherifhed. The *clergy* muft be *inde-*

pendent, and the PULPIT FREE. Books written without party views, intending to promote no interests but thofe of truth and philanthropy, muft not only not be checked by *crown* lawyers, but induftrioufly diffeminated among the people. Religion muft be confidered by the GREAT, not merely as a ftate engine, but as what it is, the fource of comfort and the guide of confcience. Its profeffional teachers muft be advanced from confiderations of real merit and fervices, and not from borough intereft, and the proftitution of the pulpit to the unchriftian purpofes of minifterial defpotifm.

No writings of fceptical or infidel philofophers do fo much harm to chriftian faith and practice, to religion and morality, as the ufing of CHURCH *revenues* and CHURCH *inftruction* as inftruments of court corruption. The very means appointed by God and the laws, for checking the depravity of the people, contribute to it, when they appear to be confidered by the GREAT as little more than artifices of politicians, defigned to keep the vulgar (as they are often unjuftly called) in fubjection to wicked upftarts, poffeffed of temporary and official power, by intrigue and unconftitutional influence.

It is certainly in the power of a well regulated government, by rendering the CHURCH effective, and by good examples and fincere attachment to virtuous men and virtuous principles, to correct the levity, effeminacy, and want of principle in private life, which leads to the lofs of liberty. The church will be effective, as foon as the people are convinced that all preferments in it are beftowed on thofe who have preached the gofpel faithfully ; and not on time-fervers, and the friends and relarelations of parafites, who have no other view in feeking feats in the fenate, but to ferve a minifter for their own advantage. Till the people are convinced that an *adminiftration is fincere in religion*, they will be too apt to confider not only *religion*, but common *honefty*, as an empty name.

The religious principle being thus deftroyed by the greedy afpirants at worldly grandeur, no wonder the people lapfe into that diffolute conduct, which feeks nothing ferioufly but felfifh pleafure and private profit. Levity of manners both proceeds from, and produces, *defect of moral principle*. Effeminacy, the natural confequence of vice and luxury caufed by *defect of moral principle*, precludes courage, fpirit, and all manly, virtuous exertion. Ignorance muft follow; for to obtain knowledge requires a degree of labor and laudable application, which thofe who are funk in indolence and fenfuality will never beftow. When ignorance is become general, and vice reigns triumphant, what remains to oppofe the giant Defpotifm, who, like a Coluffus, ftrides over the pigmy and infignificant flaves of oriental climes, from trampling on MEN in countries once free ?

Farewell, then, all that truly ennobles human nature. Pride, pomp, and CRUELTY domineer without control. The very name of liberty becomes odious; and man, degenerated, contents himfelf with the licence to eat, drink, fleep, and die at the will of an ignorant, bafe, libidinous fuperior. The fword rules abfolutely. Reafon, law, philofophy, learning, repofe in the tomb with departed liberty. The fun of the moral world is extinguifhed; and the earth is overfhadowed with darknefs and with death. Better had it been for a man not to have been born, than born in a country rendered by the wickednefs of government, corrupting and enflaving a *whole people*, a HELL anticipated.

SECTION XIX.

Certain Paffages in Dr. Brown's *" Eftimate"*
which deferve the ferious Confideration of all
who would oppofe the Subverfion of a free
Conftitution by Corruption of Manners and
Principles, and by undue Influence.

FEW books have been more popular
than Brown's *Eftimate of the Manners and
Principles of the Times.* He wrote with fincerity and ability ; but his unfortunate end, occafioned by mental difeafe, had a very unfavorable influence on the circulation of his
book, and his pofthumous fame. Nothing
can, however, be more unreafonable, than to
depreciate a book, allowed by all, at its firft
appearance, to contain indifputable and important truth, becaufe of the misfortune, or even
mifconduct, of its author fubfequent to its
publication. I confidently recommend the following paffages to the confideration of every
true lover of that free conftitution, which renders our country confpicuoufly happy and honorable among the nations which furround it.

" The reftraints laid on the royal prerogative at the revolution, and the acceffion of
liberty thus gained by the PEOPLE, produced
two effects with refpect to parliaments. One
was, that inftead of being *occafionally*, they
were thenceforward *annually* affembled ; the

other was, that whereas on any trifling offence
given they had ufually been *intimidated* or *dif-
folved*, they now found themfelves poffeffed of
new dignity and power; their confent being
neceffary for raifing *annual fupplies.*

" No body of men, except in the fimpleft
and moft virtuous times, ever found *themfelves
poffeffed of power*, but many of them would
attempt to turn it to their OWN PRIVATE AD-
VANTAGE. Thus the parliament, finding
themfelves of weight, and finding, at the fame
time, that the difpofal of all *lucrative employments* was vefted in the crown, foon bethought
themfelves, that in exchange for *their* concurrence in granting fupplies, and *forwarding the
meafures of government*, it was but equitable
that the crown fhould concur in vefting them
or their dependents with the *lucrative employments* of ftate.

" If this was done, the wheels of government ran fmooth and quiet; but if any large
body of claimants was difpoffeffed, the public
uproar began, and public meafures were ob-
ftructed or overturned.

" William the Third found this to be the
natural turn, and fet himfelf like a *politician*,
to oppofe it; he therefore filenced all he could
by places and penfions, and hence the origin
of MAKING OF PARLIAMENTS."

This *making of parliaments*, I contend, is
fundi noftri calamitas, the origin of all our
prefent political evil; it defeated the good

purpofes of the revolution, and tended to introduce the defpotifm of the Stuarts, under the mafk of liberty. It arofe from the corruption of the people ; and has gone on augmenting it to this very day.

" Vanity, luxury and effeminacy (proceeds Dr. Brown) increafed beyond all belief within thefe thirty years ; as they are of a *felfifh*, fo are they of a craving and unfatisfied nature. The prefent rage of pleafure and UNMANLY DISSIPATION hath created a train of *new* neceffities, which in their demands outftrip every fupply.

" And if the great principles of religion, honor, and public fpirit are weak or loft among us, what effectual check can there be upon the GREAT, to control their unwarranted purfuit of LUCRATIVE EMPLOYMENTS, for the gratification of thefe unmanly paffions ?

" In a nation fo circumftanced, it is natural to imagine that, next to GAMING and RIOT, the *chief attention* of the GREAT WORLD muft be turned on the bufinefs of ELECTION JOBBING, of SECURING COUNTIES, controling, bribing or BUYING BOROUGHS ; in a word, on the poffeffion of a great parliamentary intereft.

" But what an aggravation of this evil would arife, fhould ever thofe of the *higheft rank*, though PROHIBITED BY ACT OF PARLIAMENT, infult the laws, by interfering in elections, by foliciting votes, or procuring others to folicit them, by influencing elections in an avowed defiance of their country, and

even *selling* vacant feats in parliament to the
BEST BIDDER."

Would not this be TREASON *against the
constitution?* a more dangerous and heinous
political crime than any that have been profecuted by attornies-general? Does not this
directly destroy the democratical part of the
fystem, and establish a power, independent
both of the monarch and the people? Are not
both, therefore, interested in putting a stop to
fuch grofs violations of law and equity?

"What (continues Dr. Brown) can we fuppofe would be the real drift of this illegitimate
wafte (among the GREAT) of time, honors,
wealth, and labor? Might not the very reafon
publicly affigned for it be this: ' that they
may ftrengthen themfelves and families, and
thus gain a lafting interest (as they call it)
for their dependents, fons, and pofterity?'———Now, what would this imply but
a fuppofed *right or privilege* of DEMANDING
LUCRATIVE EMPLOYS, as the chief object of
their views?—We fee then, how the political
fystem of felf-interest is at length completed.

" Thus faction is establifhed, not on ambition, but on AVARICE: on AVAIRCE and
RAPACITY, for the ends of DISSIPATION.

" The great contention among thofe of
family and fortune, will be in the affair of
ELECTION INTEREST: next to effeminate
pleafure and *gaming;* this (for the fame end
as gaming) will of courfe be the capital purfuit;
this interest will naturally be regarded as a

kind of *family fund*, for the provision of the younger branches.

" In a nation so circumstanced, many high and important posts, in every public and important profession, must of course be filled by men, who, instead of *ability* and *virtue*, plead this *interest* (in elections) for their BEST TITLE.

" Thus, in a time when science, capacity, courage, honor, religion, public spirit are rare, the remaining FEW who possess these virtues, will often be *shut out* from these stations, which they would fill with honor ; while every public and important employ will abound with men, whose manners and principles are of the *newest* fashion.

" Is not the *parliamentary interest* of every powerful family continually rung in the ears of its branches and dependents? And does not this inevitably tend to relax and weaken the application of the *young men* of quality and fortune, and render every man, who has reliance on this principle, *less qualified* for those very stations, which by this very principle he obtains. For why should a *youth of family or fashion*, (thus he argues with himself), why should he submit to the *drudgery of schools, colleges, academies*, voyages, campaigns, fatigues, and dangers, when he *can rise to the highest stations* by *the smooth and easy path of parliamentary interest?*

" Where effeminacy and selfish vanity form the ruling character of a people, then those of *high rank* will be of all others moſt vain, moſt ſelfiſh, moſt incapable, moſt effeminate.

"Such are the effects of the prevailing principle of ſelf-intereſt in *high life*. But if we take into the account all that *deſpicable train* of political managers, agents, and borough-jobbers, which hang like *leeches* upon the GREAT, nor ever quit their hold till they are full gorged, we ſhall then ſee this reigning evil in its laſt perfection. For here, to *incapacity* and *demerit*, is generally added INSOLENCE. Every low fellow of this kind looks upon the man of genius, capacity, and virtue, as his *natural enemy*. He regards him with an evil eye; and hence *undermines* or defames him; as one who thwarts his views, queſtions his title, and endangers his *expectations*."

In another place, the ſame anthor very plainly deduces the corruption of the *youth of the nation*, the young nobility and gentry in particular, from *parliamentary corruption*.

"Notwithſtanding the privilege veſted in the commons of commanding the purſes of their conſtituents, it is not difficult to point out a ſituation, where this privilege would be nothing but a *name*. And as in the laſt century the regal and democratic branches by turns bore down the conſtitution, ſo, in ſuch a ſituation as is here ſuppoſed, the real danger, though hidden, would lurk in the *ariſtocratic* branch, which would be ſecretly bearing down the power both of the king and the people.

"The matter may be explained in a ſmall

compafs. Cannot we put a cafe, in which the *parliamentary interest* of the *great nobility* might fwallow up the houfe of commons? Members might be elected, indeed; and elected in *form* too. But by whom might they be *really* elected? By the free voice of the people? No impartial man would fay it. It were eafy to fuppofe thirty or forty men, who, if wanted, might go nigh to command a majority in the lower houfe. The members might *feem* to be the reprefentatives of the people; but would be, in truth, a great part of them, no more than the *commiffioned deputies* of their refpective *chiefs*, whofe fentiments they would give, and whofe *interefts* they would purfue.

" Thus, while power would, in appearance, be centering in the lower houfe, it would in reality be lurking in the higher.

" This ftate of things might not perhaps refult from any defign in the ariftocratic branch to deftroy the conftitution. They might have no farther views than thofe of *gain, vanity, or pleafure*. Notwithftanding this, their conduct might have thofe effects which their intentions never afpired to. Let us confider the moft probable effects.

" The firft fatal effect which offers itfelf to obfervation is, that the confcioufnefs of fuch an increafing and exorbitant power, which the lords might acquire in the houfe of commons, would deftroy all *honeft ambition* in the *younger gentry*. They would know, that the utmoft point they could hope to arrive at would only be to become the *deputy* of some *great lord*, in a county or borough.   All the intentions of such a post can be answered by *ignorance and servility, better* than by *genius and public spirit.* People of the latter stamp, therefore, would not naturally be appointed to the task ; and this, once known, would check the *growth of genius and public spirit* throughout the nation.   The few men of ability and spirit that might be left, seeing this to be the case, would naturally betake themselves to such *private amusements* as a free mind can honestly enjoy.   All *hope*, and therefore, by degrees, all *desire* of serving their country, would be extinguished.

"Thus HONEST ambition would naturally and generally be quenched. But even where ambition *continued*, it would be *perverted*.   Not useful, but *servile* talents would be applauded ; and the ruling pride would be, not that of freemen, but of slaves."

The above remarks were made long before American independence was established, the French revolution thought of, or the discussions on the subject of parliamentary reform became general.   The author wrote the pure result of impartial observation ; and what he wrote deserves the serious attention of all HONEST *men*, all good members of the community.   I will make no comments upon it, but leave it to operate on the mind with its own force.

SECTION XX.

On several Subjects suggested by Lord Melcombe's *" Diary," particularly the Practice of bartering the Cure of Souls for the Corruption of Parliament.*

IT is very defirable, that country gentlemen, who are often inclined to fhew a blind attachment to minifters, as if LOYALTY were due to the *fervants* of a court as well as to the mafter, would perufe, with attention, the Diary of Lord Malcombe. There they are admitted behind the curtain, and even under the ftage, to fee the machinery. There they behold filthy workmen, dirty wheels within wheels, every thing offenfive to the eye, and all bufy for hire to produce a fpecious, outfide fhew on the ftage, for the amufement of the fpectators, while the fhew-men pocket the pence. It would have been worth the while of courtiers to have paid the price of a campaign in Flanders, and the fubfidy of a German prince, to have fuppreffed the publication of Lord Malcombe's Diary. The fecrets of the minifterial conclave are there laid open; and the fight and ftench are no lefs difguftful than thofe which ftrike the fenfes on the opening of a jakes or a common fewer. Nothing but the moft felfifh covetoufnefs, the weakeft vanity, the meaneft, dirtieft, moft villainous of the paffions! No regard *for the happinefs of the nation*, much lefs *for the happinefs of mankind*; one general ftruggle, by artifice and intrigue, not by honorable and ufeful exertions, for power, profit, and titles! It might be fuppofed, that the parties concerned were banditti, contending in a cave about the divifion of plunder. How are the words *lord* and *duke* difgraced and proftituted, when prefixed to mifcreants warmly engaged in fuch tranfactions! Such men are truly levellers, the enemies of the peerage, the involuntary promoters of equality! In a greedy rapacioufnefs for themfelves, they forget not only the good of their country and mankind, but the intereft of their own privileged order.

When little and bafe minds, like the heroes of *Bubb Doddington*'s Diary, be a rule, every thing, even religion itfelf, becomes an inftrument of corruption. It is well underftood by every body, that church preferments, even with *cure* of *fouls*, have long been ufed to fecure the intereft of courts in venal boroughs; but the following paffage contains a curious proof of it, under the hand of Lord Malcombe, and under the authority of the then prime minifter, the Duke of Newcaftle.

"December the 11th, 1753," fays Lord Melcombe, "I faw the Duke of Newcaftle. I told him, that in the election matters (of Bridgwater and Weymouth) *thofe who would take money I* would pay, and not bring him a bill; thofe that would not take, *he muft pay*;

and I recommended *my two parfons* of Bridg-water and Weymouth, Burroughs and Frank-lin :—he entered into it *very cordially*, and af-fured me they fhould have the firft *crown livings* that fhould be vacant in thofe parts, if we would look out and fend him the firft intelli-gence.—I faid, I muft think, that fo much of-fered, and fo little afked, in fuch hands as theirs, and at a time when *boroughs* were par-ticularly *marketable*, could not fail of removing, at leaft, refentments, and of obtaining par-don..... His Grace was very hearty and cordial.

" 29th. Went to the Duke of Newcaftle, and got the living of Broadworthy for Mr. Burroughs.

" March 21. Went to the Duke of New-caftle—told him I was come to affure him of my moft *dutiful* affection and fincere attach-ment to him, having no engagements to make me look to the right or the left .... I *engaged to choofe two members* for Weymouth, which he defired might be a fon of the Duke of Devonfhire, and Mr. Ellis of the admiralty. I fuppofed he would confirm that nomination— *but that was nothing to me.** He might name whom he pleafed.—Mr. Pelham told me the KING afked him if I ferioufly defigned to en-deavor to keep Lord Egmont out of Bridgwa-ter. Mr. Pelham told his Majefty that he thought I would ; that I defired him *to lay me*

---

* ———————— *Tuus, O dux magne, quid optes*
Explorare labor ; MIHI *juffa capeffere fas eft.* VIRG.

at the king's feet, and tell him, that as I found it would be *agreeable* to his *majesty,* I would spare neither pains nor expence to exclude him. The Duke of Newcastle said he had seen *how handsome my proceedings had been*; that this was the *most noble* that could be imagined! ... I said, What if I came into the place Sir Thomas Robinson left? He considered a little, and said, Very well, pray go on. I said I would particularly support him in the house *where* he would chiefly want it. He said he knew I would. I said, There is my old place—Treasurer of the Navy; I should like that *better than any thing.* But I added, Why should I enter into these things; I leave it wholly to your grace. He said the *direction* of the *house of commons* was fallen upon him—therefore he could not chuse by affection, but must comply with those who could support him *there.* I said I understood so; and that I thought I might pretend to some abilities *that way*; that in the opposition, I was thought of some use *there*; that in court, indeed, I never undertook much, *because he knew I never was supported*: but now, *when I should be supported*, I hoped I might pretend to be as useful there as my neighbors. He said it was incontestably so. I said, that considering that I chose *six members for them* at my own great expence, I thought the world in general, and even the gentlemen themselves, could not expect that their pretensions should give me the exclusion. He said, that what I did was *very great*! that he often thought with furprife at the eafe and cheapnefs of the election at Weymouth ! that they had nothing like it ! I faid, I believed there were few who could give *his majefty fix members for nothing.* He faid he reckoned five, and had put down five to my account.... I faid I muft be excufed from talking any more about myfelf; that I left it entirely to him and to the King ; that I was fully determined to make this facrifice to his Majefty ; that I knew I had given no juft caufe of offence, but that I would not juftify it with his Majefty ; that it was *enough* that he was difpleafed, to make me think that I was in the wrong, and to beg him to forget it : *I would not even be in the right againft him*; and I was very fure I would never again be in the wrong againft him, for which I hoped his Grace would be my caution. He faid he would with all his heart. *He took me up in his arms,* and *kiffed me twice,* with ftrong affurances of affection and fervice."

A few days after, this *honeft man* went to Bridgwater to manage the election, and thus proceeds his Diary.

"April 14, 15, 16. *Spent in the infamous and difagreeable compliance with the low habits of venal wretches,*" the electors of Bridgwater.

If the men of Bridgwater, urged perhaps by want, were *venal wretches,* what muft we think of the Duke of Newcaftle and Lord Melcombe ? I hope my reader will paufe, and ponder the words of the preceding paffage.

They furnish a great deal of matter for very ferious reflection to thofe who regard the true interefts either of church or ftate.

Lord Melcombe's Diary was much read when it firft came out; but it has fince fallen into neglect. Events, however, have happened in the political world, which render it extremely interefting at the prefent period. In confequence of the French revolution, much pains have been taken to decry the people, and extol the ariftocratical part of fociety. The tide has run wonderfully, in confequence of *falfe alarms* and minifterial artifices, in favor of courts and courtiers. The people have been called, not only *venal wretches*, but the fwinifh multitude. Long and tirefome books have been written to run down the people, as deftitute of virtue, principle, of every thing honeft and honorable, and that can give them any right to interfere with the grand myfteries of a cabinet. But he who reads and confiders duly the very ftriking anecdotes and converfations in Lord Melcombe's Diary, will fee, that, in order to find venality in its full growth, and furvey fordidnefs in its complete ftate of abomination, it will be neceffary to turn from low to high life.

The people are often turbulent and indifcreet in their tranfactions, but they are always honeft and always generous. They feel ftrongly for the caufe of humanity and juftice. They have a noble fpirit, which leads them to view meannefs and finifter conduct with deteftation.

But is there any of this manly independence, this honeſt openneſs, this regard for the rights and happineſs of man, among thoſe whom Lord Melcombe, ſo unfortunately for the great vulgar, has introduced to public notice ? There is all the deceit in his own character, which would denominate a man a ſwindler in the commercial walks of life. All the tranſactions of the junto are conducted with the timidity, ſecrecy, duplicity of a neſt of thieves, mutually fearing and fawning, while they hate and deſpiſe each other from their heart's core.

On the practice of purchaſing votes in boroughs, by bartering the cure of ſouls, the moſt ſacred charge, if there be any thing ſacred in human affairs, I ſhall expatiate more at large in a future Section.

This Bubb Doddington, after ſelling himſelf, betraying the prince, and offering his ſix members to the beſt bidder, was made a lord. He was created Baron of Melcombe Regis, as a reward for ſuch proſtitution of principles as ought to have cauſed him to be branded in the forehead with a mark of indelible infamy.

But can we ſuppoſe that there has been but one Bubb Doddington in this country ? one Newcaſtle ? I wiſh the ſuppoſition were founded in probability. It would be the ſimplicity of idiotiſm to ſuppoſe, that Bubb Doddington has not exhibited in his Diary a picture of paraſitical courtiers, in all times and countries, where corruption is the main principle of adminiſtration.

If *such men* fhould, in any country of Europe, influence the councils of princes, and manage the popular affemblies, would there not be reafon to be alarmed for the beft conftitution ever devifed by human wifdom? *Such men* hate the people. They love nothing but themfelves, the emoluments of places, the diftinction of titles, and the pomp and vanity of the courts in which they flatter and are flattered. They will ever wifh for a MILITARY government, to *awe* the faucy crowd, and keep them from intruding on their own facred privileges and perfons. The Herculean hand of a virtuous people can alone cleanfe the Augean ftable of a corrupted court formed of mifcreant toad-eaters like Lord Melcombe.

Q

SECTION XXI.

*On choosing rich Men, without Parts, Spirit,
or Liberality, as Representatives in the National Council.*

IT has been long obferved, that none
are more defirous of increafing their property
than they who have abundance. The greateft mifers are thofe who poffefs the greateft
riches. None are fonder of the world than
they who have engroffed a large fhare of it. If
they fhould acknowledge that they have enough
money, yet they cannot but confefs, at the
fame time, that they think themfelves entitled,
in confequence of their property, to civil honors,
power, and diftinction. They have a kind
of claim, in their own opinion, to court favor ;
efpecially as they are ready to ufe the influence,
which their riches give them, in fupport of any
minifter for the time being, and in the general
extenfion of royal prerogative. Are fuch men
likely to be independent members of a fenate,
honeftly following the dictates of their judgment
or confcience, and confulting no intereft but
that of MAN in general, and the people in particular, by whom they are deputed? There
are no men *greedier* of gain than fuch men, and
none more attached to thofe vain honors, which
a minifter beftows in order to facilitate the movements of his political machine. None will rake

so deeply in the *dirt* to pick up a penny as a rich miser ; none will contend more eagerly for a feather in the cap, than those whose minds are weak, empty, and attached to the world by the consciousness of being, in great measure, its proprietors.

But what is it to me, as an *elector*, that the man who solicits my vote has, by great cunning, sordid arts, and insatiable avarice, accumulated great riches ? Has wisdom, has virtue, has knowledge, has philanthropy increased with his increasing fortune ? Uncommon success, enormous wealth, acquired in the short space of half a human life, is a *presumptive* evidence of *little principle* in the means of acquiring, and as little generosity in the modes of giving or expending it. Perhaps he *inherits* his unbounded riches. What then ? His *ancestors* were probably knaves or muck-worms. In this case, he has not to plead the merit of industry. His ancestors have left him vast sums of money ; when perhaps his own talents would scarcely have earned him a penny, or kept him out of the parish poor-house.

Nevertheless, because he is rich, though totally destitute of parts and virtue, he stands forward boldly as a candidate to represent a city or a county. He finds thousands ready to clamour on his side, and to give him their vote. He can treat bountifully, open houses, and give away ribands plentifully. Therefore he is constituted a senator, a national counsellor, commiſſioned to vote away the people's money, and to decide on the moſt important queſtions of conſtitutional liberty.

What can he do but put himſelf into harneſs, and be driven his daily ſtage, by the political coachman, the prime miniſter? He cannot go alone. He has not ſenſe enough to judge for himſelf in the ſmalleſt difficulty. He has not ſpirit enough to preſerve his independence; therefore he will conſider himſelf merely as a puppet, to be moved by the higher powers, at their will; a ſtop-gap, to fill up a place which might be occupied by an abler member, whoſe virtues and talents might ſerve the public indeed, but would render him troubleſome to thoſe who gladly diſpenſe with all virtuous interference.

Let us ſuppoſe, for argument ſake, four ſuch *poor* creatures (ſuch I call them, though *rich* in gold) choſen to repreſent the city of London, the grand emporium of the world, and, from the number of its inhabitants, claiming a fuller repreſentation than any part of the nation. I own the ſuppoſition is moſt diſgraceful; for it can never happen, one would think, that ſuch a city ſhould not ſupply men of the firſt *abilities*, for a truſt ſo important and ſo honorable. But let us ſuppoſe the CITY, from a ſyſtem of manners favored by, and favorable to, miniſterial corruption, ſo far degraded as to chooſe four men of very moderate abilities and characters, merely becauſe they happen to be rich contractors, and of ſycophantic diſpo-

fitions, likely to purfue their *own* intereft by
fervilely obeying the beck of a minifter.

Suppofe them once in for feven years. The
taverns are now fhut up, the *advertifements*,
the canvaffing all forgotten, and they commence
as arrant courtiers as the meaneft tool of power,
put, by a paltry lord, into a rotten borough of
Suflex, Wiltfhire, or Cornwall.

But mark the mifchief. As they nominally
reprefent the firft city in the world, the meafures which *they* vote for, (becaufe they are
bidden, and hope for contracts and baronet-
ages), are fuppofed, by foreigners at leaft, to
have the concurrence of the moft important
part of the Britifh empire. Though the minifter may defpife them from his heart, per-
fonally, yet he avails himfelf of that weight
which the place they reprefent gives them in
the eyes of ftrangers. " The GREAT *city* is
with him," (in the only place he pretends to
know it, the houfe of reprefentatives).

Their ignorance, their meannefs, and their
fycophancy, have another effect, highly injurious to all plans of conftitutional reformation.
" Here (fays the courtier) are four men fent
by the firft city in the world. Are they better
fenators, or more refpectable men, than thofe
who are fent from Old Sarum, or any of the
boroughs inhabited by beggars, and purchafed
by lords, as a lucrative fpeculation ?" The
probability is, (he will fay of them), that,
with more *greedinefs after gain*, from the fordid habits of their youth, they have lefs of the

Q 2

accomplishments and liberality of
Their eagerness to raise their famil
them more tractable tools in the
skilful minister, than those whose
already raised, and who, howeve
place themselves under the guid
peerage, have had an education \
to have given them enlarged minc
ments of honor.

Thus the friend to despotic pri:
the oppofer of parliamentary reforn
argument from the meanness of ricl
by *great cities* to parliament mei
they are rich), against all improve;
representation. The boroughs,
send at least *gentlemen*, and well-inf
though in circumstances comparative
whereas these great commercial boc
all excellence in the poffeffion of supe
depute men as fenators, who are
for any department beyond the w
the counting-house, whose views a
and purpofes *habitually* fordid and
urges, that, from the fpecimens :
great cities, there is no reafon t
that the extenfion of the right of fu:
render the reprefentative body m·
or enlightened. He doubts wheth
be favorable to liberty. If great b·
men only for their property, finc
have moft ufually *want* moft, none
dier to fell themfelves and their coi
a minifter, for a feather or fugar-p

the reprefentatives of great bodies, delegated to parliament merely becaufe they have inhe-. rited or acquired *exceffive riches*, with fcarcely any ideas beyond the multiplication-table.

Men deputed to parliament, fhould certainly be far above want ; but I contend that riches, independent of perfonal merit, can never be a fufficient recommendation. It is the moft important truft that can be repofed in man. It requires a moft comprehenfive education, ftrong natural abilities, and, what is greater than all, a juft, honeft, upright heart, with a manly firmnefs, and an enlarged philanthropy.

Can there be any difficulty in finding, at any time, four men of fuch character in the city of London, or two fuch in any county of England ? Certainly not ; efpecially when the corrupting idea fhall be exploded, that PRO-PERTY is the beft qualification of a national counfellor and law-giver. *Able* and *honeft* men are not the moft inclined to thruft themfelves forward, and to *obtrude* themfelves, much lefs to enter into competition, when all the influence of riches and minifterial favor will be exerted to traduce their character, to fruftrate their endeavors, and fend them back to private life with their fortunes injured, and their tranquillity difturbed. The electors muft *fearch* for fuch men, and draw them from their virtuous obfcurity. Thus honored, they will go into the fenate with the pure motives of ferving their country and mankind, and return with *clean hands*, fufficiently rewarded by the bleffings of the people.

The city of London, and all great cities, as well as counties, are to be moſt feriouſly exhorted to conſider the importance of the truſt they delegate at an election, and to chooſe men of known abilities, and experienced attachment to the cauſe of the people. They ſhould beware of men, however opulent and reſpectable in private life, who can have no other motive for obtruding on public life, for which they are *unqualified*, but to raiſe themſelves, and families to fortune and diſtinction, by *ſelling their truſt* to a miniſter. Such men can never be friends to liberty and the people. They contribute, by means of their property, to the general ſyſtem of corruption, and, perhaps without knowing it, (for they *know* but little), promote, moſt effectually, the ſpirit of deſpotiſm.

SECTION XXII.

Of the despotic influence of great Merchants over their Subalterns, of Customers *over their Tradesmen, and rich trading Companies over their various Dependents, in* compelling *them to vote for* Court *Candidates for Seats in Parliament, merely to serve* PRIVATE IN-TEREST, *without the smallest Regard for* public *Liberty and Happiness, or the Fitness or Unfitness of the Candidate.*

THE rottenness of corruption, originating from ministers, intoxicated with the love of power, and greedy after the emoluments of office, is sometimes found (especially under the influence of *false alarms*) to pervade the whole mass of the people, and to infect the very heart of the body politic. The vitals of liberty become tainted, and, without great efforts, a *mortification* may be justly apprehended.

In this corrupt state, *little despots,* aspiring at court favor, hoping to draw the notice of the minister on their faithful endeavors to serve him, arise in almost every town and village of the country, and in every street of a great city. They claim and exercise a jurisdiction over certain VASSALS, as they think them, their tradesmen, their tenants, and all others, who derive emoluments from them in the way of their bufinefs, or expect their cuftom and countenance. If the VASSALS prefume to act for themfelves as MEN and freemen, they lofe their bufinefs, their dwelling places, their farms, and all chance of acquiring a competency. The vengeance of the *little defpots* purfues them; and frequently quits not the chace, till it has hunted them down to deftruction.

Even in the CITY OF LONDON, opulent as it is, and *independent* as it might be, a city which ufed to be the firft to ftand up in defence of liberty, an overbearing influence can find its way to the obfcureft diftrict, and infinuate itfelf into the blindeft alley. The *Great Merchant or Manufacturer,* who is neceffarily connected with many fubordinate traders or workmen, confiders the influence he gains from extenfive connections in bufinefs, as a very valuable and vendible commodity at the *market* of a *minifter.* Naturally wifhing to make the moft of his trade, he refolves to treat this connection as a part of his *ftock*, and caufe it to bring him an *ample* return. At leaft he will *adventure.* It may be a prize to him, as it has been to many. Much depends on his own prudential management of the commodity. It may lead to a valuable *contract*, efpecially if kind fortune fhould kindle the flames of war; it may open the path to court favors of various kinds; it may ultimately confer a feat in the houfe, and perhaps a baronettage. This laft honor is highly defirable, as it removes at once the FILTH that naturally

attaches to the very name of *citizen, dealer*
and *chapman*.

In the city of London, the majority of *electors*,
who send the *few* members of parliament allotted to it, are of the *middle*, and indeed of the
inferior rank of shopkeepers, rarely rising to the
dignity of MERCHANTS, who reside at the
houses with *great gates*, or rather in the *new
squares*, two or three miles north-west of the
polluted and polluting *city* : for such is the
insolence of little city DESPOTS who are in a
very *great way*, that they commonly *despise* the
freedom of the city where their counting-house
stands, and where they gain their plumbs.
They do not *condescend* to be FREE of the city.
They would consider it as a degradation from
their *gentility* to be LIVERYMEN and members
of a city company. Liverymen, indeed !
What ! *great men*, as *all* BANKERS are, *East
India Directors*, usurious *money-lenders*, living
magnificently in Portland-place or Portman-
square, or the grand avenues to them, to be
LIVERYMEN ! Horrid degradation ! The
very idea is shocking to the *spirit of despotism*.
It is time enough to take up their FREEDOM of
the city, when it is necessary, as candidates,
to possess that qualification. There are too
many votes to make it *worth while* to be a voter.
These *great* men, therefore, view the electors
as subordinate persons, whom they may send
on an errand to Guildhall to VOTE for the
minister's candidate, just as they would dispatch
a clerk or porter to the Custom-house to take

a Cuſtom-houſe-oath, or to do any job connected with the *low* trade or manufacture which
enables them to aſſociate with the fine folk of
St. James's.

The *elector* who goes to the huſtings *muſt*,
indeed, vote upon his *oath*, that he *has* received
and *will* receive no BRIBE.   He does not conſider the lucrative employments and the emoluments ariſing from the *great man's* cuſtom,
which would be loſt on *diſobedience*, as a *bribe*,
and therefore votes againſt his judgment, conſcience, and inclination, without a murmur;
eſpecially as his daily bread may perhaps depend on his obſequiouſneſs, and very likely the
comfort and ſecurity of a wife and large family.

This conduct of the GREAT MEN is not only
unconſtitutional and affronting to the city, but
as truly DESPOTIC in principle as any thing
done by the Grand Seignior.   It is *mean* alſo
and baſe to the laſt degree; for the great men
uſually exert not their influence from friendſhip
to the miniſter, or to a candidate, or from any
regard to a cauſe which they think connected
with the public good; but ſolely to ſerve themſelves, to provide for poor relations, to enrich
or to aggrandize an upſtart family, already rendered contemptible by fungous pride.

The glorious rights and privileges of Engliſhmen, of which we read and hear ſo much,
are then to be all ſacrificed to ſerve a man, who
perhaps went out as a *writer* to the Eaſt Indies, and returned in five or ſix years, laden
with riches; the injured widow and orphan in

vain lifting up their heads, and uttering their lamentations over the deaf ocean, while the fpoiler is haftening to Europe with that treafure which, as it was gained by extortion, is to be expended in corruption.

Male parta male dilabuntur.

A prodigious recommendation this, as a reprefentative in parliament of induftrious citizens, who have toiled all their lives at the counter, or in the manufactory, for a bare competence!

When NABOBS, as they are called, perfect ALIENS, recommended only by riches and court influence, can *feat* themfelves for *great* cities and *counties* as eafily as they ufed for Cornifh BOROUGHS, there certainly is reafon to fear that the fpirit of defpotifm has rapidly increafed, and is proceeding to deftroy all remains of public virtue among the PEOPLE. The queftion naturally arifes, if a NABOB, a perfect alien, fhould ever be elected for the city of London; whether, in fo large a body as the free-born citizens, and among the livery of London, a man is not to be found who has ferved a regular apprenticefhip, gone through all the gradations of fuccefsful trade, and become a member of the corporation, worthy to reprefent the firft COMMERCIAL body in the univerfe? Is it neceffary to IMPORT members, as we do tea and muflins, from China and Bengal? Honefty, virtue, independence, and abilities, muft indeed be rare qualities, from

R

Templebar to Whitechapel, if not enough of them can be found to conftitute a reprefentative in parliament. Muft the Englifh oak be neglected, for EXOTICS raifed rapidly in warm climates; and from the hafty growth of which, very little is to be depended upon, when the wind and weather affail them? A fad encouragement this to the young merchants, traders, and manufacturers who enter regularly on bufinefs, and become freemen and *liverymen*, to find that the moft induftrious and fuccefsful trader, and the beft character, cannot fecure the honorable appointments and important trufts, in the gift of their fellow-citizens! to find, that perfons, who never ferved apprenticefhips, never carried on trade, never became free, never were connected in the city companies, perfect *ftrangers to the corporation*, and avowed *defpifers* of them ALL, fhall be made, by the influence of a minifter, and the overbearing weight of oriental riches, LEGISLATORS for the emporium of Europe! If fuch an event were ever to happen, it would difcourage all *virtue* in the *rifing generation* of merchants, traders, and manufacturers; and teach them, that every thing bows to ALMIGHTY MONEY, however obtained, and to COURT INFLUENCE, always ready to favor overbearing and overgrown property. It would be a melancholy fymptom of degeneracy among the people. It would fhew that the *manly fpirit* begins to fade and wither, as it has long done in *Turkey* and *Ægypt*, under the fpirit of defpotifm.

It is truly alarming to all true Englifhmen, to fee great *trading companies* ufing the influence which riches beftow, in feconding the views of a *minifter*, without the leaft attention to the public good, the prefervation of *liberty*, and the happinefs of the human race. It is certain, that men united in corporate bodies, will act in a manner which they would be afhamed of in their *private* capacities ; becaufe, when fo united, the refponfibility appears to be thrown from individuals on the AGGREGATE, and fo attaching to *every one*, can be fixed on *none*. Such bodies may be truly dangerous, when, from the hope of titles and other favors, the members who compofe them, are fervilely devoted to the *minifter;* not indeed to the *man*, but to the *favorite at court*, who, from his office, has in his hands the means of corruption, contracts, loans, lottery-tickets, appointments in all the profeffions, and, above all, TITLES.

Such monopolizing fraternities attack liberty with the club of Hercules. They rife with gigantic force. Reafon, argument, the law and the conftitution yield to them, as the chaff before the wind. If they fhould not receive a powerful check from the *people* at large, who have not yet fallen down worfhippers of GOLD, they muft go on to eftablifh, on the banks of the Thames, *oriental* defpotifm : and it would not be wonderful to fee the two fheriffs riding up Cheapfide on elephants, with the Lord Mayor borne in a *palanquin*, on the necks of liverymen, haftening to *proftrate* themfelves at the feet of a *prime minifter*, now become as great as the Emperor of China : it would not be wonderful to fee BANKERS erecting an *oligarchy;* the great houfe in Leadenhall-ftreet, *a temple,* and a *golden calf* the GOD.

SECTION XXIII.

Of the Pageantry of Life ; that it originates in the Spirit of Despotism ; and contributes to it, without advancing private any more than public Felicity.

THE proud despise the people, represent them as little superior to the brutes, laugh at the idea of their rights, and seem to think that the world was made for themselves only ; yet the proud are never satisfied but when they attract the notice of this very people, by splendor, by ostentation, by the exercise of authority over them, and by insolent airs of self-importance. The people, it must be owned, in the simplicity of their hearts, gape with admiration at the passing spectacle which insults them with its glare, and feel themselves awe-struck with the grandeur of the cavalcade, which would trample them in the dirt if they did not struggle to escape.

Politicians, observing this effect of finery and parade on the minds of the unthinking, take care to dress up the idol, which they themselves pretend to worship, and which they wish the people really to adore, in all the taudry glitter of the lady of Loretto. They find this kind of vulgar superstition extremely favorable to their interested views. Accordingly, in all despotic countries, great pains are taken to amufe and delude the people with the trappings of royalty. Popery prevailed more by the gaudinefs of its priefts and altars, and the pomp of its proceffions, than from the progrefs of conviction. The people, in fuch circumftances, have indeed the pleafure of fine fights; but they ufually pay much more dearly for them than for exhibitions at the theatre; and have this mortifying reflection, as a drawback from their pleafure, that the payment is involuntary, and the fight a political delufion. It infults their underftandings, while it beguiles them of their rights; and takes from them the earnings of their induftry, while it teaches them to feel their own infignificance.

But not only defpots, courtiers, and public functionaries, think it proper to ftrike the vulgar with awe, by purchafing finery of the builder, the taylor, and the coach-painter; but the titled and the overgrown rich men, through every part of every community, where family aggrandizement is procurable without public fervices, or private or perfonal virtue. Riches, in fuch focieties, confer not only the means of luxurious enjoyment, but of civil fuperiority. They affume a value not naturally their own, and become the *fuccedanea* of wifdom, patriotifm, valor, learning, and beneficence. The great object is therefore to make an oftentation of riches, and to keep the people at a diftance, by dazzling their eyes with the blaze of equipage and magnificence. As all the minuter luminaries gravitate to the fun

in our folar fyftem, fo all thefe afpirants at
diftinction and fuperior importance gravitate to
royalty. The crown is the glittering orb round
which they ambitioufly revolve. They would
all therefore contribute, if they were able, to
add new brilliancy, new heat, new influence
and powers of attraction to their fountain of
glory. They turn to it as the fun-flower to the
fun; and feel their colors brighter, and their
leaves invigorated, when a ray of favor falls
upon them in a peculiar direction. They cannot turn a moment to the people. The popular
climate chills them. The gales from this
quarter are as the icy breezes from the frozen
regions of the north, where the genial beams
of folar influence can fcarcely penetrate.

It may then be fairly prefumed, that where
all orders of the rich are vying with each other
to make a fplendid appearance, even above their
rank and means of fupport, the fpirit of the
times, among thefe orders at leaft, is favorable
to the increafe of court influence, and therefore to the fpirit of defpotifm.

This rivalry in fplendor is, in courfe, attended with great expence; an expence, which,
by reducing independent fortunes, diminifhes
independence of fpirit. They who are ruined
in feconding the purpofes of a court, naturally
think themfelves entitled to indemnity from
court favor. They become then, merely tools
of the minifter, and dare not fpeak or act, in
any inftance, againft him, left they renounce

all hope of the glittering prize, the fecret *douceur*, the fhare of the loan, the lottery-tickets, the contract, the place, the provifion for a fon, a nephew, a coufin, or the clerical tutor of the family, who has perhaps grown grey in hungry hope, fed only by the meagre diet of a minifterial promife.

Thus the rage for outfhining others in externals, contributes to ruin both fortune and principle. Add to this, that the prevalence of pageantry erects, in fociety, a falfe ftandard of human excellence. Money becomes the deity. Money is to give confequence, confideration, power. Money engroffes honor, which is due, and has often been paid, to poverty, when adorned with art, virtue, knowledge, or any other kind of perfonal merit. The man becomes nothing, and money all. How muft the human mind fink in fuch a conjuncture ! Its nobleft energies cannot give it that eftimation with mankind, which money, inherited by a fool, or acquired by a knave, boldly claims and obtains. Then what encouragement to young men to purfue improvement with any fingular ardor ? Common attainments are perhaps the beft adapted to facilitate the acquifition of money. Common attainments and fuperficial ornaments will form the whole of education. In the mean time, MIND is neglected, and human nature degenerates. Then fteps in the *defpot*. For the confequence, take the map, and look over the countries which formed ancient Greece.

The pageantry of life, confidered in a political view, as defigned by the *grandees* to awe the people, and keep them out of the PARK of felfifh happinefs, which the grandees have fenced with high pales, and guarded with fpring-guns and man-traps, certainly may lay claim to the praife of deep cunning or worldly wifdom. The pageantry of life may anfwer the purpofe of the fcenery of the play-houfe, and keep the vulgar from beholding the grandees of the world, before they are dreffed and *made up* for public exhibition. The galleries would certainly lofe much of their veneration for the theatrical kings, queens, and nobles, if they were to fee them behind the fcenes, unbedizened. The pageantry of life is therefore highly efficacious in deluding the vulgar. When not carried too far, and abufed for the purpofes of oppreffion, it may fometimes have its ufe. But is it, in general, conducive to the happinefs of man ; either of thofe who are the actors in the pageant, and gratify their pride by attracting the eyes of beholders ; or of thofe who are led by it to a foolifh admiration and a tame acquiefcence? Chains of gold and filver are no lefs galling than fetters of iron.

Pageantry has contributed perhaps more than any other caufe to the prevalence of war, the bane of happinefs, the difgrace of human nature. The grand operations of war, the fplendor of arms, the finery of military drefs, have been the amufements which defpots have chiefly delighted in, whenever they could behold them in perfect confiſtence with their own perſonal ſafety. The pageantry of war dazzles young minds, and ſupplies both armies and navies with willing victims. The uglineſs of ſlaughter, the deſolation of fertile plains, the burning of peaceful villages, have all been unnoticed, amid the *pride, pomp, and circum-ſtance of glorious war.* The taſte for falſe glare and deceitful appearances of happineſs and glory, has then been one of the moſt prolific parents of human calamity. It has palliated robbery, and covered foul murder with a glittering veil of tinſel.

All impoſture is ultimately productive of evil. Pageantry, in a wretched world like this, aſſumed by infirm mortals doomed ſhortly to die, cannot but be deceitful. Its object is to put off falſe and counterfeit goods for true. There is nothing in human affairs that will juſtify or ſupport that glare of happineſs which the pageantry of the rich and great ſeek to diſplay. The maſk is too ſmall and too tranſparent to conceal the face of woe, the wrinkles of decay and imperfection. In times of great ignorance, when ſcarcely any could read, and very little communication was preſerved among the different orders of ſociety, the mummery of courts and courtiers taught the vulgar to believe that the internal organization of beings, ſo decorated externally, muſt be of a ſuperior nature. Princes and prieſts dreſſed themſelves in groteſque garbs, in a kind of maſquerade habit, to carry on the delufion. But the reign of great wigs, fur gowns, hoods, and cloaks, is nearly at its clofe. Gilded coaches, horfes richly caparifoned, gaudy hammer-cloths, fine footmen, endeavor to fupply their place; but they have loft much of their influence; and at laft it will be found, that to obtain the refpect of the people, it will be neceffary to deferve it. No longer will the public admire the poor creature who rides *within* the coach, for a fplendor which he owes entirely to the manufacturer of carriages, the painter, the carver, the gilder, the harnefs-maker, the horfe-dealer, and the groom. No longer will men unjuftly transfer the praife due to the taylor and hair-dreffer, to the proud beau, who ftruts as if the earth were not good enough to tread upon, nor the people whom he meets, to look at as he paffes them.

The pageantry difplayed by contractors, by placemen, by penfioners, by commiffaries, by all who fatten on the public fpoils, may juftly be confidered as an infult on the people. In times of great profperity it might be winked at; but in times of diftrefs and adverfity, it is offenfive. It anfwers no good end. It merely gratifies the vanitiy of thofe who make the oftentation. How can they find in their hearts to throw away fums that would maintain thoufands, in fetting off themfelves, and making a figure, during an hour or two every day, in Bond-ftreet and Pall-Mall, while they pafs hundreds who are ready to perifh with cold and hunger, and cannot but know that the world abounds with inſtances of extreme want and miſery? The pageantry of the unfeeling great in France aggravated the ſenſe of ſuffering under its deſpotiſm; but, on the other hand, in provoking the people by the inſult, it accelerated and completed the glorious revolution.

It is probable that every little wretch who decorates himſelf, and all that belongs to him, with finery to the utmoſt of his power, would be a *deſpot*, if he could, and dared. He ſhews all the diſpoſitions to aſſume ſuperiority without merit. He certainly has a narrow and vain mind. He cannot be a philoſopher or philanthropiſt. With all his ſtyle and ſplendor in eating, drinking, dwelling, dreſſing, and riding, we cannot admire him; then let us pity, or deride.

Mere folly might be laughed at and neglected; but the folly I deſcribe is miſchievous. It delights in oppreſſion and war; and is one of the principal promoters of the *deſpotic ſpirit*.

SECTION XXIV.

Insolence of the higher Orders to the Middle Ranks and the Poor ; with their affected Condescension, in certain Circumstances, to the lowest of the People.

PUBLIC corruption must produce private. When PRIDE is a ruling principle in the conduct of state affairs, it must display itself in every part of domestic life, accompanying its lordly possessor from the palace at St. James's and the levee in Downing-street, to the rural mansion in the distant province, to the convivial table, to the fire-side, to the stable, and to the dog-kennel.

A due degree of self-respect, a dignified behaviour, a demand of what is due to one-self, attended with a cheerful payment of what is due to others, are highly laudable, and have no connection with that senseless, sullen, cruel pride, which marks the spirit of despotism.

This latter sort of pride is totally destitute of feeling for others. It scarcely acknowledges the common tie of humanity. It stands alone, completely insulated from all human beings below it, and connected only by a narrow isthmus with those above it. It seems to think the world, and all that it contains, created for its own exclusive gratification. The men and

S

women in it are merely inftruments fubfervient to the will and pleafure of ariftocratic infolence.

With this idea of its own privileges and claims, it is no wonder that it fhews fymptoms of extreme forenefs and exceffive irritation on the leaft oppofition to its *will and pleafure.* Accordingly, thofe of the human race, whofe unhappy lot it is to be domeftic or menial fervants to perfons of either fex who fwell with the felfifh pride of ariftocracy, are kept in a ftate of abject fervility, compelled to watch the looks and motions of the demigod or demigoddefs, and fpoken to with a feverity of language feldom ufed to the horfes in the ftable, or the dogs in the kennel. No attendance, by night or by day, can be fufficient. Such fuperior beings cannot perform the moft ordinary operations of nature without affiftance, which degrades both the giver and receiver. They cannot put on their own clothes; but like eaftern tyrants, furrounded by flaves, ftretch themfelves on the couch of indolence, while their fellow-creatures, equals by nature, with trembling folicitude faften a button, or tie a fhoe-ftring. The flighteft error, delay, or accident, draws down imprecations on the head of the offender, more terrible than the anathemas of a pope.

If the *little Mogul* affect fpirit, then he talks, in his ire, of horfewhips, kicking down ftairs, breaking every bone in the fkin of the wretched operator, who, as human nature is prone to error, may have deviated, in adjufting a curl, from the ftandard of court propriety. When he has occafion to fpeak of one of his fervants, he commonly fays, " one of my rafcals did this or that ;" and when he fpeaks to them, efpecially on the flighteft neglect or miftake, his choler breaks out into oaths, curfes, and epithets, expreffive of bitternefs and venom, for which language has not yet found adequate terms. The genius of Homer, which defcribed the wrath of Achilles, can alone paint in color black enough, the atrocity of the *great man*'s ire. If it were not for that vulgar thing *law*, which, on fome occafions, makes no diftinctions, the great man would trample the little man who has buckled his fhoe awry, out of exiftence.

To maintain that accuracy of drefs and fplendor of appearance, which fo fuperior a being thinks abfolutely neceffary, certain vulgar people, called tradefmen, muft inevitably be employed ; and in this country of plebeian liberty, they will no more work for a nabob, or a rich contractor, or a peer of the realm, without payment, than for a French *fans culottes*. But woe betide them, if they have the infufferable infolence to prefent their bills uncalled, though their families are ftarving, and their landlords are ejecting them from their habitations. " The infolence of the rafcals ! (exclaims the great man), let them wait, let them call again, and think themfelves well off if I do not chaftife them with a horfewhip, or kick them down ftairs, for knocking at my door, and bringing bills without order. But, d'ye hear : pay the fcoundrels this time, and mind, I never deal with them any more !" Then follows a volley of oaths and curfes on the heads of all fuch blackguards, low-lived wretches, fcum of the earth, thieves, and pickpockets, that do not know how to keep their diftance, and treat a *gentleman* with due refpect. " Aye, (he adds), there we fee the fpirit of the times, the effect of thefe curfed doctrines, which thofe *mifcreants* *, the philofophers, have broached, to the deftruction of all law, order, and religion, throughout Europe."

The middle rank of people, who refide in his vicinity, he takes no more notice of, than if they lived at the arctic or antarctic pole. He keeps them at a diftance, becaufe, though not fo rich as himfelf, yet claiming and fup- porting the rank of *gentlemen*, they would be likely to approach too near, and perhaps pre- fume upon fomething of an equality, not only by nature, but by felf-efteem and inftitution. He paffes his next-door neighbors in his car- riage or on horfeback, in his daily rides, with- out condefcending to turn his eyes upon them. He does not recollect even their names. They may be very good fort of people, for any thing he knows to the contrary ; but really he has not the honor of knowing them. A defpot will not bear a rival near his throne ; and

---

* Lord Auckland's expreffion, when fpeaking of mo- dern philofophers.

therefore he cannot bear any who, with inferior fortunes, might happen to equal him in
ſpirit, in ſenſe, in behaviour, and in education.
But if there is any body in the neighborhood
very low indeed ; ſo low, as to be removed
from all poſſibility of claſhing with his importance, ſuch an one he will make a companion,
and ſhew him moſt marvellous marks of humility and condeſcenſion. Indeed, for the ſake
of obtaining a little popularity, he will notice
cottagers and poor children at play, and make
extremely free with clowns, jockies, grooms,
huntſmen, and all who have any thing to do
with dog and horſe fleſh. But keep your diftance, ye little ſquires, parſons, and profeſſional men, who make ſaucy pretenſions to
knowledge or ingenuity. However, he can
never be at a loſs for company, while he and
his equals drive phaetons and four, to dine
with each other at fifteen miles diſtance, and
while officers are quartered in the vicinity. He
is abjectly ſervile to his ſuperiors, inſolent and
neglectful to the middle ranks, and free and
eaſy to the humble ſons of poverty, who will
bear a volley of oaths whenever he thinks proper to diſcharge them, and who, if ſpit upon,
will not ſpit again, becauſe they are his workmen or tenants.

He who can eradicate ſuch inſolence from a
neighbourhood, by treating it with the contempt and ridicule which it deſerves, certainly
contributes to the happineſs of ſociety. It is

confined in its fphere of action; but it is the fame fort of defpotifm which ravages Poland, and deluges the earth with human gore. In a free country like this, where law and liberty flourifh, it is a vulture in a cage, but ftill it is a vulture; and the little birds, to whom nature has given the free air to range in, ought to unite in endeavoring to deftroy it.

Does any fenfible man believe that fuch perfons, if their power were equal to their will, would fuffer freeholders of forty fhillings a-year, to vote for members of parliament; or juries of twelve honeft plebeians to decide in ftate trials, where minifters are anxious (as they value their places) for a verdict favorable to their adminiftration? They would not permit, if they could help it, the middle ranks to breathe the common air, or feel the genial fun, which God has given to fhine indifcriminately on the palace and the cottage. They are as much enemies to kings as to the people, becaufe they would, if poffible, be kings themfelves; but as that is impoffible, they crouch, like fawning fpaniels, to the hand which has it in its power to throw them a bone.

This defcription of perfons is peculiarly formidable to liberty, becaufe they are infatiably greedy of *power*. From their order chiefly arife the purchafers of boroughs, in which they traffic on fpeculation, like dealers in hops, determined to re-fell their commodity, as foon as they can, to the beft bidder. They are alfo of that hardened effrontery which pushes its way to public employment, stands forward at court, and, on all occasions, assumes that importance, which, from the general diffidence of the better part of mankind, is but too easily conceded to the most impudent pretensions. In consequence of this unblushing assurance, this arrogant, audacious presumption, this hardened temper, which can bear repulse without being abashed or dispirited, they oftenest rise to the highest posts; and such as would be posts of honor, if they were not filled by men who have not one quality of a beneficent nature, or which deserves the esteem of their fellow creatures. But though they have no inclination to do good; they acquire the power, which they fail not to exercise, of doing much evil. They encourage arbitrary principles. They depreciate the people on all occasions; and add weight and confidence to the aristocratical confederacy. They may sometimes be men of parts. They are seldom deficient in the graces of Lord Chesterfield. But they are hard-hearted, selfish wretches, attached to the childish vanity of the world, and preferring a title or a riband to the peace, the lives, the property, and the liberty of their fellow-mortals; all which they are ready to sacrifice, even for the *chance* of pleasing a prime minister, and obtaining some bauble, which reason ever despises, when it is not the badge of experienced virtue. "One of these (says

an old writer*) values being called His Grace,
or Noble Marquis," (*unideal* names as they
are), " more than a million of lives, provided
that in fuch a general deftruction he can fave
ONE ; and to confirm themfelves in their ill-
gotten honors, they generally hatch plots,
fuborn rebellions, or any thing that they think
can create bufinefs, keep themfelves from being
queftioned, and THIN mankind, whereby they
lofe fo many of their enemies."

* Samuel Johnfon ; not the *Lexicographer*, whofe *religion* was *often* Popifh fuperftition, and whofe *loyalty* the
moft *irrational* Toryifm. I venerate his abilities ; but
deteft his politics. He would have difplaced the *Brunfwick family* for the *Stuarts*, if his power had kept pace
with his inclinations.

SECTION XXV.

Of a Natural Aristocracy.

Nobility, according to the idea of the vulgar, both in high and low life, is nothing more than RICHES that have been a *long time* in *one* family : but it often happens that riches have been originally gained and preferved in *one* family by fordid avarice, by mean and difhoneft arts ; fuch arts as are utterly incompatible with true nobility, with fuperiority of intellects, united with generofity of difpofition.

Moft of the *titles* of *nobility*, and other civil diftinctions, were taken from WAR : as a marquis, a duke, a count, a baron, a landgrave, a knight, an efquire. The inventors of arts, the improvers of life, thofe who have mitigated evil and augmented the good allotted to men in this world, were not thought worthy of any titular diftinctions. The reafon is indeed fufficiently obvious : titles were originally beftowed by defpotic kings, who required and rewarded no other merit but that which fupported them by *violence* in their arbitrary rule. In fome countries they are *now* given, for the fame reafons, to thofe who effect the fame purpofes, not by war only, but by CORRUPTION.

Perſons thus raiſed to civil honors, thus enriched by the long-continued favor of courts, would willingly depreciate all dignity which is derived from GOD and virtue only, unindebted to patents royal. They would create an artificial preference to a diſtinguiſhed few among the human race, which nature is for ever counteraſting, by giving ſuperior abilities to thoſe who are puſhed down among the deſpiſed and negleſted many. This conduſt is both unjuſt and unnatural. It cannot be favorable to human happineſs, becauſe it is adverſe to truth, and does violence to the will of God manifeſted in the operations of nature. In France it was carried to that extreme which brought it to its termination. There is a tendency to carry it to extremes in all countries where courts predominate. The friend of reaſon and of man will therefore endeavor to convince the people, that an ariſtocracy, founded on caprice or accident only, without any regard to ſuperior abilities and virtues, is a fertile cauſe of *war*, and all thoſe evils which infeſt a great part of civil ſociety.

That the BEST and *ableſt* men ſhould govern the worſt and weakeſt, is reaſonable: and this is the *ariſtocracy* appointed by God and nature. But what do we mean when we ſay the beſt and ableſt men? Do we mean men of the BEST families; that is, men in whoſe families riches and titles have long been conſpicuous? By the ABLEST men, do we mean men who poſſeſs the greateſt *power*, by undue influence, in borough and county elections, though the exertion of that *power* be ſtrictly forbidden by the law and conſtitution? Or do we mean men of honeſt, upright, and benevolent HEARTS; of vigorous, well-informed, well-exerciſed underſtandings? Certainly the latter ſort, which forms the *ariſtocracy* eſtabliſhed by God and nature. This is gold; the king's head ſtamped upon it may make it a *guinea*. The other is only copper; and though the *ſame* impreſſion may be made upon it at the mint, it is ſtill intrinſically worth no more than a half-penny.

But Mr. Burke has favored mankind with a deſcription of what he calls a *true* natural ariſtocracy.

The firſt *requiſite* *, according to him, is "*To be bred* in a PLACE of *eſtimation*." Mr. Burke is a good claſſical ſcholar, and often writes *Latin* in Engliſh †. PLACE here is the Latin LOCUS, which every polite ſcholar has obſerved to ſignify FAMILY. If I were to tranſlate this little ſentence into Latin, I might venture to render it in this manner: *honeſto oportet oriundus ſit loco*—you muſt, as the common people would expreſs it, be a *gentleman born*. The accident of *birth* therefore is placed at the head of the qualifications neceſſary to give

* See Appeal from the *new* to the *old* Whigs, page 128.

† Thus he uſes the word VAST, which the common reader underſtands VERY GREAT, in its claſſical ſenſe, for *deſolate*. Many other inſtances might be given.

a man *pre-eminence* in fociety. This doctrine is certainly confiftent with the whole tenor of the book; but whether it contributes to the general happinefs of mankind, or tends to the fpirit of defpotifm, let impartial obfervers determine. Mr. Burke had faid a few lines before, *fatis eft equitem mihi plaudere*—" It is enough for me that *gentlemen or nobles* approve my doctrine;" and there is therefore little doubt but that he *is* fatisfied; for their approbation muft be fecured by opinions fo favorable to their *importance* in fociety, independently of laborious, virtuous, and *ufeful* exertion.

The next *requifite* is, " to SEE nothing low or fordid from one's infancy;" that is, to be kept at a diftance from the fwinifh multitude, fo as not to know thofe *wants* which it is the bufinefs of fuperiors, or of a *natural* ariftocracy, to fupply or alleviate.

The third *requifite* is, " to be *taught* to *refpect onefelf.*" This feldom requires any great *teaching* among perfons who have the two preceding *requifites.* Pride and felfifhnefs are the very principles of defpotifm.

The fourth *requifite* to natural ariftocracy, " is to be *habituated* to the *cenforial* infpection of the public eye." Yes; fo habituated as to be hardened by effrontery, and to fay that *a king holds his crown* * *in contempt of the people;* and, *fatis eft equitem mihi plaudere,* which may be rendered, paraphraftically, " I care nothing

---

* Mr. Burke's doctrine.

for the *people*'s *cenforial* eye or tongue, if the GREAT honor me with their applaufe, for defending their exclufive privileges from being trodden under the hoof of the fwinifh multitude.".

I pafs over fome very proper *requifites*, to proceed to the laft. The laft is, " to be among RICH traders, who, from their SUCCESS, are prefumed to have *fharp* and vigorous underftandings, and to poffefs the virtues of diligence, order, conftancy, and regularity, and to have cultivated an habitual regard to commutative juftice.—Thefe are the circumftances of men who form what I fhould call a natural ariftocracy, without which there is NO NATION. Without this," (the writer intimates in a few fubfequent lines), " HE cannot recognize the *exiftence* of the PEOPLE."

Refpecting Mr. Burke greatly, as I do, and agreeing with him in many particulars in this very paffage, I cannot help thinking that he has laid too much ftrefs on riches and BIRTH, in pointing out the men intended by NATURE to take the lead in all human affairs, and to form what he calls a *true* natural ariftocracy.

Nam genus et proavos et *quæ non fecimus ipfi*
Vix ea noftra voco.

I think it injurious to fociety and mankind at large, to lavifh honors and confer power on accidental qualities, which may exift in their greateft degree and perfection without the leaft particle of *perfonal merit*, without wifdom or

T

benevolence. It difcourages induftry. It ftifles all virtuous emulation. It makes RICHES the grand object of purfuit ; not for their own intrinfic value, not for their power of fupplying neceffaries, and even luxuries, but for the *political confequence* they beftow, independently of the mode of acquifition or expenditure. I would have no IDOLATRY. God has fhewn his peculiar indignation againft it. I would not worfhip a *calf*, though a *golden* one. KINGS LOG, and *Gods* made of ftocks and ftones, can only command reverence from men *really* funk to a ftate *below* the fwine.

I know Lord Bolingbroke's doctrines of liberty are difliked, by thofe who fee their own confequence increafing in the increafing fpirit of defpotifm. But I will cite a paffage from him, which may counterbalance the *fervile* ideas which fome men entertain of the ariftocracy conftituted by NATURE.

" It feems to me, (fays he), that in order to maintain the moral fyftem of the world at a certain point, far below that of *ideal perfection;* but however fufficient upon the whole to conftitute a ftate eafy and happy, or, at the worft, tolerable ; I fay, it feems to me, that the Author of Nature has thought fit to mingle, from time to time, among the focieties of men, a few, and but a few, of thofe, on whom he is gracioufly pleafed to beftow a larger portion of the ætherial fpirit, than is given, in the ordinary courfe of his providence, to the fons of men.***

" You will find that there are fuperior fpirits, men who fhew, even from their infancy,
though it be not always perceived by others,
perhaps not felt by themfelves, that they were
born for fomething more and better. Thefe
are the men to whom the part I mentioned is
affigned. Their talents denote their *general
defignation.*

"I have fometimes reprefented to myfelf
the VULGAR, who are accidentally diftinguifhed
by the titles of KING and SUBJECT, of LORD
and VASSAL, of nobleman and peafant; and
the FEW who are diftinguifhed by nature fo
effentially from the herd of mankind, that
(figure apart) they feem to be of another fpecies. The *former* loiter or trifle away their
whole time; and their prefence or their abfence
would be equally unperceived, if caprice or
accident did not raife them often to *ftations*,
wherein their ftupidity, and their vices, make
them a PUBLIC MISFORTUNE. The latter
come into the world, or at leaft continue in it,
after the effects of furprife and inexperience are
over, like men who are fent on more important errands. They may indulge themfelves in
pleafure; but as their induftry is not employed
about trifles, fo their amufements are not made
the bufinefs of their lives. Such men cannot
pafs unperceived through a country. If they
retire from the world, their fplendor accompa-
nies them, and enlightens even the obfcurity
of their retreat. If they take a part in public
life, the effect is never indifferent. They either

appear like minifters of divine vengeance; and their courfe through the world is marked by defolation and oppreffion, by poverty and fervitude; or they are the guardian angels of the country they inhabit, BUSY to avert even the moft diftant evil, and to maintain or procure PEACE, plenty, and the greateft of human bleffings, LIBERTY."

Such men, when they take the latter courfe, and become the guardian angels of the country they inhabit, are the *ariftocracy* appointed by God and nature. Such men, therefore, fhould be felected by kings for civil honors, and public functions of high importance. If kings were *republicans* in the proper fenfe, all the people would be royalifts. But when brilliant honors and minifterial employments are beftowed on fools and knaves, becaufe they were begotten by anceftors whom they difgrace, or poffefs riches which they abüfe, government becomes a nuifance, and the people feel an *ariftocracy* to be little better than an *automaton machine*, for promoting the purpofes of royal or MINISTERIAL defpotifm.

SECTION XXVI.

The exceſſive Love of Diſtinction and Power which prevails wherever the Spirit of Deſpotiſm exiſts, deadens ſome of the fineſt Feelings of the Heart, and counteracts the Laws of Nature.

IN a ſyſtem of manners, which renders the poſſeſſion of riches more honorable than the poſſeſſion of virtue, which attaches a degree of merit to hereditary rank and nominal diſtinctions, above all that perſonal exertions can poſſibly acquire, the natural ideas of right and wrong are confounded; and man, become a depraved, artificial animal, purſues pre-eminence in ſociety, by *counteracting nature,* as well as by violating juſtice.

That he *counteracts nature,* under ſuch a ſyſtem, will be evident, on conſidering the preſent ſtate of conjugal union among thoſe who appear to place the chief good of man in riches, ſplendor, title, power, and courtly diſtinctions. Love is every day ſacrificed, by the lovelieſt of the ſpecies, on the altar of PRIDE.

The fine ſenſibilities of the heart, if ſuffered to influence the choice of a companion for life, might lead to family degradation. " Nature, then, avaunt (exclaims Ariſtocracy). Love is a vulgar paſſion. The ſimpleſt damſel, that

T 2

flumbers under the roof of ftraw, feels it in all its ardor. Daughter, you have nobler objects than mere nature prefents. Remember your birth. You muft make an alliance which may aggrandize the family, which may add title to our riches, or new brilliancy to our title."

In vain have the Loves and the Graces mould. ed her fhape and face with the niceft fymmetry. In vain has art added her fineft polifh to the work of nature. Poor IPHIGENIA muft be facrificed. Her heart, peradventure, has chofen its mate, and happy would fhe be, if fhe could renounce all the embarraffments of high fortune, and emulate the turtle-dove of the vale. But no; fhe muft not tell her love. Perhaps the object of it is only a *commoner*; perhaps he is only a younger brother; perhaps he has little to recommend him but youth, beauty, honor, and virtue. He cannot keep her an equipage. He has no manfion-houfe. Yet, her heart inclines to him, and both, God and nature approve her choice; but neither her heart, nor God, nor nature, will be heard, when pride and ariftocratical infolence lift up their imperious voice, and command her to remember her rank, and keep up the family dignity.

Lord ***** is introduced as a fuitor, under the father's authority. Lord ***** influences five or fix boroughs, and the junction of fuch an intereft with that of the family muft, in all human probability, fecure a riband, and perhaps a marquifate.

His lordſhip is ten years older than poor
Iphigenia. His life has been ſpent, from infancy, in the midſt of luxuries and pleaſures,
to ſpeak of it in the ſofteſt terms. He has a
lively juvenile pertneſs about him; but his face
is that of of an old man—pale, or rather yellow, except his noſe, which is decorated with
a ſettled redneſs, and his forehead, which is
variegated with carbuncles. Several of his
front teeth are gone, having been ſacrificed to
Venus by the god Mercury. His breath—ye
poets, bring your roſes, your honeyſuckles,
your jaſmines—not for compariſon—but, if
poſſible, to drown the ſtench which, while he
ſolicits Iphigenia's hand, is like that which
iſſues from a putrid carcaſe, or the apertures of
a boghouſe. Nothing offenſive, however,
oozes from his neck, the deep holes of the
king's evil having lately been completely cica-
trized by a ſkilful quac doctor, as a meaſure
preparatory to his approaching nuptials.

Behold, then, the ſuitor, alighting from a
high phaeton, beautifully adorned with coats
of arms, not only on the ſides and back, but
on the lining, drawn by four cream-coloured
ponies, and followed by two fine figures of
men in white liveries, with horſes richly capari-
ſoned, and diſplaying, in every part, where it
is poſſible, coronets of ſilver.

Iphigenia appears delighted at the honor of
his propoſal, though her heart, when ſhe re-
clines on her pillow, feels a pang of regret
which no language can deſcribe. The ſtruggle

between love and pride is violent; but it paſſes in ſecret. She hears of nothing among her companions, but of the great alliance ſhe is going to make with an ancient and illuſtrious family. Splendid manſions, glittering carriages, birth-day dreſſes, flit before her imagination. Above all, the delightful idea that ſhe ſhall take precedence of thoſe who now think themſelves her equals and ſuperiors, diſpels every thought of LOVE. As to the MAN, the huſband, he is ſcarcely conſidered at all, or he muſt be conſidered with diſguſt. But his title, his houſe in town, his manſions and parks in the country, his parliamentary intereſt, the favor in which he ſtands at court, the brilliant appearance he makes in the realms of faſhion; theſe, added to a father's influence, determine Iphigenia at once to forget the object of her love, and give her hand to deformity, diſeaſe, putreſcence, and folly. She marries: the family eſtates and iefluence are united, and the battered, worn-out bridegroom becomes, in time, a MARQUIS.

The puny offspring of ſuch connubial alliances are trained in the ſame idolatrous veneration of rank, title, and grandeur; and WOMAN, formed to love and be loved, ſacrifices her happineſs to family pride, and lives and dies a legal proſtitute, without once taſting the exquiſite and natural delight of virtuous, equal, and ſincere affection.—Taught from the cradle to believe herſelf a ſuperior being, ſhe is cheated of the happineſs which falls to the lot of thoſe who view their fellow-creatures as one great family, and are not too proud to partake of the common banquet of life, and to choofe a *part-ner* like the *turtle of the vale.*

Now mark the confequence. In no rank of fociety is conjugal happinefs more rarely found than among thofe who have imbibed moft copi-oufly the ariftocratical principles of felfifh pride. The prefent age abounds with public and noto-rious inftances of infelicity of this fort in the higheft ranks of fociety. It would be painful to dwell upon them. I drop a tear of pity on the lovely victims to defpotifm, and let the cur-tain fall.

But furely that degree of PRIDE, nurfed by ill-conftructed fyftems of fociety, which leads to the violation of the firft law of nature, and produces mifery of the fevereft kind ought to be difgraced and reprobated by all who have hearts fufficiently tender to fympathize with the fufferings of their fellow-mortals. Love, and the natural affections between human creatures, are the fweet ingredients which Providence has thrown into the cup of life, to fweeten the bit-ter beverage. And that ftate of fociety, which divefts man of his nature, which renders him a factitious creature, which hardens his heart with felfifhnefs, and fwells him with the morbid tumors of vanity, deferves execration. It increafes all the natural mifery of man, and withholds the anodyne.

Something may be faid in excufe for the more amiable part of the fpecies, when they difcard

love from their boſoms to indulge pride. Their
haughty fathers too often inculcate the leſſon of
pride from the earlieſt infancy ; and teach them
to think nothing really beautiful and lovely,
which is not marked by faſhion, or varniſhed
by titles, riches, and heraldic honors. The
men in general ſet them the example. They
laviſh their *love* on the courtezan, and follow
prudence in the choice of a wife ; that is, they
ſeek not a heart that beats in uniſon with their
own, but a legal connection which increaſes
their fortune, or aggrandizes their ſituation.
A marriage of love, at an age when the heart is
moſt prone to it, is conſidered as a folly and a
misfortune, unleſs it advances the man in
ſociety. The women learn to retaliate, and to
give their hands without their hearts ; gratifying pride at the expence of love.

When truth, juſtice, reaſon, and nature are
little regarded, in competition with the DESIRE
of diſtinction, which is the caſe wherever the
ſpirit of deſpotiſm has inſinuated itſelf, all true
and ſolid happineſs will be ſacrificed for the
appearance of ſuperiority in birth, in poſſeſſions,
in houſes and carriages, and above all, in court
favor. The tendereſt ties of conſanguinity,
affinity, and friendſhip, ſnap aſunder when op-
poſed to the force of any thing which is likely
to contribute to perſonal ſplender or family
pride, political conſequence, influence at elections, and finally, to the honors conferred by
royalty. The little aſpirants at ſubordinte
degrees of deſpotiſm, are continually crawling

up the hill, ever looking at the brilliant object on the fummit, and leaving below, all that love and nature teach them to embrace.

From this principle, unnatural as it is, arifes the anxious defire of ariftocratical bigots to *make*, as they exprefs it, an ELDEST SON; to ftarve, or at leaft to diftrefs, a dozen fons and daughters, in order to leave behind them one great reprefentative, who may continue to toil in the purfuit of civil pre-eminence, for the gratification of *family pride*. The privileges of primogeniture eftablifh petty defpots all over the land, who are interefted, and fufficiently inclined, from pride as well as intereft, to promote the fpirit of defpotifm. They would have no objection to the feudal fyftem, in which the only diftinction was that of lords and vaffals. Not contented with engroffing the property which ought to be fhared among their brothers and fifters, they claim privileges in confequence of their property, and would *appropriate* the birds of the air and the beafts of the foreft for their recreation in the field, and their luxury at the table.

When the laws of nature, and eternal truth and juftice, are violated, no wonder that defpotifm advances, and man is degraded.

SECTION XXVII.

On the Opinion that the People are annihilated or abforbed in Parliament; that the Voice of the People is no where to be heard but in Parliament; and on fimilar Doctrines, tending to depreciate the People.

THERE is no doctrine fo abfurd but pride and felfifhnefs will adopt and maintain it with obftinacy, if it be conducive to their gratification. Alexander, it is faid, *really* believed himfelf a god. The vileft of the Cæfars demanded divine honors. Many inftances are on record of wretched beings, with hardly any thing worthy of *man* about them, forgetting, in confequence of a little elevation above others, that they were mortals; behaving with the wickednefs and cruelty of devils, and at the fame time arrogating the power and dignity of the celeftial nature. It is related of Hanno, the Carthaginian, that he taught ftarlings to fay " *Deus Hanno** ;" and that when a very large number had learned their leffon, he turned them loofe into the woods, hoping that they would teach the wild beafts on the trees to repeat the fame words, and that thus the divinity of Hanno might be wafted into the remoteft regions, and become the worfhip of the univerfe. Such conduct appears to refemble the

* Hanno is a God.

the ravings of the poor lunatic, who crowns himfelf, as he fits in his defolate cell, with a crown of ftraw, and imagines, while he fways a fceptre of the fame materials, that he is an emperor. But in truth, the pride of defpots, I mean thofe who have all the difpofitions of defpots, though they may not have the diadems, difplays many of the fymptoms of downright lunacy. Pride is allowed by the phyficians to have a powerful effect in turning the brain ; and though it may not always fit the unhappy fufferer for Bedlam, yet commonly renders him unfit for the offices of focial life.

Shocking as madnefs is, it fometimes behaves in a manner which turns pity into laughter. Can any thing be more ridiculous, than the in-folence of fome perfons, who, having adopted high ariftocratical notions, to correfpond with their high birth, high titles, and high rank, declare that they know not what is meant by the people out of parliament ; that they do not acknowledge the political exiftence of the peo-ple, but on the benches of St. Stephen's cha-pel ? Individuals of low degree they may know, and employ in their fervice, but they know nothing of the people, as *millions* of MEN, pof-feffing rights or power. " The conftitution (fay they) knows nothing of the people confi-dered as individuals." King, lords, and com-mons conftitute the nation ; but what is meant by the people they cannot divine. A mob they know, and would always have them dif-perfed by the military, as foon as two or three are gathered together ; but the people, as a part of the conſtitution, they never could diſcover.

Mr. Burke, the great Coryphæus of ariſtocracy, ſays, " As a *people* can have no right to a corporate capacity without *univerſal conſent,* ſo neither have they a right to hold excluſively any lands in the name and title of a corporation. On the ſcheme of the preſent rulers in our neighboring country, regenerated as they are, they *have no more right to the territory called France* than I (Edmund Burke) have. *Who are theſe inſolent men, calling themſelves the French nation,* that would monopolize this fair domain of nature ? Is it becauſe they ſpeak a certain jargon ? Is it their mode of chattering ? The crowd of men on the other ſide of the Channel, *who have the impudence to call themſelves a* PEOPLE, can never be the lawful excluſive poſſeſſors of the ſoil." How truly laughable to hear an individual, Mr. Edmund Burke, taxing twenty-ſix millions of human creatures with IMPUDENCE, for preſuming to call themſelves a PEOPLE ! I muſt ſmile at ſuch abſurdity, while I ſincerely lament that this ingenious man has miſſed the opportunity of raiſing his family to the peerage, the grand objeᴄt of ſo many years indefatigable labor, by a loſs never to be repaired, and in which every feeling heart muſt ſympathize. Ambition, what art thou to the feelings of a father, exclaiming, like David, " O Abſalom, my ſon, my ſon !" The great teacher Death ſhews the

l human afpirations at fublunary
who lofes a fon in the prime of life
er of honor, may learn to weep
houfands, whofe deareft relatives
at off by the fword of war, in con-
doctrines which he maintained by a
y of his eloquence, without fore-
garding the calamities they had a
produce.

writer goes on and obferves, that
multitude (from the context he
JORITY *of the people*) are not under
focial difcipline of the wifer, more
more *opulent*, they can fcarcely
E in civil fociety.... When you
common fort of men from their pro-
as, fo as to *form them* into an
y, I no longer know that venerable
the PEOPLE, in fuch a difbanded
ters and *vagabonds*. For awhile
e terrible indeed; but in fuch a
ild beafts are terrible. The mind
n no fort of fubmiffion. They are,
re always been reputed, rebels.
lawfully be FOUGHT WITH and
r, whenever an advantage offers."
ve rife to thefe elucidations he has
w pages before. " The factions
amongft us, in order to diveft men
of their country and to remove
minds all duty with regard to the
vor to propagate an opinion that
E, in forming their *commonwealth*,

have by no means parted with their power over it !" Horrendum dictu !

" Difcufs any of their fchemes—their anfwer is—it is the act of the PEOPLE, and that is fufficient !—The people are mafters of the commonwealth; becaufe in fubftance they are the commonwealth ! The French revolution, fay they, was the act of the majority of the people; and if the majority of any other people, the people of England for inftance, wifh to make the fame change, they have the fame right.— Juft the fame, undoubtedly. That is, NONE AT ALL."

Such is the doctrine of this warm partifan to ariftocratical diftinction. But what fay feven or eight millions of good people, who wifh nothing, in their interference in politics, but to fecure and extend their own happinefs, and to make all others happy within the fpheres of their influence ? Let them fay what they pleafe, their remonftrance muft not be heard. They are political *non-entities*; they are, as pride commonly calls inferiors in private life, NOBODY, or *people whom nobody knows.*

But now comes the tax-gatherer. Thefe non-entities muft find *real* tangible money to pay for the falaries of places, to pay penfions, and the intereft of money advanced for the waging of wars, faid to be in defence of law, order, and religion. It will not do to plead that they have no political exiftence. A very confiderable part of their property, the produce of their labor, muft be annually paid for the support of those who have the effrontery to say they are not *visible*, as a majority of individuals, in the eye of the constitution.

At a general election, would any candidate for a considerable city or county dare to advance such opinions respecting the insignificance, or rather non-existence, of the people, as have been advanced by borough members, in their zeal for power and prerogative? The *People* would deny the doctrine with a voice loud enough to silence the most obstreperous declaimer.

Mr. Burke will make no new converts to this opinion. The Tory party had adopted it, previously to the instruction of their sanguine advocate. It was always one of their principles. The people themselves will certainly reprobate ideas which lead to their political *annihilation*, in *every* respect, but in the privilege of contributing to the public revenue. But one cannot be surprised at any wild assertions of a man who writes under the impulse of passion. Anger, inflamed by mortified pride, seems to animate almost every sentence of his late invective. And what are we to think of the WHIGISM of one, who, in the commencement of the alarm concerning French principles, is said to have proposed to Mr. Fox to join together (these are the very words of the proposal) in " FROWN-ING DOWN THE DOCTRINES OF LIBERTY *." The proposer must have no small opinion of

* See Mr. Wyvill's Letter to Mr. Pitt, page 108.

himſelf, when he imagined that, aſſiſted by *one*
more, he could *frown down the doctrines of
liberty*. Jupiter ſhook Olympus with a nod;
and Burke was to diſcountenance liberty, and
annihilate the political exiſtence of a people,
with a FROWN.

Diviſum imperium cum Jove, Burkus habet.

I revere the private virtues of the man. I feel
and admire his excellence as a writer. I deplore the miſtake which has led him to gratify
the *few* in power, at the expence of millions
of his fellow-creatures, who would have rejoiced in ſuch an advocate againſt the influence
of the deſpotic ſpirit. Imperial power has
means enough to maintain itſelf. Genius ſhould
ever eſpouſe the cauſe of liberty, and of thoſe
who have no ſtanding armies, no treaſury, no
tribe of dependents, nothing to ſtand their
friend, but a good cauſe, which, in a corrupt
ſtate of ſociety, is too often defeated by a bad
one.

May the people, in all climates which the
ſun views in his daily progreſs, prove their political exiſtence by their public virtue! May
deſpots learn to fear the power of thoſe whoſe
happineſs they have dared to deſtroy. In our
own country, we have a king who rules in the
hearts of his people, and who would therefore
be the firſt to reject the doctrines of Mr.
Burke, which tend to ſink the people, as a
majority of individuals, into a ſtate of inſigni-
ficance. May the people claim and preſerve

their rights, in defiance of all overruling influence, and all fophiftical declamation. But let
them purfue their philanthropic ends with
fteady coolnefs. Let them refpect themfelves,
and act confiftently with their dignity. Let
not a fingle drop of blood be fhed, nor a fingle
mite of property unjuftly feized, in correcting
abufes, and recovering rights. Let them pafs
a glorious act of amnefty, and generoufly forgive the Pitts, the Burkes, the Loughboroughs,
the Aucklands, the Mansfields, the Wynd-
hams; proving to an admiring world, that a
great PEOPLE can be gentle and merciful to
frail, erring individuals, while it explodes their
errors, and calmly evinces, by virtuous energies, its own *political exiftence* and fupreme
authority.

SECTION XXVIII.

The fashionable Contempt thrown on Mr. Locke, and his Writings in Favor of Liberty; and on other Authors and Books espousing the same Cause.

I T is an infallible proof of great abilities in a writer who espouses the cause of the people, when he is cavilled at, written against, and condemned by the persons whose despotic principles he has endeavored to expose and refute. It is a sign that he has touched them to the quick, and left a sore place, the smart of which is continually urging them to murmur. Their affected derision and contempt of him are but transparent veils to hide the writhings of their tortured minds; an awkward masque to cover the ugly features of impotent revenge, struggling, through pride, to conceal the painful emotions of rage.

It is amusing to observe what mean and little arts are used by these angry persons, to lower the character of any writer, whose arguments they cannot refute. They hire a venal tool to write his life and crowd it with every falsehood and calumny which party malice can invent, and popular credulity disseminate. They relate, without examination into a single fact, and decide, without the smallest attention to candor or justice. The man is to be hunted

down. The minifter and his creatures cry
havoc, and let flip the vermin of corruption.
The newfpapers, in daily paragraphs, difcharge
the venom of abufe on his name. *Venal cri-
tiques* pour their acrimonious cenfure, in general
terms, on his compofitions, which they could
not equal, and dare not examine with impartiality. Nicknames are faftened on him ; and
whenever he is fpoken of, all additions of re-
fpeȼt are omitted, and, in their place, fome
familiar and vulgar abbreviation of his chriftian
name is ufed to vilify his furname. Poor artifices indeed ! for while they expofe the malice
and weaknefs of thofe who ufe them, they
leave the arguments and doȼtrines of the writer
rather confirmed than fhaken by an attack fo
feeble.

It is not furprifing, indeed, that *cotempo-
rary* writers in favor of the people, whatever
their abilities, and however convincing their
arguments, are treated with affeȼted contempt,
as often as they excite real admiration. Envy
always ftrikes at *living* merit. The policy of the
afpirants at arbitrary power unites with envy,
to deprefs all who are rifing to public efteem
by perfonal exertion, by their own virtue, independently of court patronage and hereditary
diftinȼtion. But it might be fuppofed that
departed genius, elevated, by the confpiring
voice of nations, to the higheft rank, would
be furrounded with a fanȼtity which would
defend it from profanation. It is not fo. The
love of power, in the hearts of mean and felfifh

men, acknowledges no reverence for genius. It has no reverential feelings beyond the purlieus of a court. The falfe brilliancy of what is called high and fafhonable life, is preferred by it to the permanent luftre of all folid perfonal virtue.

Mr. Locke, therefore, one of the chief glories of Englifh literature, is to be depreciated, for he wrote on the fide of liberty. Poffeffing *reafon* in greater perfection than moft men, he naturally inclined to efpoufe the caufe of MAN, without confining his regard to thofe who boafted adventitious honors, the fantaftic diftinctions of birth, or the fortuitous advantages of fortune. Thefe are few, compared with the millions who conftitute the mafs of a commonwealth. His underftanding, greatly elevated above the ordinary ftandard, clearly faw, that the purpofes of real philanthropy can be accomplifhed folely by improving the condition of the MANY. *They* muft be taught to know and value their rights. They muft learn to reverence themfelves, by feeling their importance in fociety. Such an improvement of their minds will lead them to act confiftently with their dignity as rational creatures, and as members of a community which they love, and the welfare of which they find to depend on their own virtue.

Mr. Locke was certainly ftimulated to write his book on government by thefe philofophical and philanthropic ideas. In purfuance of thofe ideas, he wifhed to fupport, by doctrines favorable to general liberty, the REVOLUTION. Let us attend to his own words in his Preface.

" Thefe papers, (fays he), I hope, are fufficient to eftablifh the throne of our great Reftorer, our prefent King William; to make good his title, in the CONSENT OF THE PEOPLE, which, BEING THE ONLY ONE OF ALL LAWFUL GOVERNMENTS, he has more fully and clearly than any prince in Chriftendom; and to juftify to the world the people of England, whofe love of their juft and natural rights, with their refolution to preferve them, faved the nation when it was on the very brink of flavery and ruin."

Mr. Locke's book then tends directly to ftrengthen the foundation of the throne on which the prefent royal family is feated. It is equally favorable to the king and the people. Yet becaufe it is *at all* favorable to the people and the general caufe of liberty, it is the fafhion, in the ariftocratical circles, to revile it. It is faid to contain the elements of thofe doctrines which the philofophers of France have dilated, which gave independence to America, and rendered France a republic. It is faid, very unjuftly, to contain the feminal principles of Mr. Paine's matured and expanded tree. Mr. Locke, therefore, the great defender of the Revolution and of King William, is reprobated by Tory courtiers, and numbered, by the afpirants at enormous power and privileges, to which they have no juft and natural claim, among Lord Auckland's " *mifcreants called philofophers.*"

Men who undertake to defend any thing contrary to the common fenfe and common intereft of mankind, ufually hurt the fide they intend to defend, by promoting a *difcuffion,* and calling forth common fenfe, excited by the common intereft, to defend its own caufe. Thus Sir Robert Filmer's book gave rife both to Sydney's and Locke's defence of liberty. Thus Mr. Burke's Reflections on France drew forth Mr. Paine's Rights of Man, in which is much excellent matter, mingled with a blameable cenfure of limited monarchy. Thus Salmafius's mercenary invective againft the republicans of England in the laft century, provoked the great Milton, fcarcely lefs eloquent in profe than in poetry, to defend the right of the people of England to, manage, in their own country their own concerns, according to their own judgment and inclination.

Milton and Locke are great names on the fide of liberty. But Milton has been treated contemptuoufly; and fome have fhewn a fpirit illiberal enough to detract from his poetry in revenge for his politics. His laft biographer, Dr. Johnfon, who had many early prejudices which his moft vigorous reafon could not to the laft fubdue, was, by early prejudice, a violent Tory and Jacobite. I think there is reafon to believe, that he would have been eafily made a convert to popery. I venerate.

his abilities and virtues; but I cannot help remarking, that his high-church and high-prerogative principles led him to speak less honorably of Milton than he must have done if he had viewed him through a medium undiscolored. Milton was a greater man than Johnson; and though I think he went too far in his hatred to monarchy and episcopacy, yet, in extenuation, let it be considered how much monarchy and episcopacy had been abused in his time, and how much more friendly to freedom they both are in our happier age. Milton discovered a noble spirit of independence, and his writings contain some of the finest passages that ever were written in vindication of civil liberty. They contributed to raise that spirit which afterwards produced our happy revolution; and I have no doubt but that Milton would have rejoiced under a *limited* monarchy. It is to writings and to a spirit like his mankind are indebted for the limitation. If honest and able minds like Milton's had not appeared on the part of the people, it is probable that no such thing as a limited monarch would have been found on the face of the earth; and the family now on the British throne, would have been known only in the petty dynasties of the German empire.

Free spirits are therefore to be pardoned in some errors, which the propensity of human nature to err must ever render *venial;* and the general tendency of their writings to make the

X

mafs of mankind free and happy, ought to fecure attention to their doctrines, and honor to their names. The enemies to the fpirit of defpotifm have feen, with pain, the attempts to leffen thefe great men in the eyes of the world extended to writers of lefs renown, but of more recent date. They have feen men, *good men in private life*, and philofophers, whofe difcourfes and letters have gained the notice and efteem of every enlightened country, re-proached, vilified, perfecuted, and almoft de-ftroyed, becaufe, in confequence of that fine underftanding which had done fo much in phi-lofophy, they made fome difcoveries in politics which muft for ever militate powerfully againft the fpirit of defpotifm. Voltaire, Rouffeau, Raynal, Price, Prieftley, Paine, however dif-ferent their characters, attainments, and abili-ties, are all vilified *together*, (becaufe they have written admirably on the fide of liberty), all involved in one indifcriminate torrent of oblo-quy. The partifans of unlimited power would perfuade us, not only that they were knaves, but fools. Some of them have very exceptionable paffages in their works; but where they treat of civil liberty, they plead the caufe of human nature. They have not pleaded it unfuccefsfully. Political artifices cannot ftifle truth and common fenfe.

The independent part of mankind, who de-teft parties and faction, and mean nothing but the happinefs of their fellow-creatures, will do

well to be upon their guard againſt the miſre-
preſentations of thoſe who would vilify a Locke,
a Milton, a Sydney. Let them read and judge
for themſelves. The men who are anxious to
withhold or extinguiſh the light, may fairly be
ſuſpected of intending to do evil.

SECTION XXIX.

Of the Defpotifm of INFLUENCE; *while the Forms of a free Conftitution are preferved.*

THE words of a great lawyer, in-ftructing the youth of a nation at a celebrated univerfity, muft be fuppofed to be well confi-dered. Blackftone, the grave commentator, after expatiating on the advantages derived from the Revolution, proceeds to remark, that " though thefe provifions have *nominally* and in *appearance*, reduced the ftrength of the execu-tive power to a much lower ebb than in the preceding period; yet if, on the other hand, we throw into the oppofite fcale the vaft acqui-fition of force arifing from the RIOT ACT, and the annual expedience of a STANDING ARMY; and the vaft acquifition of PERSONAL ATTACH-MENT, arifing from the magnitude of the *national debt*, and the manner of levying thofe yearly millions that are appropriated to pay the intereft; we fhall find that the CROWN has gradually and imperceptibly gained almoft as much INFLUENCE as it has apparently loft in prerogative."

Blackftone, confiftently with the habits of his profeffion, expreffed himfelf cautioufly. He fays the Crown has gained *almoft* as much influence as it has apparently loft in preroga-tive. There are men of great political judgment who think that it has gained more. The Houſe of Commons has, in an auſpicious hour, reſolved, and it can never be too often repeated, that the influence of the crown has increaſed, is increaſing, and ought to be diminiſhed. Influence is more dangerous than prerogative. It is a ſubtle poiſon that acts unſeen. Prerogative can be reſiſted, as a robber; but influence is as an aſſaſſin.

Lord Bolingbroke tells us, that " we have loſt the ſpirit of our conſtitution; and therefore we bear, from little engroſſers of delegated power, what our fathers would not have ſuffered from true proprietors of the royal authority."

Such ſuggeſtions are certainly alarming. They come from high authority, and are abundantly confirmed by recent tranſactions. The magnitude of the national debt, and the ſhare that almoſt every family in the kingdom, directly or indirectly, poſſeſſes in the public funds, contribute, more than all other cauſes, to increaſe the influence of the Crown among the maſs of the people. But the debt is ſtill increaſing, in conſequence of war. Property in the funds is ſtill more widely diffuſed; the influence, in conſequence, more extended. Liberty may be more effectually invaded by the influence of the *ſtocks*, than it ever was invaded, in the days of the Stuarts, by the abuſe of prerogative.

We are happy in a king, who, making the happineſs of the people his firſt object, certainly would not avail himfelf of any advantages afforded by circumftances, to intrench upon their liberty. But be it remembered, that *minifters* in this country, with their favorites, often conftitute an OLIGARCHY.

This minifterial OLIGARCHY may certainly abufe the influence of the Crown, fo as to render itfelf virtually fuperior to the limited and conftitutional monarchy. Should fuch ever be the cafe, the *oligarchy* will be a fpecies of defpotifm, the more formidable as the more infidious, poffeffing the power, but denying the form. By a judicious diftribution of favors, by alluring all the rich and great to its fide, either by hope or by fear, it may erect a rampart, which the independent part of the people, acting from no fyftem, and difunited, may vainly feek to demolifh. The monarch and the people may join hand in hand, without effect, againft a *minifterial oligarchy*, thus buttreffed by a faction compofed of rank and wealth, artfully combined, in the meaneft manner, for the bafeft purpofes. Falfe alarms may be fpread on the danger of *property* from the diffufion of new principles, fo as to drive all who poffefs an acre of land, or a hundred pounds in the public funds, within the minifterial pale. *Religion* may be faid to be in danger, in order to bring in the devout and well difpofed. *Order* may be declared in jeopardy, that the weak, the timid, and the quiet may be led, by their fears, to unite with wealth and power. Plots and confpiracies are common expedients of

They have been ufed, by profligate
with fuch a total difregard to truth
.bility, that they now begin to lofe
ît. But how dreadful, if influence
r prevail with JURIES, to gratify the
of falfe plots, treafons, and confpi-
bringing in verdicts favorable to the
the villainous fabricators! Englifh
indeed ftill uncorrupted. They are
ed with courts and minifters. And
rupt part of our fyftem, in cafes of
, is able to prevent the mifchief which
caufed by the corrupt part of it.
t juries, in the late trials for treafon,
only done honor to our country and
nature, but added great ftrength to
of truth, juftice, and the conftitu-

s truly alarming, to hear the verdicts
obliqely impeached by GREAT MEN
lative affemblies. There has appeared
:r fymptom of the fpirit of defpotifm,
attempts of courtiers and crown law-
he public fenate, to vilify juries and
licts, given after a more folemn and
*r*eftigation than ever took place on
als. Perfons acquitted after fuch an
ave been faid to be no more innocent
itted felons. That the people have
:h an infult on their moft valuable
with patience, is a proof that a tame
ice has been produced among them,
to their virtuous anceftors. It is to

be hoped the infult will ftimulate future juries to preferve their rights with jealous vigilance, and render them impregnable by miniſterial influence, directly or indirectly applied. If the men who difapprove the verdicts of the virtuous juries, on the late occafions, had themſelves been the jurors, they would have given different verdicts, pronounced the prifoners guilty, and affigned them over to the refentment of irritated, ariftocratic pride. So mighty is the defpotifm of influence, that neither juftice nor mercy can check it in the breaft of a proud parafite.

There is every reafon to believe, (and the belief is highly confolatory), that juries will long continue to preferve their integrity; becaufe they are indifcriminately felected from the *middle* rank and the mafs of the *people*. Influence cannot reach every individual in the millions that conftitute a great nation. But we muft remember that influence is *increafing*; and that its nature is to diffufe deadly poifon, without giving alarm. Like the air loaded with infection, it filently and fecretly wafts difeafe into the ftrongeft abodes of health, and penetrates the caftle, which is impregnable to the fword of the open invader. Therefore, as influence increafes, the jealoufy and vigilance of the uninfected part of the community fhould increafe in proportion. Though undue influence may never operate on juries, yet is there no danger left it fhould, at fome diftant period, contaminate the minds of judges and *crown lawyers*, for whofe obfequious interpretations of law may be held up prizes moft glittering in the eyes of imagination, and moft alluring to avarice and vanity ?

But granting that the foul ftain of corruption fhould never fpot the white robe of *juftice ;* that the religion of an oath fhould ftill be revered, and confcience hold the balance with an even hand ; yet is there no danger left the *defpotifm of influence* fhould deftroy the vitals of a *free conftitution*, and leave nothing behind but the form, the *exuviæ,* the name ? There was a *fenate* under the vileft of the Roman emperors. The Britifh houfe of commons might become, under a *minifterial oligarchy*, the mere levee of a prime minifter. They might meet merely to " *bow and bow*," receive their orders and *douceurs*, and then depart in peace.

The *prefent* ftate of the houfe of commons cannot be too generally known ; and I therefore tranfcibe the following paffage from the Proceedings of the Society of the Friends of the People.

" The condition of the Houfe of Commons is *practically* as follows :

" Seventy-one *peers* and the *Treafury* NOMINATE ninety members, and procure the return of *feventy-feven*, which amount to one hundred and fixty-feven. Ninety-one commoners nominate eighty-two members, and procure the return of fifty-feven, which amount to one hundred and thirty-nine."

So that the peers, the *Treasury*, and *rich* commoners with influence equal to peers, return three hundred and six members out of five hundred and thirteen, which is the whole number of *English* representatives in the House of Commons. The *Scotch* members are not considered in this part of the Report.

The Society give the names of the different patrons at full length, to authenticate their statement; and I believe its accuracy and authenticity have never been controverted.

After observing that *seventy-one* PEERS and the *Treasury* nominate or procure the return of one hundred and sixty-seven members of parliament, who may vote away the *people*'s money, and make laws, with the other branches, to bind many millions, let us remember, that at the commencement of every session, the following resolutions are entered on the Journals:

" Resolved, that no peer of this realm hath any right to give his vote in the election of any member to serve in parliament. Resolved, that it is a high infringement upon the liberties and privileges of the Commons of Great-Britain, for any lord of parliament, or any lord-lieutenant of any county, to concern themselves in the elections of members to serve for the Commons in Parliament."

The committee of the Friends of the People say, " they have been the more disposed to take notice of these resolutions, because the power of the House of Lords, in matters of election, has been prodigiously increased, within the *last ten years*, by the creation of *nine peers*, who return, by nomination and influence, no less than TWENTY-FOUR members to the House of Commons. If, therefore, the interference of the Lords in the election of the Commons be, as the latter uniformly declare, a *high infringement* of their liberties and privileges, the Committee must report those liberties to have been of late subject to the most alarming and frequent attacks."

After producing facts that defy denial, I confidently leave every honest and sensible man in the kingdom, unblinded by prejudice, unwarped by interest, to determine whether the cause of liberty is not on the decline, and the spirit of despotism likely to avail itself of the general corruption of the aristocracy, and the tame acquiescence of the people.

I leave the question to be determined by such men, whether it is not possible that INFLUENCE may create a complete *despotism* in a country, even while the *forms* of a free constitution are preserved inviolate?

SECTION XXX.

The Spirit of Despotism delights in War or systematic Murder.

"THE *people* of England are industrious, they are peaceful, they wish to enjoy the fruits of their industry without a *war*, and to recover their lost weight in our mixed frame of government, without the hazards of a *revolution*.

"It is from the prevalence of *Mr. Burke's politics* alone, among the *upper classes* of society, that the rise of any *dangerous disaffection* in this country is to be apprehended. To the plain sense of Englishmen, a war commenced with France, on *his* principles, must appear to be a war on French liberty, to beat down the equitable claims of reformation *here*, and *eventually to destroy every valuable right of the people.*

"Such will be the suspected motives for plunging this country in a war, in which our *fleets* may be victorious, but in which even our successes must be ruinous. For views thus wild and chimerical, the nation, whose wounds received in the late war with America are hardly yet closed up, must prepare to bleed afresh. For objects thus odious and destable, *the industrious classes of the people must forego their comforts;* the shoulders, already galled with taxes, the pernicious consequence of *for-*

mer INJUSTICE and FOLLY, muſt ſubmit again to new and heavier impoſitions.

" They will be cheerfully voted, no doubt, by the *faithful Commons*; but the Commons will no longer enjoy the confidence of the public. Every vote of credit or ſupply will then increaſe the general diſguſt; and ſhould no greater diſaſter befal us, the mere protraction of the war muſt exhauſt the patience of a diſabuſed people.

" But what may be the contagious effect of French opinions on a nation *ſick of the war of kings*, groaning under an intolerable load of taxes, and hopeleſs of redreſs from men, *whom they will ceaſe to conſider as repreſentatives*, it is needleſs to ſtate. To foreſee it, is eaſy; to prevent it, may be impoſſible."

Thus far the excellent WYVILL, in a letter to Mr. Pitt, in which he wiſely diſſuaded him from the unfortunate and diſgraceful war, of which that miniſter muſt ſoon repent, though power and repentance do not uſually unite. No diſſuation could cool Mr. Pitt's heroic ardor, or check his juvenile impetuoſity. War was haſtily commenced. The conſequences were foretold, and the prediction is fulfilled.

But to an accurate obſerver it is an alarming proof of the ſpirit of deſpotiſm, when the GREAT are eager to ruſh into *war*; when they liſten to no terms of accommodation, and ſcorn to negociate, in any mode or degree, previouſly to unſheathing the dreadful inſtrument of ſlaughter. If war, inſtead of being what it

Y

has been called, the *ratio ultima*, becomes the *ratio prima regum*, it is a proof that *reafon* has loft her empire, and force ufurped her throne.

FEAR is the principle of all defpotic government, and therefore defpots make war their firft ftudy and delight. No arts and fciences, nothing that contributes to the comfort or the embellifhment of human fociety, is half fo much attended to, in countries where the fpirit of defpotifm is eftablifhed, as the means of deftroying human life. Tigers, wolves, earthquakes, inundations, are all innocuous to man, when compared with the fierceft of monfters, the GORY DESPOTS. Fiends, furies, demons of deftruction! may the day be near, when, as wolves have been utterly extirminated from England, defpots may be cut off from the face of the whole earth; and the bloody memory of them loaded with the execration of every human being, to whom God has given a heart to feel, and a tongue to utter!

Wherever a particle of their accurfed *fpirit* is found, there alfo will be found a propenfity to war. In times of peace, the *grandees* find themfelves fhrunk to the fize of common mortals. A finer houfe, a finer coach, a finer coat, a finer livery than others can afford, is all that they can difplay to the eye of the multitude, in proof of their affumed fuperiority. Their POWER is inconfiderable. But no fooner do you blow the blaft of war, and put armies under their command, than they feel themfelves indeed great and powerful. A hundred thoufand men, in battle array, with all the inftruments of deftruction, under the command of a few *grandees*, inferior, perhaps, in bodily ftrength, to every one of the fubject train, and but little fuperior in intellect or courage, yet, holding ALL, on pain of death, in abfolute fubjection; how muft it elevate the *little defpots* in their own opinion! " This it is to live," (they ex-claim, fhaking hands with each other), " this is to be great indeed. *Now* we feel our power. Glory be to us on high ; efpecially as all our fame and greatnefs is perfectly compatible with our perfonal fafety ; for we will not rifque our precious perfons in the fcene of danger, but be content with our *extended patronage*, with the delight of commanding the movements of this human machine, and with reading of the blood, flaughter, and burnt villages, in the Gazette, at our fire-fide."

All the expence of war is paid by the peo-ple, and moft of the perfonal danger incurred by thofe, who, according to fome, have no political exiftence ; I mean the *multitude*, *told by the head*, like fheep in Smithfield. Many of thefe troublefome beings, in human form, are happily got rid of in the field of battle, and more by ficknefs and hardfhip previous or fubfequent to the glorious day of butchery. Thus all makes for the fpirit of defpotifm. There are, in confequence of a great carnage, fewer *wretches* left to provide for, or to oppofe its will ; and all the honor, all the profit, all the *amufement*, falls to the fhare of the *grandees*, thus raifed from the infignificance and inglorious indolence of peace, to have their names blown over the world by the trumpet of Fame, and recorded in the page of hiftory.

But a ftate of war not only gives a degree of perfonal importance to fome among the great, which they could never obtain by the arts of peace, but greatly helps the caufe of defpotifm. In times of peace, the people are apt to be impertinently clamorous for reform. But in war, they muft fay no more on the fubject, becaufe of the public danger. It would be ill-timed. Freedom of fpeech alfo muft be checked. A thoufand little reftraints on liberty are admitted without a murmur, in a time of war, that would not be borne one moment during the halcyon days of peace. Peace, in fhort, is productive of plenty, and plenty makes the people faucy. Peace, therefore, muft not continue long, after a nation has arrived at a certain degree of profperity. This is a maxim of Defpotifm. Political phlebotomy is neceffary in a political plethora. " Bleed them *ufque ad deliquium*," (fays the arbitrary doctor), " and I will undertake that in future the patient fhall be more tractable."

Erafmus, the friend of man, the reftorer of civil and religious liberty, has the following paffage in a Differtation on War, lately tranflated into Englifh under the title of *Antipolemus*?

" There are kings who go to war for no other reafon than that they may with greater eafe eftablifh *defpotic authority* over their own subjects at home. For in time of peace, the power of parliaments, the dignity of magistrates, the vigor of the laws, are great impediments to a prince who wishes to exercise arbitrary power. But when once a war is undertaken, the chief management of affairs devolves on a *few*, the ministers of executive government, who, for the general safety, assume the privilege of conducting every thing according to their own humor, demanding unlimited confidence. The prince's favorites are all exalted to places of honor and profit. Those whom he dislikes are turned out and neglected. *Now* —(the time of war) is the time for raising as much money upon the people as the despot's heart can wish.—In short—now—the time of war, is the time that they feel themselves despots in very deed and truth, not in name only, but despots with a vengeance. In the mean while, the grandees play into one another's hands, till they have eaten up the wretched PEOPLE, root and branch. Do you think that men of such dispositions would be backward to seize any, the slightest occasions for war, so lucrative, so flattering to avarice and vanity * ?"

---

* " *Sunt qui non aliam ob causam bellum movent, nisi ut hac via facilius in* SUOS TYRANNIDEM *exerceant. Nam pacis temporibus,* senatus auctoritas, magistratum dignitas, legum vigor, *nonnihil obstant, quo minus liceat principi, quicquid libet. At,* bello suscepto, jam omnis rerum summa ad paucorum libidinem devoluta est. Evehuntur quibus bene vult princeps; dejiciuntur quibus infensus est. Exigitur pecunia quantum libet. Quid multis?* TUM DEMUM SENTIUNT

Language has found no name fufficiently expreffive of the diabolical villany of wretches in high life, who without perfonal provocation, in the mere wantonnefs of power, and for the fake of increafiing what they already poffefs in too great abundance, rufh into *murder!* Murder of the innocent! Murder of myriads! Murder of the ftranger! neither knowing nor caring how many of their fellow-creatures, with rights to life and happinefs equal to their own, are urged by poverty to fhed their laft drops of blood in a foreign land, far from the endearments of kindred, to gratify the pride of a FEW at home, whofe defpotic fpirit infults the wretchednefs it firft created. There is no greater proof of human folly and weaknefs than that a whole people fhould fuffer a *few worth-lefs grandees,* who evidently defpife and hate them, to make the world one vaft flaughter-houfe, that the grandees may have the more room to take their infolent paftime in unmo-lefted ftate. A man, a reafonable being, a chriftian, plunging the bayonet, without paf-fion, into the bowels of a man, for hire! The poor creatures who actually do this (in defpotic countries) are but mechanical inftruments of knaves in power. Their poverty, and not their will, confents. May Heaven's fweet mercy, then, wafh off the blood-ftains from

SE VERE MONARCHAS *effe. Colludunt interim duces, donec infelicem populum ufque ad radicem arroferint. Hoc animo qui fint, an eos putas gravatim arrepturos, oblatam quam-cunque belli occafionem?"* ERASMUS.

their hands, and referve its wrath for thofe whofe thirft of power, which they never had a wifh to ufe for the good of man, leads them to wade to it through feas of human gore!

Let any difpaffionate man, uninfluenced by placemen, penfioners, contractors, and expectants of court favor, impartially confider, from the earlieft ages to the prefent, the hiftory of war. He muft obferve that fcarcely any wars have been *juft* and *neceffary*; though they almoft all have claimed thefe epithets, with a perfevering formality which would excite ridicule, if ridicule were not loft in abhorrence. He will find that folly, extreme folly, wearing a crown inftead of a fool's cap, has in many countries, from the mere wantonnefs of mifchief, cried, " Havoc, and let flip the dogs of war." He will find that in moft countries (our own, of courfe, always excepted) war has been eagerly fought, from *policy*, to divert the people's attention from domeftic abufe, to aggrandize thofe who build the fabric of their grandeur on the ruins of human happinefs, and to deprefs, impoverifh, and humble the people.

There is nothing from which the fpirit of liberty has fo much to fear, and confequently the fpirit of defpotifm fo much to hope, as from the prevalence of military government, fupported by vaft ftanding armies, and encouraged by alliances with military defpots on the continent of Europe. The whole energy of the found part of our free conftitution fhould be exerted in its full force to check a proud minifter, who rafhly runs into a war, and notwithftanding accumulated difafters, perfeveres in its profecution. He cannot hope for victory. He muft have fome other motive for perfevering againft all rational hope. Let the PEOPLE inveftigate the motive; and if it be inimical to LIBERTY, let them fuccour her in diftrefs, by calling in her beft auxiliary, PEACE.

SECTION XXXI.

On the Idea that we have arrived at Perfection in Politics, though all other Sciences are in a progressive State.

THOSE who have been fortunate enough to have gained poffeffion of honors and profits, under a corrupt fyftem, well pleafed with *things as they are*, boldly contend that they cannot be better. But thefe, compared with the mafs of the community, are few and ultimately of little confequence. Their opinion therefore muft not weigh againft any improvement which is likely to promote the melioration of human affairs. Let them enjoy unmolefted the luxuries of the table, the fplendor of equipages, large houfes, and every other external advantage, which makes *little man* fwell into fancied importance. In the mean time let every honeft, benevolent member of the community, who is fatisfied with being happy himfelf, without defiring to entrench on the happinefs of others, endeavor to reform abufes, and promote every improvement which can render human life (fhort as it is, and full of calamity) more comfortable, and lefs expofed to the injuries and contumelies of the proud oppreffor.

Rewards are offered for the difcovery of the longitude at fea. Men are not only allowed but encouraged to profecute their enquiries into all other arts and fciences. But the grand art, the art of government, that is, the art of fecuring the civil happinefs of millions, is to be confidered as facred and infcrutable. Thofe very millions whom it more immediately interefts, dare not, if the defpots could prevail, to lift up the awful veil. Racks, gibbets, bowftrings, chains, and prifons, are prepared, in moft of the kingdoms of the world, to awe the curious, and check the fpirit of political improvement. OPTIMISM has long been eftablifhed in the courts of defpotic princes. *Whatever is, is right*, fay they; for knowing that they ftand on a rotten foundation, they fear that the very fixing of the fcaffold for repair would precipitate the downfall of the whole fabric.

Mankind might, at the clofe of this century, juftly celebrate a general jubilee; for arbitrary government, in Europe at leaft, has received its death blow by the revolution in France. And it is devoutly to be wifhed, for their own fakes, that in limited monarchies, the voice of truth and virtue, calling for the reform of abufes, exifting evidently as the meridian fun, will never be filenced by the terrors of the law in the hands of crown lawyers, or the fabre of dragoons, under the command of a defpotic minifter.

Is it to be believed that governments were brought to *perfection* in early and dark ages, when the minds of the great as well as the little were enveloped in the mifts of ignorance, and fhackled by the chains of fuperftition? Is it reafonable to fuppofe that they who were nar-

row-minded, ill-informed, childifh, and bar-
barous in all other parts of knowledge and of
conduct, were liberal, wife, and illuminated
in the fcience and practice of government; fo
liberal, fo wife, fo illuminated, as to ftrike
out at once a fyftem *complete* in all its parts,
and fuch as could in no fubfequent age, in no
variety of circumftances, admit of correction,
addition, or melioration? Did this wonderful
fagacity, approaching to infpiration, produce
any thing elfe, in any other department, which
defies all improvement, and challenges the refpect and veneration of the lateft pofterity?
Reafoning from analogy, we muft conclude,
that men, capable of eftablifhing at once a perfect fyftem of government, muft have produced
other inventions for the accommodation and fecurity of life, worthy to be preferved inviolate,
and handed down unaltered, till time itfelf be
abforbed in the ocean of eternity. But where
fhall we look for it? The very queftion implies
a doubt of its exiftence; for fingular excellence, fuch excellence as approaches to perfection, cannot be concealed, but will fhine
with its own luftre and force, obfervation and
wonder. Is the *architecture* of thefe paragons
of wifdom fuperior to the modern, in beauty
or convenience? Let us only walk the ftreets
of London, and mark thofe houfes which were
fpared by the great fire, and which may fairly
be fuppofed improvements on the more antient
fabrics. We fee them, contrary to every principle of common fenfe, with ftories projecting

over each other. · We fee them ugly, mean, inconvenient. Let us proceed to the north-weft parts of that great town. Take a view of Portland-place. Contraft the fymmetry, the accommodation, the magnificence, with the old edifices of Holborn or Alderfgate, and be per-fuaded that modern improvements in govern-ment might be as much fuperior to the work of antient bunglers, as the elegant buildings of an Adams or a Wyat to the old manfions now converted into inns, in the dirtieft ftreets, in the moft decayed diftricts of the metropolis.

· · Man is a progreffive animal, and his advance towards improvement is a pleafurable ftate. Hope cheers his path as he toils up the hill that leads him to fomething better than he has yet experienced, on its gay fummit gilded with funfhine. The labor of the afcent is a delight. But if he cannot help conceiving, from a fenfe of grievances which he feels, fomething EXCEL-LENT, to which he is prohibited by coercion from approaching, hope fickens, and ill-humor fucceeds to complacency. Hence arifes a dif-agreement between the governed and the go-vernors ; and the governors being poffeffed of prefent power, ufe force and rigor to ftifle the murmurs of complaint. Coercion but increafes the ill humor, which often lies latent, like the fires of a volcano, for a confiderable time, but at laft burfts forth with irrefiftible fury. It is wife, therefore, as well as juft, in all governors, who have a regard for any thing but their pre-fent and private intereft, to encourage difcuffion, to feek improvement of the fyftem, and to reject no reform propofed by great numbers, without a cool, a temperate, and a long deliberation. The reafons for rejection fhould be clearly ftated, with the utmoft regard to open and ingenuous behaviour; and thofe who remain unconvinced, after all, fhould not be treated with afperity. Every individual, in a free country, has a right to approve or difapprove the fyftem under which he lives, without peril or control, while he preferves the peace. His peaceable deportment and acquiefcence in the opinion of others, contrary to his own conviction, renders him a very meritorious character. He may be won over by gentlenefs; but force only tends to excite the violence which it would imperioufly repel.

But to tell a man of fenfe, reading, and reflection, that he muft not venture to entertain an opinion on political matters, or the exifting government, different from that of the minifter and the herd of courtiers, is an impotent endeavor to exercife a defpotifm over his mind, againft which nature revolts, and a manly fpirit muft rebel. Such a man can ufually judge of governments, and all the inftitutions of focial life, better than mere men of bufinefs, however high their rank or important their employments; far better than courtiers, occupied in vain ceremonies, and ufually as little able as inclined to enter into deep difquifition.

Indeed it is difficult to avoid laughing at the extreme ignorance of crowned heads them-

Z

felves, in defpotic countries, when one contrafts it with the importance they affume, and the pomp and fplendor with which they transfer their royal perfons from place to place. The fight is truly ludicrous. Are thefe the men, occupied, as they ufually are, in the meaneft trifles and the moft degrading pleafures, who tell us that the government over which they prefide, is a perfect fyftem, and that the wifeft philofopher knows not how to govern mankind—that is, to confult their happinefs and fecurity—fo well as themfelves, neglected as they have been in youth, and corrupted in manhood by panders to their vices, and flatterers of their foibles, their pride, and their ambition? There is reafon to believe that many kings, in defpotic kingdoms, have been lefs well educated, and poffefs lefs abilities, than a common charity boy, trained in a parifh fchool to read and write. Yet thefe are the men who, with their upftart creatures, prefume to call philofophers wretches, and to condemn the Voltaires, the Rouffeaus, the Sydneys, the Harringtons, and the Lockes.

There are perfons, even in countries where limited royalty is eftablifhed, who are for ever extolling the CONSTITUTION, with all the abufes that have infinuated themfelves into it, in terms of extravagant and unqualified praife. They talk againft better knowledge, and may therefore be fufpected of fome finifter motive. They can fee defects as well as others; but they affume the worft of all blindnefs, that which is voluntary.

The truth is, thefe men, for the moft part, are fuch as would not like the *conftitution in its purity*, becaufe in its purity the conftitution is really excellent, and highly favorable to the liberty which they hate. The conftitution, in its purity, renders the people of *confequence*, whofe political exiftence they are inclined to controvert or deny. But the conftitution, in its ftate of corruption, is favorable to preroga-tive, to ariftocratical pride and influence, to Tory and jacobitical principles; therefore it is, in their eyes, criminal to handle it, to hint at its improvement, to remove a grievance, or reform an abufe. The whole, together, though violated every day by corrupt influence, they affect to confider as a written charter, dropt down from heaven, like the old Roman *Ancilia*, and therefore fcarcely to be viewed by vulgar eyes, and certainly not to be touched by the hand of the profane PEOPLE.

Defpotifm is fo ugly in its form, and fo hof-tile, in its nature, to human happinefs, that no wonder thofe who wifh to diffufe its fpirit are inclined to check and difcourage among the people all political inveftigation. But let it be a rule among thofe who really value liberty and the conftitution, to ufe the more diligence in political difcuffions, in proportion as courtiers and minifters difplay a wifh to fupprefs political writings and converfations, and diffeminate the doctrine, that things are fo well conftituted as neither to require nor admit any improvement.

SECTION XXXII.

On POLITICAL ETHICS ; *their chief Object is to throw Power into the Hands of the worst Part of Mankind, and to render Government an Institution calculated to enrich and aggrandize a few, at the Expence of the Liberty, Property, and Lives of the many.*

IN the *schools* of early difcipline, where youth is ufually initiated in the ftudies of humanity, men are taught to believe, that virtue is founded on *eternal truth*, and that the diftinctions of right and wrong are as clearly definable as thofe between the meridian funfhine and the midnight fhade. They are told, from the higheft authority, that happinefs is to be found in rectitude of conduct ; and that under all circumftances, whatever may be the confequence, nothing can juftify the dereliction of integrity. The facred fcriptures, the antient philofophers, parental authority, the laws of their country, and the PROCLAMATIONS of kings, all combine to convince them, that morality is founded on the rock of truth, and that governments are *fincere* in their profeffions to encourage thofe who do well, and be a terror only to the EVIL.

Why was a national *church* inftituted and fupported at a great expence, but to enforce among the people the laws of God, as paramount to all human laws, and fuperceding the wretched devices of ftate policy ? Government, by entering into a ftrict alliance with the church, certainly engages to fupport the doctrines of Chriftian morality : and it is no lefs impious in a king or a minifter to promote or increafe any public meafures repugnant to Chriftian morality, than it would be in the bench of bifhops.

When we enter our *libraries*, we find ourfelves furrounded with authors, celebrated for ages by the moft enlightened part of the world, who teach the immutability of truth, enforce the pureft doctrines of morality, and endeavor to found the dignity and happinefs of human nature on the bafis of virtue.

But let us leave a moment the fchool, the church, the library, and enter a court and a cabinet. There *Machiavelian* ethics prevail; and all that has been previoufly inculcated appears like the tales of the nurfery, calculated to amufe babes, and lull them in the lap of folly. The grand object of counfellors is to fupport and increafe the POWER that appoints to fplendid and profitable offices, with little regard to the improvement of human affairs, the alleviation of the evils of life, and the melioration of human nature. The reftraints of moral honefty, or the fcruples of religon, muft feldom operate on public meafures fo as to impede the accomplifhment of this primary and momentous purpofe. A little *varnifh* is indeed ufed, to hide the deformity of Machiavelifm ; but it is fo very thin, and fo eafily diftinguifhed from the native color, that it contributes, among thinking men, to increafe the deteftation which it was intended to extenuate.

Thus, for inftance, treaties between nations commence with a moft folemn avowal of good faith, in the name of the Father, the Son, and the Holy Ghoft. Great and mighty nations, profeffing Chriftianity, maintaining a church, united moft intimately with the church, enter into agreements, under this awful fanction, and break them without the leaft reluctance, whenever a *cabinet* minifter finds it in his inclination, or imagines it his intereft to caufe a rupture. The Father, the Son, and the Holy Ghoft are little thought of ; but the great object is to ftrike a blow with advantage, before the adverfe nation is on its guard, and while it is relying on the treaty.

Another inftance of *political religion* is confpicuous in the prevailing practice of rendering the emoluments of the church fubfervient to the *minifter,* in fecuring him a majority, and facilitating what is called his principal duty, the *management* of the SENATE.

The Roman pontiffs, while in the rank of inferior clergy, and even of cardinals, have exhibited the appearance of great piety, and a religious regard to truth and juftice ; but when advanced to the *triple mitre,* and become, in fact, KINGS, they have ufually become perfectly fecular in their public conduct at home, and in their connections with furrounding nations, and have pleaded, in excufe, ftate neceffity. But can any *neceſſity* arife to violate the eternal laws of truth and juſtice? Is religion a leaden rule, in the *hands* ſtrong enough to bend it to their various purpofes? Pope JULIUS the Second appears to have been one of the very worſt princes that ever reigned. He delighted in WAR, while he profeſſed to be the repreſentative of the Prince of Peace. He was guilty of oppreſſion and injuſtice; and while he pretended to be feeding the *ſheep* of Chriſt, gave himfelf no other concern but how he might fecure the fleece. Yet all his conduct was palliated, by the politicans around him, from the plea of ſtate neceſſity. Morality and religion gave way to the fyſtem of POLITICAL ETHICS ; and he, who ought to have bleſſed mankind, and to have preached peace, became their oppreſſor, defpot, and unrelenting murderer. I mention JULIUS only as a ſtriking inſtance, and hundreds may be adduced, of the depraved fyſtem which rules cabinets, and which, for the gratification of the FEW, renders the MANY miferable. No Machiavels can ever juſtify, in the eyes of God, or of *men* uninfluenced by corruption, any politics, however fubtle and able, which, for the fake of aggrandizing a *nation,* (an *abſtract idea*), much lefs of gratifying a court, renders all the individuals of the *nation* fo to be aggrandized, poor, wretched, infecure, and flaviſh.

Let us fuppofe a nation entering moſt eagerly, and without liſtening one moment to terms of accommodation, into a moſt dangerous war, *professedly* to exterminate the bad *principles* and morals of a neighboring people, and to defend *law*, *order*, and *religion*. It is impossible to imagine but that a nation acting in this manner, and with this profession, *must* regulate all its *own* public conduct, especially in a war of this kind, according to the *strictest* law, order, and religion.

Will that nation oppose an armed *neutrality*, instituted to prevent the interruption of *neutral* commerce? Will she maintain her reputation for *justice*, if she should be the first and most violent in destroying this neutrality? Will she break the *law* of nations, by insulting ambassadors? Will she take up arms, and actually fight in defence of popery, after professing herself at the head of protestantism, and the opposer of all intolerant superstition? Will she, after declaring herself the friend of order, religion, and liberty, enter into alliances with and subsidize the plunderers and oppressors of Poland? Will she, pluming herself upon the love of order and religion, and detesting the cruelty of the nation with whom she is at war, suffer Asia to be pillaged, and its inhabitants to be slaughtered by her own sons; or encourage the Indians to attack her brethren in North America; or hire mercenaries of German princes to do the work of death, in a contest in which they have no immediate concern? Will she endeavor to *starve* a *whole* nation, with whom she is at war, not only the rulers and warriors, but infants, women, and old people;

by preventing the importation of *corn?* Will she FORGE aſſignats? Will ſhe continue the ſlave trade?

A conduct like this appears to be not only inconfiſtent with the pretended defence of *law*, *order*, and *religion*, but at once proceeding from the ſpirit of defpotiſm, and promotive of it. It is certain that a man in private life, acting in this manner, would be thought a bad man, a man deſtitute of principle, and with whom it would be ſcarcely leſs dangerous to be on terms of profeſſed friendſhip than of open enmity. But actions do not alter their nature with the paucity or multiplicity of the actors; and a *nation* may be guilty of perfidy as atrocious and contemptible in its nature as an individual, and infinitely more miſchievous. Certainly the adviſers and abettors of ſuch conduct do not take the moſt effectual means of recommending to mankind that *monarchy* which they wage war to re-eſtabliſh. They are hurting the cauſe of KINGS in the minds of independent men and of poſterity, while they blindly appear to themſelves to be promoting it with the greateſt energy.

Whatever may be urged by ſophiſts or politicians, it is certain that the great eternal laws of truth and juſtice cannot be violated with impunity. The violation may anſwer ſome ſordid and temporary purpoſe; but in the end, it muſt be injurious, if not fatal. Truth, like the ſun in the heavens, is one. The clouds indeed are variegated; but then they are infubftantial, and of momentary exiftence. So is falfehood. It can affume any color. But time caufes the hues to fade ; and truth burfts forth with new effulgence. We fee defpotifm gradually withdrawing from the fineft countries of Europe. It muft depart, at laft, from all, for it is oppofed by reafon and nature. They who endeavor to render it permanent, labor in vain ; but at the fame time, they may detain it a while, and caufe, in the interval, mifery and CARNAGE.

Let us rejeft all Machiavelifm, all *political ethics*, that contradict the acknowledged principles of truth and moral honefty. There can be no legitimate government which is not founded and fupported by fyftems of conduct favorable to the happinefs of human creatures—the great mafs of the people. Good government cannot be formed on the bafis of falfhood and chicanery. Let the government of England ever ftand on the fquare, folid, upright pedeftals of truth and juftice, and it muft defy every fhock, but the convulfion of the world's diffolution.

SECTION XXXIII.

On trafficking with the CURE OF SOULS *(Cura Animarum,) for the Purpose of political,* i. e. moral *Corruption.*

THE parish priests of a proteftant country, when they are, what they ought to be, and what they would ufually be, if it were not for political influence, CHRISTIAN ORATORS and CHRISTIAN PHILOSOPHERS, are the moft ufeful body of men, considering their numbers and their power, in the whole community. The good they are able to do is beyond all eftimate; but unfortunately, it is a fort of good not always taken into the account of thofe who are in purfuit of more palpable advantages, SOLID GOLD, high ftation, and DOMINION OVER THEIR FELLOW-CREATURES. The proper bufinefs of the clergy is to mortify this very pride, the indulgence of which is to their courtly patrons, the *fummum bonum,* the chief good of exiftence.

Thefe perfons, not having time or inclination to attend to religion, or any thing but the pomp and vanity of the world, idolizing themfelves, and unwilling to acknowledge any other Deity, confider religion and the church merely as ftate engines; powerful engines, in conjunction with military force, to prefs down the elaftic fpirit of the people. They think, indeed, the emoluments attending ecclefiaftical functions *too much*, if confidered as recompences for religious fervices, which, in their minds, are no fervices at all, but *fcarcely enough*, when converted into *douceurs* for the bufinefs of corruption, the grand object of modern minifters.

Ambitious noblemen, therefore, buy boroughs, and, like Lord Melcombe, fend their myrmidons to the fenate; and minifters pay the expenfe of the purchafe, by conferring the higheft ecclefiaftical dignities, with ftipends of many thoufands a-year, defigned originally to be fpent in charity, on the younger brothers, the coufins, the tutors, or the agents of thefe patrician borough-mongers. It is indeed deemed *politic*, now and then, to raife a very ingenious, learned, and pious man to the MITRE; but feldom without contriving to promote, at the fame time, the grand bufinefs of corruption. This ingenious, learned, and pious man, *un eveque de la fortune*, is highly fatisfied with the dignity and emolument of his office. What need has he of the *patronage* appendant to it? In this age, it were a childifh weaknefs, fomething fimilar to the fimplicity recommended in the gofpel, to give away good things to modeft merit. But, though *he* has no need of the patronage, there are thofe, to whom he is bound, by every tie of gratitude, who want it all. He therefore underftands that the CURE OF SOULS is to be given to perfons whom the prime minifter may recommend; as the Duke of Newcaftle recommended Burroughs and

Franklin, whom he had never feen or known, to the patronage of the lord chancellor. A *tranflation* may be impeded, if fcruples of confcience fhould prevent an obfequious compliance with a minifter's *congé d'elire.* " As to fitnefs or unfitnefs," (cries the friend of corruption), " any man that can read is *fufficient*, for both prayers and fermons are ready made; and even if it were fuppofable that a man could not read, a parifh, that pays the rector a thoufand a-year, may be fupplied with an ingenious curate for forty."

Formerly learning was fcarce among the laity. The clergy engroffed what little there was in the world, and made themfelves neceffary to the ftate, not only in ecclefiaftical, but political offices and employments. " Before the Reformation," (fays a learned writer), " the canon law was in great ufe and efteem, and of great ufe; and while the laity were in general unlettered, or employed in a military life, the king made ufe of clergymen, fkilled in this law, in the offices of the chancery, privy feal, fecretary of ftate, in the courts of juftice, and in embaffies. The king rewarded men thus qualified to do him fervice, with benefices and other ecclefiaftical preferments; and the LORD CHANCELLOR or Lord Keeper, in particular, was furnifhed with many advowfons, to which, as they became vacant, he might prefent worthy mafters and clerks in Chancery, who were *then all clergymen;* which advowfons ftill continue in his gift, though the reafon thereof hath long ceafed." But *one* reafon having ceafed, *others* may have rifen ftill more weighty. We have already remarked, more than once, how that prime minifter, the Duke of Newcaftle, ufed the advowfons in the gift of the Chancellor. We know how preferment is beftowed in Ireland as well as England. We remember the *old manner* of appointment to the provoft-fhip of Trinity-college, Dublin.

The excellent divine from whom the laft quotation was taken, fpeaking of clergymen honored and enriched with *two cures of fouls,* proceeds thus : " I do not deny but there are *pluralifts* of great ecclefiaftical merit; but I do deny that in general *pluralifts* have greater merit than unalifts, or than many in orders who have no living at all; or that pluralifts in general, become pluralifts for their ecclefiaftical merit.

" Read over the lift of pluralifts in England, and fee whether this fort of merit be univerfally, or generally, or COMMONLY, regarded in the *difpenfations* granted them to hold pluralities. See whether the *judge* of this fort of merit hath power, if he were ever fo well inclined, to regard it univerfally, or generally, or *commonly:* fee whether the motive of the patron to prefent a clerk to a fecond living, hath, in one inftance out of twenty, been his eminent ecclefiaftical merit; or whether the fame favor would not have been beftowed on the *fame* perfon, had his merit *been inferior;* nay, in many cafes, upon the *fame* perfon, although inftead of merit there had been demerit; and very often alfo, if not the more likely, if inftead of want of a competence, there had been affluence. See whether the MERIT, which hath been *fometimes* confidered in this cafe, hath not, *inftead of ecclefiaftical merit*, been *political opinions, ferviceablenefs in elections*, private treaties, domeftic negociations, and other *mean offices*, below the confideration and interpofition of ecclefiaftics, and hurtful to the ecclefiaftical character. With fome patrons, there is not one of thefe qualifications that is not a ftronger motive than parts, and learning, and piety, and prudence, and virtue put together." Thus faid Dr. Newton, the founder and head of a college in Oxford, at a time when the *cure of fouls* was not confidered as fo trifling a care as it has been by more recent minifters, who have feemed ready to facrifice both foul and body to the gaining of a majority in the fenate. The CHURCH once preferved her own dignity with a noble independence; but now fhe muft bow, like a lacquey, to the vileft minifter of ftate.

But what is this *cura animarum*, this office of watching over the fpiritual ftate of populous diftricts? Is it not, on the hypothefis that the Chriftian religion is true, the moft important office that can be undertaken by man on this fide the grave? Is not the power of appointing to that office a truft moft facred, if there be any thing facred here below? What is SACRILEGE? the ftealing of a cufhion or filver chalice from a church? And is it no facrilege to fteal the church itfelf, and all its emoluments, defigned to *prevent* the increafe of corruption, in order to reward and to promote corruption? Is the *cura animarum* to be the laft confideration in the patron's mind, though the firft in the eye of reafon and religion? And is all this injuftice, facrilege, impiety, and blafphemy to be endured, becaufe the gift of the ftipend, the endowment, the tithes, the fees, *buy an elector*, who *fwears*, at the time of giving his vote, that he has not received a bribe? Is it to be wondered, if, under fuch abufes, religion fhould be on the decline? Do the writings of infidels, or the venal practices of patrons, contribute *moft* to exterminate Chriftianity? What has a fimilar fyftem in France effected, carried indeed to ftill greater lengths, but ftill fimilar? The greedy rapacioufnefs of court fycophants in England is doing the work of ANTICHRIST, and deftroying civil liberty.

But I am chiefly concerned at prefent to confider the ufing the church, or the *cure of fouls*, for the corruption of the *ftate* and the *violation* of the *conftitution*, as a POLITICAL enormity. It certainly contributes to the fpirit of defpotifm. It naturally tends to make all the youth in the nation, who enter on this facred profeffion, look up to court favor, and not to depend on their own merit or exertions, for promotion. It prevents them from voting freely at elections. It prevents them from preaching freely from the pulpit. Its natural tendency is to make them what they ought particularly to avoid, adulators, worldly wife, parafitical, and *acceptors of men's perfons for the fake of advantage.* They muft know, under fuch a fyftem, that if they vote according to confcience, or preach or write according to the truth as it is in Jefus, they muft forego all thofe profpects of rifing in their profeffion, which, if merit were rewarded, are a ftimulus to every thing that can benefit human nature. Clerical men, infirm, like others, often fink under this temptation. Few can renounce great temporal advantages for the fake of promoting public good, efpecially when they are fure of perfecution as well as neglect. Now, what muft be the confequence to liberty, of a whole national clergy rendered expectant on the favor of a court, and a proud ariftocracy? May we not hear again from the *pulpit*, the doctrines of divine right and paffive obedience; the fame doctrines in effect, under names lefs offenfive to the people? Have we not *lately* heard them?

There is no mode of promoting the purpofes of corruption, and the aggrandizement of thofe who already engrofs the pomp of grandeur, more injurious to liberty, and more villanoufly bafe, than that of feizing the appointments and rewards of piety and virtue, to beftow them on thofe, whofe worldly wifdom is their chief recommendation, and who feem ready to worfhip God only in the *fecond* place, if they worfhip him at all.

A a 2

The Tindals, the Collins's, the Boling-brokes, the Humes, the Gibbons, the Voltaires, the Volneys, the *miscreant* philosophers of France, never did so much injury to the cause of Christianity, as those English ministers of state, who, while they shed the blood of thousands for the sake of law, order, and *religion*, prostitute the church and the CURE OF SOULS to the corruption of the senate.

SECTION XXXIV.

Of Mr Hume's *idea, That* abfolute Monarchy
is the eafieſt Death, the Euthanaſia *of the*
Britiſh Conſtitution.

THE very ingenious fpeculatiſt, Mr.
Hume, feems to wiſh as well as think, that as
death is unavoidable by the political as well as
the animal body, the Britiſh conſtitution may
die in the arms of defpotifm. His words are,
" I would much rather wiſh to fee an abfolute
monarch than a republic in this iſland. Abfolute monarchy is the eaſieſt death, the true
euthanaſia of the Britiſh conſtitution."

His opinion, that our free government will
terminate in defpotifm, feems founded on the
following argument, which he has inferted in
his Eſſay on the Britiſh Government.

" The Britiſh fpirit and love of liberty,
however great, will never be able to fuppoit
itfelf againſt that immenfe property which is
now lodged in the king, and is ſtill increafing.
Upon a moderate computation, there are near
three millions annually at the difpofal of the
crown. The civil liſt amounts to near a million ; the collection of all taxes to another million ; and the employments in the army and
navy, along with ecclefiaſtical preferments, to
above a third million. A monſtrous fum ! and
what may fairly be computed to be more than

a thirtieth part of the whole income and labor of the kingdom. When we add to this immenfe property the increafing luxury of the nation, our pronenefs to corruption, along with the great power and prerogatives of the crown, and the command of fuch numerous military forces, there is no one but muft defpair without EXTRAORDINARY EFFORTS, of being able to fupport our free government much longer under all thefe difadvantages."

But why fhould not ' *extraordinary efforts*' be made, when the object is extraordinary— no lefs than the prefervation of human happinefs, by the prefervation of civil liberty ? No efforts fhould be declined in fuch a caufe ; nor fhould MEN, fenfible of their bleffings, and defirous of handing them down as they received them, fink, with daftardly indolence, into a ftate of defpair.

Mr. Hume, with all his penetration, could not forefee the revolution in France ; and how much the eftablifhment of liberty, in that extenfive and enlightened country, would contribute to defeat the purpofe of defpots in all the nations of Europe. It is certain that the minds of the *people* in all countries are opened to the light of truth, by the emancipation of four or five and twenty millions of men, from the flavery of prejudice and arbitrary dominion. There is now very little occafion for that defpair of preferving the freedom of the Britifh government, if the people will but be true to their own caufe. Defpotifm, in its laft ftruggles, may make great efforts; but even they will exhauſt its ſtrengh, and accelerate its diſſolution. Firmneſs and perſeverance in the people will ultimately triumph over the unnatural exertions of deſpotiſm, driven to madneſs by deſpair.

The ſpirit of liberty, it has been ſaid, is a ſpirit of jealouſy. It ought to be ever-waking and circumſpect; for the ſpirit of deſpotiſm never ſlumbers, but watches every opportunity to increaſe prerogative, and diminiſh popular authority. During thoſe late alarms which cowardly and ſelfiſh ariſtocracy labored to diffuſe, in its panic fear for its own privileges, many inſtances occurred of men who would willingly have ſacrificed all the boaſted freedom of Engliſhmen, to the ſecurity which they flattered themſelves grandeur, titles, and riches would enjoy under an abſolute government. Their pride was ſtung to the quick, by the idea of equality, while their avarice trembled for their property, and their cowardice for their perſonal ſafety. They ſaw ſpectres in the ſhapes of Truth, Juſtice, and Liberty, triumphing over an enſlaved and deluded world; they knew that they had little intereſt or connection with ſuch *perſonages*, and ſhuddered at their fancied approach. They ſhrieked with terror; and would gladly have haſtened to the greateſt deſpot on earth for protection. England had no deſpot on the throne to afford them an aſylum; and therefore they placed all their hopes on the *military* arm. War was the cry;

victory was fure. Baftiles were already built in imagination, and chains fabricated for the millions that people the provinces of Gaul

Had it been poffible for thefe men to prevail, in the moment of their confternation, the fceptre of England would have been converted by them into an iron rod, and its king into the *grand monarque* of the old French tyranny. Defpotifm, expelled from France, would have croffed from Calais to Dover, and been received with open arms by devoted vaffals, the flavifh alarmifts of an Englifh ariftocracy. The free government of England might have found at this period, as Mr. Hume prophecies it will hereafter do, an eafy death in abfolute monarchy.

But though the high *church and king alarm-ifts* did not fucceed at that time, which feemed aufpicious to their defigns, yet ftill they continue on their pofts, watching opportunities to infringe on liberty, to feduce the people from their love of it, and gradually to reconcile them to arbitrary rule.

Strange as it is, as a moral phenomenon, that men fhould wifh to be flaves, yet it is certain, that the tribe of perfons devoted to the pomp and power of uncontrolled royalty, whom I call Tories or Ariftocrats, for want of a more appropriate and precife appellation, are ftill extremely zealous to make our KING a far fuperior potentate than he is allowed to be by that REVOLUTION, which gives him all the royal rights he poffeffes, and places him on the throne.

Many circumſtances favor the wiſhes of theſe perſons ; and nothing oppoſes them ſo much as the French revolution, and thoſe liberal opinions on the rights and happineſs of man which begin to prevail, wherever courts and miniſters have little influence. Among the circumſtances which flatter them moſt with the extenſion of royal power, the elevation of themſelves, and the depreſſion of the people, is the intereſt which almoſt every man and woman in the nation poſſeſſes in the public funds, and which they are all taught to believe would be depreciated, or even annihilated, if the parliament were reformed, the people reinſtated in their rights, and the influence of the crown diminiſhed. This has communicated the *panic* of the alarmiſts among multitudes too remote from courts, and too inconſiderable in ſtation, to be influenced by miniſterial bribes; who, otherwiſe, could not but have ſided with the cauſe of juſtice and humanity. The terror of anarchy, occaſioned by the *ill-judged*, impolitic, as well as cruel conduct of ſome among the firſt leaders of the emancipated French, has increaſed the number of miniſterial partiſans and favorers of *extended* power and prerogative.

Were it poſſible that a *panic* could be permanent, or falſhood and artifice ultimately victorious over truth and juſtice, there might be reaſon to fear, from the ſpirit which the *alarmiſts* diffuſed, that Engliſh liberty might ſoon ſicken, and at laſt die *paralytic* in the arms of deſpotiſm. But notwithſtanding a temporary lethargy, the mafs of the people, thofe who are quite out of the reach of courtiers and grandees, ftill retain the healthy vigor of their fathers' virtue, and would roufe themfelves effectually to prevent the accomplifhment of Mr. Hume's prediction. They muft indeed be lulled with the Circèan cup of corruption to fleep on, and take their reft, when the giant Defpotifm is at their doors, ready to crufh, with his mace, all that renders life valuable to MEN ; to men who have learned to think that mere vegetation is not life. But Circè's cup is not capacious enough to contain opiate for a whole people. All the douceurs of a minifter, all the patronage in the profeffions, all the riches of the caft and the weft, are infufficient to bribe the obfcure *millions*, who conftitute the *bafe* of the political fabric, into complete acquiefcence under the preffure of defpotic power, or under the apprehenfion of it. The light of reafon and of learning is too widely diffufed to be eafily extinguifhed. There is every reafon to believe, that it will fhine more and more unto *a perfect day*.

But as popular commotion is always to be dreaded, becaufe bad men always arife to miflead its efforts, how defirable is it that it may be prevented, by conciliatory meafures, by a timely conceffion of rights, by redrefs of grievances, by reformation of abufes, by convincing mankind that governments have no other object than faithfully to promote the comfort and fecurity of individuals, without facrificing the folid happinefs of living men to *national* glory, or royal magnificence. True patriotifm and true philofophy, unattached to names of particular men, or even to parties, confider the happinefs of man as the firft object of all rational governments; and, convinced that nothing is more injurious to the happinefs of man than the fpirit of defpotifm, endeavor to check its growth, at its firft and flighteft appearance.

If the free government of England evinces, by its conduct, that the happinefs of the people is its fole object, fo far from dreading the late Mr. Hume's prophecy, that it will die in the arms of defpotifm, we may venture to predict, that it will never die. My orifons fhall be offered for its perpetuity; for I, and all who think with me, on this fubject, are its *true* friends; while the *borough-mongers*, under the cloke of loyalty, are enemies both to the king and the people.

B b

SECTION XXXV.

The Permiſſion of Lawyers *by Profeſſion, aſ-
piring at Honors in the Gift of the Crown, to
have the greateſt Influence in the Legiſlature,
a Circumſtance unfavorable to Liberty.*

WHEN advocates addreſs each
other at the bar, they always adopt the appellation of *learned* brother. There certainly is
a neceſſity for great learning in the profeſſion
of the long robe. But of what *kind* is the
learning required? It is, undoubtedly of a kind
very little connected with philoſophy or enlarge-
ment of the mind. It is, in its wideſt range,
confined to local cuſtoms, and the ſtatutes of
a ſingle nation. It pores upon the letter of the
law, and ſcarcely dares to contemplate the ſpirit.
It is for the moſt part employed in minute
diſquiſitions, in finding exceptions, in ſeeking
ſubterfuges, and often in making the great
eternal rules of equity give way to the literal
meaning of a narrow and unjuſt ſtatute, framed
by ignorant men in times little removed from
barbariſm, and certainly both ſlaviſh and ſuper-
ſtitious.

Is the *education* of profeſſional and *practiſing*
lawyers particularly calculated to expand the
intellect, or to fill the heart with ſentiments
of peculiar honor and generoſity; ſuch ſentiments as alone can conſtitute a worthy law-

giver, and an all-accomplished statesman? Is
it not confined to particular and minute objects,
instead of taking in the whole horizon of human
concernments? A few, and but a few, of
those who have risen to the first honors and
emoluments, have had a truly liberal education.
The rest have been trained either in the office
of an attorney, or in studies and exercises that
contribute no more to liberalize or improve
the heart, than the copying of instruments,
the perusal of statutes, the knowledge of *forms*.
Some of the finest faculties of the human constitution, the imagination and sentimental affections, have little room for play, where the eye
and memory are chiefly concerned; and where
the mind is obliged to labor in the trammels of
dismal formalities, like the horse in harness,
dragging a heavy vehicle in the wheel-ruts
made by those who have gone before, without
the liberty of deviation. A hard head, a cold
unfeeling heart, with a tenacious memory, are
likely to succeed best in such toil, which requires
less of speed than of patient plodding perse-
verance.

A dull man, trained in this dull manner,
may become a very useful *lawyer*, and certainly
deserving of all the *fees* and emoluments of his
profession. But does it follow, that he must
be a statesman, a senator, a cabinet counsellor,
fitted to determine on questions of peace and
war, and to consult and promote the happiness
of human nature? A lawyer, by singular felicity of genius and disposition, may be fit for

the momentous tafk ; and I only afk whether his *education*, and the ftudies and employments of his profeffion, are fuch as to render him *pre-eminently* a ftatefman, and director of the meafures of government? Becaufe he may, for a fee, plead fuccefsfully on any fide, conduct a trial, and affift a jury in determining a queftion of *meum* and *tuum* or may be able to expound a ftatute, is he *therefore* more likely than all others to *frame* laws of the moft *beneficent* kind, having a view, not to particular cafes only, but to the general welfare? All his ftudies of jurifprudence have been *merely* for the fake of lucre, and not free and difinterefted, like thofe of the general fcholar, the philofopher and philanthropift.

The lawyer has, however, better opportunities for *difplaying* his knowledge and abilities than the members of other profeffions. Men have recourfe to him on matters very dear to their hearts ; matters of property. With the fagacity of a very moderate intellect, and a knowledge acquired by dint of mere labor and long practice, he may be able to tranfact their *pecuniary* bufinefs with fkill and fuccefs. He becomes, therefore, a favorite with *men of property* in the nation, which, whenever corruption prevails, will contribute much to pufh any afpirant up the ladder of promotion. He foon pants for rewards extraneous to his profeffion. It is not enough to be a judge or chancellor ; he muft be a peer of the realm, a counfellor of ftate, a chief director in the *upper* houfe. It is painful to behold all the old nobility, educated, as they have been, at the greateft expence, improved by private tutors and by travel, crouching to a man, who has acquired effrontery in the courts below, and whofe unblufhing audacity has been the chief caufe of the elevation, at which himfelf is furprifed.

Men like thefe, emboldened by fuccefs, and, accuftomed, from their earlieft entrance into active life, to browbeat and overbear, affume a right to guide the opinions of the fenate and the council in the moft important meafures of ftate. They become, in fact, the rulers of the nation; but owing their elevation to the favor of a *court*, and placing all their expectations of farther honors on its continuance, they become devoted to its purpofes. They are, in fact, ftill ATTORNIES AND SOLICITORS, ready to exert all their powers of fophiftry, and to exhauft all their ftores of chicanery, to defend the meafures of the minifter, by rendering law, as far as they can, a leaden rule. The old peers fit in filent admiration; while men, furnifhed with all the fubtleties of practifing lawyers, long hackneyed and hardened in the paltry bufinefs of private individuals, prefume to dictate peace or war, to impede or prevent falutary reform, and keep the church, the army, and the navy under their fupreme control. Such is their habitual volubility and confirmed affurance, that men of more liberal minds, but of lefs felf-conceit and lefs notoriety, ftand in awe of them, and fuffer them, with abject acquiefcence, to *domineer*. But however they may oppofe the *people's* right, and the happinefs of the public, they are fure to efpoufe the caufe of thofe from whom comes their promotion. They therefore contribute to diffufe the fpirit of defpotifm, more than any other profeffion.

" But" (fays the minifter) " we cannot do without them. We muft have *able* men in the Houfe of Lords; therefore we muft have *new* men; and they muft be felected from a profeffion accuftomed to public bufinefs, and which gives thofe who belong to it opportunities of making an open difplay of their abilities." This is a fad compliment to the hereditary nobility; as it feems to argue that they are totally unfit to conduct the bufinefs that comes before them, without *attornies* and *folicitors* from below, who are ennobled merely to fave the credit of the peerage. But the truth is, the minifter wifhes to have fome *fharp* and tractable *tools*, by which he may do his dirty work, uninterrupted by the interference of thofe who, poffeffing a conftitutional *right* to examine it, would perhaps often cenfure it, if they were not overawed and overborne by thofe who pretend to be initiated in the *myfteries* of law.

In confequence of this management, a *whole profeffion*, with few exceptions, extremely bufy both with tongue and pen, is conftantly enlifted in the fervice of a minifter. A great number of *attornies* and *folicitors*, befides the gentlemen

officially honored with thofe names, are conftantly *retained* on the fide of the court, and
confequently lean, for their own fakes, and
with a hope of making their families, to the
extenfion of crown influence and prerogative.
A fet of men, fo fubtle, fo active, fo attentive
to intereft, muft ferve any caufe which they
choofe to efpoufe; and there is no doubt but
that they greatly ferve (in the hope of ferving
themfelves) the caufe of defpotifm.

Let anyone who is unacquainted with the pains
taken by modern minifters to retain the lawyers
on the fide of prerogative, infpect the *court
calendar*, and remark how great a portion of
the modern peers have owed their coronets
entirely to their profeffion as lawyers, to their
qualifications as mere men of bufinefs in *detail*,
with very fcanty knowledge of any thing elfe,
and with fmall claims to excellence as patriots,
philofophers, or philanthropifts. Mere men
of bufinefs commonly fix their eyes on objects
of private lucre or temporal elevation *alone*.
They are apt to laugh at the names of patriotifm, liberty, and difinterefted virtue. They
have commonly been too long hackneyed
among the loweft of mankind, not perhaps in
rank only, but in fpirit, knowledge, liberality,
to retain any very *fcrupulous* delicacy in their
own bofoms, or to believe its exiftence in
others. They confider the good things of the
world as a fcramble, where every man is to
get what he can by addrefs, and bold preten-
fion, fince the law will not allow the ufe of

violence. Certainly there can be no hope of reform, or what the French call a *regeneration* of human affairs, while men fo verfed in corruption, fo enriched by it, and fo well pleafed with it, bear fway in fenates, and direct the councils of princes*.

* Several of the Crown Lawyers concerned in the profecution of Hardy, &c. in which fo much pains was taken to fhed innocent blood, were put into Parliament by PEERS or *grandees*, as their members or agents, contrary to law and the conftitution.

The Marquis of Bath nominates Sir JOHN SCOTT, (the Attorney General,) to reprefent his Lordfhip in the Houfe of Commons.

Lord Beverley nominates Sir JOHN MITFORD (the Solicitor General,) to reprefent him.

Earl Fitzwilliam nominates SERJEANT ADAIR.

The *Earl of Lonfdale* nominates Mr. ANSTRUTHER.

Mr. Buller nominates Mr. BEARCRAFT.

See Petition prefented to the Houfe of Commons, 6th of May, 1793.

SECTION XXXVI.

Poverty, when not extreme, *favorable to all Virtue, public and private, and confequently to the Happinefs of human Nature.; and* enormous Riches, *without Virtue, the general Bane.*

SUPERFLUITY of riches, like fuperfluity of food, caufes ficknefs and debility. *Poverty*, or mediocrity of fortune, is the nurfe of many virtues; of modefty, induftry, fobriety. But, in this age, the very name of poverty is odious. Poverty is a haggard phantom that appals half the world, and drives them over feas, into torrid zones, to difeafe and death ! Life itfelf is thought by many a gift fit to be thrown back again into the face of the Almighty Donor, if it is not accompanied with the *means* of luxury, the means of making *a figure* beyond *others;* in a word, the means of indulging the *fpirit of defpotifm.* Things are fo managed, in a ftate of deep political corruption, that the honors due only to virtue are paid exclufively to MONEY; and thofe who want not riches for the fake of indulgence in pleafure, or from the love of money itfelf, grow complete *mifers,* in the hope of obtaining together with opulence, civil *honors,* feats in the fenate-houfe, and ROYAL FAVOR. They hope to make themfelves of *confequence* enough to be *corrupted* or rather *purchafed* by the ftate.

What is the confequence to the *people*, the laborer, the manufacturer, the retail trader, to poor families with many children, women with fmall patrimonies, annuitants, dependents, and all the numerous train of perfons who are compelled to live, as the common phrafe expreffes it, from *hand to mouth?* Their gains or means are *fixed*, and by no means rife with the rifing price of neceffaries. But, in confequence of this rage for riches, the neceffaries of life become not only dearer, but worfe in quality; lefs nourifhing, lefs commodious, and lefs durable. *Landlords* raife their rents to the utmoft poffible extent; each determining to make his rent-roll as refpectable as fome opulent neighbors favored by a lord lieutenant for his INFLUENCE. They will not let their farms in little portions, to poor induftrious tenants; but to fome *overgrown monopolizer*, who is in as much hafte to grow rich as the *landlord* himfelf; feeing that as he becomes rich he becomes a *man of confequence* in the *county*, and that not only efquires, but even lords, take *notice* of him at the approach of a general election. He is a *wholefale* farmer, and will breed but few of the animals of the farm-yard, and thofe only for his own family confumption. His children are too proud to carry the productions of the hen-rooft or dairy to the market. He fcorns fuch *little* gains. He deals only in a *great way;* and keeps up the price by withholding his ſtores when the market is low. The neighboring ruſtics, who uſed to be reſpectable, though little farmers, are now his day-laborers, begging to be employed by the great man who has engroſſed and conſolidated half a dozen farms. The old farm-houſes are pulled down. One *capital manſion* is ſufficient for a large territory of meadow and arable land, which uſed to diſplay ſmoking chimnies in every part of a cheerful landſcape, with a healthy pro- geny of children, and tribes of animals, enli- vening the happy ſcene. The *tenant* now reigns over the uninhabited glebe a ſolitary deſpot ; and ſomething of the ancient *vaſſalage* of the feudal *ſyſtem* is reſtored, through the *neceſſities* of the ſurrounding cottagers, who live in hovels with *windows ſtopt up*, hardly enjoy- ing God's freeſt gifts, light and air. A mur- mur will exclude them even from the HUT, com- pared with which the neighboring dog-kennel is a palace.

The *little tenants* of former times were too numerous and too inconſiderable to become objects of *corruption*. But the *great tenant*, the engroſſer of farms, feeling his conſe- quence, grows as ambitious as his landlord. He may have ſons, couſins, and nephews, whom he wiſhes to provide for by places ; and therefore it becomes a part of his *prudential* plan, to ſide, in all county elections, and at all public meetings, with the *court party*, the lord lieutenant, and the ariſtocratical toad-eaters of the miniſter.

In like manner, the GREAT *manufacturer*, finding that riches tend to civil HONORS and political confequence, as well as to plenty of all good things, cannot be contented with the *flow progrefs* of his grandfathers, but muft *whip and fpur*, in his career from the temple of Plutus to the temple of Honor. His work-men therefore, are paid, not by the *day*, in which cafe they would endeavor to do their work *well*, though flowly, but by the *piece*. The public, perhaps, *muft* of neceffity purchafe his commodity, however bad, and it is probably as good as others fabricate, becaufe *all* are purfuing the fame glorious end, by fimilar means. The materials, as well as the work-manfhip, are of inferior quality. For, the great monopolizers and dealers can *force* a trade, and get *vent* among the little retailers, by giving credit, and by various other contrivances, for the moft *ordinary* ware. The *great man*, whofe forefathers felt little elfe but *avarice*, now burns with AMBITION ; and, as *city honors* and rural dignities, fenatorial confequence and even magiftracy, are beftowed by minifterial favor, he muft be *devoted* to a minifter, and carry all the little traders and artifans to fecond the views of a court at the general election, or at public meetings, appointed for the promotion of a minifter's project to *keep himfelf in place*.

Thefe, and a thoufand fimilar caufes, vifible enough in the various departments of manufac-ture, commerce, and agriculture, are at this moment urging on the great machine of corruption, and diffufing the fpirit of defpotifm. The revolution of France will indeed check it, throughout Europe, by the influence of princi-ples, favorable to the freedom and happinefs of man; but at prefent, even that event is ufed by fhort-fighted politicians, to increafe arifto-cratical arrogance, to deprefs popular fpirit, and to give unnatural influence to the poffeffion of MONEY, however acquired and however abufed.

An indignant writer of ancient Rome ex-claims :

Nullum crimen abeft, facinufque libidinis ex quo
PAUPERTAS ROMANA perit.*　　　　JUVENAL.

Prima peregrinos obfcœna PECUNIA mores,
Intulit et turpi fregerunt fecula luxu,
Divitiæ molles.——

The virtuous ancients, by the light of nature and the evidence of experience, were taught that, when riches obtained a value and efteem beyond their *proper ufe*, merely for the fake of fplendor, oftentation, and ariftocratic op-oppreffion, a fatal blow was given to liberty. The human race, they thought, degenerated under the *defpotifm of money*. In fuch a corrupt fyftem, there was no encouragement given in the ftate to excel in virtue for its own fake:

* Since Poverty, our guardian god, is gone,
Pride, lazinefs, and all luxurious arts,
Pour like a deluge in from FOREIGN PARTS,† &c.
　　　　　　　DRYDEN.

† Viz. The Eaft Indies at prefent.

C c

even generals and admirals went on *expeditions*, not even for falfe and vain-glory, far lefs from motives of patriotifm; but to fill their coffers with plunder, and render war a cloke for pillage.

Cauponantes bellum, non belligerentes.

They made a *trade*, and a *fordid* trade, of *legal bloodfhed*, not conducting it with the difinterefted fpirit of foldiers, animated with the love of their country, but with the cunning and avarice of Jew ufurers in Duke's Place.

And have we had no inftances of generals or admirals making war, a trade, in recent times, and in Chriftian nations; ufing the fword, to which the idea of *honor* has been attached, as an implement of lucre, and rendering it far lefs *honorable* than the knife of the butcher, exercifing his trade in the market of Leadenhall? If it fhould ever be true, that fhips of war are made merchantmen in the vileft merchandize, *the barter of human blood for gold*, will it not prove, that the attaching honor to the poffeffion of *money*, is deftroying, not only the national virtue, but its honor and *defence?* Have towns in the Eaft Indies *never* been given up to plunder, contrary to the law of nations, as well as juftice and humanity, to make the fortune of European officers?

It is a noble and virtuous ftruggle, to ftand up in defence of the rights of nature, true honor, liberty and truth, againft the overbearing dominion of *pecuniary* influence. MAN will fhine forth in his genuine luftre; when *money* can no longer *gild* the bafe metal of folly, knavery, pride, and cruelty. While the corrupt Ganges flows into the Thames, it will contaminate its waters, and infect the atmofphere of freedom. When Britifh freeholders, yeomen, merchants, manufacturers, generals, admirals, and fenators, become flaves to *pelf* only, forgetting or defpifing the very name of *public virtue* and difinterefted exertion, nothing can oppofe the fpirit of defpotifm but *the fpirit of the common people.* *That* fpirit, indeed, may at once refcue human nature from mifery, and perpetuate the bleffings of a pure and free conftitution. But when they who fatten on the blood of their fellow-creatures, are alfo permitted to *domineer* by the influence of their ill-gotten MONEY, over free countries, to command majorities at elections, and drive all oppofition before them, what chance of happinefs can remain to virtuous independence? What, in fuch circumftances, can preferve liberty, but a *convulfive struggle,* attended, perhaps, with the horrors of the firft French revolution, which God, in his mercy, *avert!*

SECTION XXXVII.

On the natural Tendency of making Judges and Crown Lawyers, Peers; of translating Bishops and annexing Preferments to Bishopricks, in what is called, commendam.

IF there is any part of the constitution of England, in the praise of which eloquence may employ her most glowing colors, without entrenching upon the confines of truth, it is the JUDICIAL part of it. The purity of public justice in England, is unequalled in any country which the sun illuminates in his diurnal progress. The reason is obvious. The *verdict* is given by juries of men usually beyond the reach of corruption. No ministerial influence can descend to all the individuals, in middle and humble life, who may be called upon to sit in judgment, and ultimately decide, as jurors, on the property, the fame, and the life, of their fellow-citizens. We have lately had a most glorious instance of the virtue of private citizens, exercising this most important office. The *verdicts* given in the state trials, in one thousand seven hundred and ninety-four, do *more honor* to the British character, than all the military exploits in the reign of George the Third. Such verdicts make our constitution truly enviable to the nations of Europe. Twelve honest men, on each of these trials, proved to the world, that no power, no authority, no terror, nor even the factitious rage of aristocratical principles, which had been artfully foftered, could lead them to fwerve from the right line of juftice. They *feared God, but not man;* and pofterity will *honor* them, when the names of fubtle politicians, clothed with a brief but lucrative authority, if mentioned at all, fhall be mentioned with deteftation. It was well obferved by a zealous and honeft advocate on the occafion, that he could not *defpair* of the cafe, when it was brought from the corrupt to the uncorrupt part of the conftitution. The days of acquittal were the jubilees of truth, the triumphs of virtue; and, in a time of dejection, revived the hopes of patriotifm and philanthropy.

Official judges, not having the final determination of the caufe, but feeling the check of the JURIES, commonly conduct themfelves, even in *ftate trials*, with fome degree of candor and moderation. Indeed, we are fo happy as to fee men appointed to this office, in our time, whofe tried integrity gives reafon to believe, that, if they were not thus wifely checked, they would, with *few* exceptions, preferve impartiality.

Neverthelefs, though much has been faid on the independence of judges, and though great praife is due to our king, who placed them in their offices for life, and not removable at his pleafure, yet it muft be confeffed, that there ftill remain temptations, which might have great influence on men lefs virtuous than our *prefent* judges are. It is obferved, that PEERAGES, in modern times, have been beftowed, with peculiar bounty, on lawyers; and fome have ventered to fay, that the expectation of this fplendid reward may fruftrate all endeavors to fecure, efpecially in *ftate trials*, the perfect independence of the judges who prefide. It is not enough that they do not fear *removal* from their dignified office. Their *hopes* may influence, more than their *fears*. They may *hope* to add to opulence the dignity of family diftinction, efcutcheons, coronets, and hereditary feats in the legiflature. If themfelves have feen too much of the vanity and folly of worldly pomp to admire it, (which, however, is not often the cafe with men who may be great lawyers, without any philofophy or religion,) yet they may have fons, wives, daughters, relatives, and friends, to whom the fplendor of life, (as *they* have, poffibly, little *folid* merit,) is valuable in the *higheft* degree. A peerage is therefore, for the moft part, a very powerful allurement, I will not fay, to difguife the truth or pervert the law, but obfequioufly to feek minifterial favor.

When peerages are lavifhed on lawyers high in place, it is a circumftance viewed with fome degree of jealoufy by thofe who are willing to guard conftitutional liberty with unwinking vigilance. Perhaps it might afford fatisfaction to fuch men, if judges were by law *excluded* from all higher elevation; if they were indeed *moft amply* paid and moft refpectfully revered;

but, for the fake of preventing the poffibility of a wrong bias, where the happinefs of the people is moft intimately concerned, were prevented from viewing a brilliant dazzling coronet, fufpended as their *reward*, over the fcales of juftice.

But here an objector will urge, with ferious folicitude, that, as the Houfe of Lords is a court of judicature, in the laft refort, a court of appeal from every court in the kingdom, it is neceffary that it fhould be well fupplied with lawyers of eminence.

On this fubject Mr. PALEY fays; " There appears to be nothing in the conftitution of the Houfe of Lords; in the education, habits, character, or profeffions of the members who compofe it; in the mode of their appointment, or the right by which they fucceed to their places in it, that fhould qualify them for their arduous office; except, *perhaps*, that the elevation of their rank and fortune affords a fecurity againft the offer and influence of SMALL bribes. Officers of the army and navy, courtiers, ecclefiaftics; young men who have juft attained the age of twenty-one, and who have paffed their youth in the diffipation and purfuits which commonly accompany the poffeffion or inheritance of great fortunes; country gentlemen, occupied in the management of their eftates, or in the care of their domeftic concerns and family interefts; the GREATER part of the affembly *born to their ftation*, that is, placed in it by CHANCE; moft of the reft advanced to the peerage for fervices and from motives *utterly* unconnected with legal erudition ;— *thefe men* compofe the tribunal to which the conftitution entrufts the interpretation of her laws, and the ultimate decifion of every difpute between her fubjects ! "

From this *very degrading* reprefentation of the Houfe of Lords, the Reverend Archdeacon proceeds to juftify the practice of conftantly placing in it, fome of the moft eminent and experienced lawyers in the kingdom. He would, I think, with more propriety have argued againft rendering one part of the *legif-lature* a court of juftice, defigned both to make and execute the laws ; becaufe every folid politician has agreed in the propriety of keeping the legiflative and judicial powers as feparate and as diftant from each other as it is poffible.

I leave this point for the difcuffion of future political writers, and fatisfy myfelf with fuggefting, that it is neceffary to the perfect contentment of a people jealous of their liberty and the purity of judicial proceedings, that all temptations whatever fhould be removed from the fight of frail human beings, fitting in the feat of judgment, which may lead them to court the favor of ruling powers at the expence of juftice. It is not MONEY alone which BRIBES. Title and rank have more influence on the univerfal paffion, *vanity ;* efpecially when avarice has been already gratified with ample falaries and the emoluments of a lucrative profeffion.

The confideration of the *poffible* rewards which may diminifh the independence of *judges*, naturally leads to the confideration of thofe which may *fecularize* the *bifhops*, and injure the caufe of religion, for *which alone* epifcopacy itfelf could be eftablifhed.

But, as this is a fubject of fome delicacy, I fhall ufe the authority and words of Dr. Watfon, the prefent Bifhop of *Llandaff*, who, having been in the minority at the time he wrote upon it, ventured to fpeak the *whole* truth, with that freedom which becomes an honeft man in every rank, and is particularly expected from a Chriftian bifhop.

" I know," fays Bifhop Watfon, " That many will be ftartled. I beg them not to be offended, at the furmife of the bifhops not being independent in the Houfe of Lords ; and it would be eafy enough to weave a *logical cobweb*, large enough and ftrong enough to cover and protect the conduct of the Right Reverend Bench from the attacks of thofe who diflike epifcopacy. This, I fay, would be an eafy tafk ; but it is far above my ability to eradicate from the minds of others (who are, notwithftanding, as well attached to the church eftablifhment as ourfelves,) a SUSPICION THAT THE PROSPECT OF BEING TRANSLATED *influences the minds* of the BISHOPS too powerfully, and induces them to pay too great an attention to the BECK of a *minifter*. The fufpicion, whether well or ill founded, is *difreputable to our order;* and, what is of worfe confequence, it hinders us from doing that good which we otherwife might do ; for the laity, while they entertain fuch a fufpicion concerning us, will accufe us of avarice and ambition, of making a *gain of godlinefs*, of *bartering the dignity of our office* for the *chance* of a TRANS-LATION.

" Inftead then, (proceeds the Bifhop), of *quibbling* and difputing againft the exiftence of *minifters influence over* US, or recriminating and retorting the petulance of thofe who accufe us on that account, let us endeavor to remove the evil; or, if it *muft not* be admitted that this evil has any real exiftence, let us endeavor to remove the *appearance* of it.

" The difparity of income and patronage might be made fo fmall, or fo apportioned to the labors, that few bifhops would be difpofed to wifh for tranflations; and confequently the bifhops would, in *appearance* as well as in *reality*, be INDEPENDENT.

" But, in rendering the bifhops independent, you will reduce the power of the crown in the Houfe of Lords.—I do not mean to deny this charge; nay, I am willing to admit it in it's full extent.—The influence of the crown, when exerted by the cabinet over the public counfellors of the king, is a circumftance fo far from being to be wifhed by his true friends, that it is as dangerous to the real interefts and honor of the crown itfelf, as it is odious to the people, and DESTRUCTIVE OF PUBLIC LIBERTY.

" It may contribute to keep a *prime minifter* in his *place, contrary to the fenfe of the wifeft and beft part of the community;* it may contribute to keep the king himfelf unacquainted with his people's wiſhes, but it cannot do the king or the ftate any fervice. To maintain the contrary is to fatirize his majefty's government; it is to infinuate, that his views and interefts are fo difjoined from thofe of his people, that they cannot be effectuated by the *uninfluenced concurrence of honeft men.*

" I cannot admit the circumftance of the biſhops being rendered *independent* in the Houfe of Lords, as any real objection to the plan propofed; on the contrary, I think it a very ftrong argument in its favor; fo ftrong an one that, if there was no other, it would be fufficient to fanctify the meafure."

The corruption of the church for the purpofe of corrupting the legiflature, is an offence far more injurious to the general happinefs of mankind and the interefts of a Chriftian community, than any of thofe which have baniſhed the offenders to Botany Bay, or confined them for years within the walls of the prifon-houfe. Both the corruptors and the corrupted, in this cafe, are more injurious to Chriftianity than all the tribe of fceptics and infidels; than Tindal, Toland, Bolingbroke, Hume, Rouffeau, Voltaire, and Gibbon. The *common people* do *not read* them, and perhaps could fcarcely *underftand* them. But the common people *do* read the newfpapers daily, and fee the names

and qualities of thofe who divide in the fenate-
houfe, on queftions of the laft importance.
They muft therefore entertain a SUSPICION,
as the Bifhop of Llandaff expreffes it, that religion itfelf, as well as its official, opulent, dignified fupporters, is but an inftrument of ftate,
a tool in the hand of a minifter. They muft
naturally confider *venalty* as *doubly* bafe, when
clothed in the fanctified robes of religion.
What has happened in France, in confequence
of the corruptions of the church by the ftate,
ought to afford a ftriking admonition.

I wifh to point out, in *thefe times*, *writings*
of LIVING BISHOPS in favor of Chriftianity,
becaufe they would be oppofed with the beft
grace againft the writings of LIVING INFIDELS.
But, to the reproach of my want of intelligence,
I know not the names of the majority, till I
find them in the COURT CALENDAR. The
printed works of even this *majority* I cannot
find, either in the fhops or the libraries: the
few I do find, even of the *minority*, are not
adapted to the wants of the people at large.
Their *occafional* fermons, after they have ferved
their *day* become, like almanacks, out of date:
a collection of old *court calendars* would be
nearly as edifying and more entertaining to the
multitude.

It is indeed certain, that the archiepifcopal
mitres received more luftre than they gave,
from the fermons of Dr. Tillotfon and Dr.
Secker. It would give me pleafure to place
the fermons of LIVING ARCHBISHOPS by their

fide ; and I would mention them had they come to my knowledge. The fermons, however, of the *few* living bifhops who are *known* at all to the PUBLIC will, I hope, prove to mankind, that fome among the bifhops, in this happy ifle, do not think it a fufficient return for princely revenues, to *vote always with a minifter*, or to increafe, with lawn fleeves, the pageantry of a birth-day. To perform the occafional duties of ordination, confirmation, and vifitation, cannot fatisfy the minds of men who receive the honors and emoluments of Durham, WIN-CHESTER, York, or Canterbury. That it is fo, is happy; for if ever the prelatical clergy fhould be SUSPECTED of becoming merely minifterial inftruments; if, for inftance, they fhould ever be fuppofed fo far fecularized, as to concede to the minifter that made them bifhops, the right of nominating to all the moft valuable preferments in their gift, in order to enable *him* the better to corrupt that parliament in which themfelves alfo have engaged to give a VENAL VOTE ; from that time, they would contribute more to the downfal of the church, than all the writings of all the unbelievers, from Frederic, late King of Pruffia, to the American Republican, Thomas Paine. The *fin of fimony* in a private man, who pays a *fair price* for a profitable appointment, with his *own* money, honeftly earned by virtuous induftry, and *does the duties of it*, is as nothing when compared to the *fimony* of him who buys a high and important ftation, greatly lucrative, with

D d

a corrupt VOTE and a bafe dereliction of thofe rights of patronage, which were intended to encourage merit only, and to prevent that very corruption which he feeds and cherifhes, to gratify his own fordid avarice and childifh vanity.

The bifhops, in their charges, are now founding an alarm. They very juftly affirm, that the exiftence of Chriftianity is now in danger. They wifely urge the INFERIOR clergy to the moft vigilant activity. Thus far they certainly do honor to the epifcopal function. But ftill, while the public SUSPECTS the bare poffibility of the bench being, as Bp. Watfon fays, at the *beck of the minifter*, they will confider all this zeal as little better than that of Demetrius, who made filver fhrines for Diana.

When indeed we add to the *probable* effect of *tranflations* from a poorer to a richer bifhopric, the holding of rich *pluralities with* bifhoprics, under the name of COMMENDAMS, it is difficult not to think with Bifhop Watfon, that epifcopal independence is endangered, and that we muft look rather in *cathedrals*, than in the Houfe of Lords, for epifcopal integrity. Confcientious diffenters are fhocked, and libertines and infidels *laugh*, when they view the bench, as if they were fpectators of a folemn mummery, or a mock-heroic farce. All this danger, offence, and reproach, might poffibly be prevented, if *tranflations* and *commendams* were utterly prohibited.

But, fetting afide the effect of tranflations and commendams on the ftate of *religion*, let

us ferioufly confider them as they operate on
the increafe of prerogative and the fpirit of defpotifm. Thefe things influence not only thofe
who have attained mitres, but a numerous tribe
of expectants; and thofe expectants POSSESS
THE EAR OF THE PEOPLE. Is it reafonable to
fuppofe that the doctrines of the pulpit will
not, under thefe circumftances, be fafhioned to
the inclinations of the minifter? What can
contribute more to diffufe the fpirit of defpotifm, than the employment of many thoufand
pulpits, at leaft once in each week, in obliquely
preaching doctrines, that favor its prevalence,
under the *fanction* of DIVINE AUTHORITY?

SECTION XXXVIII.

*That all Oppofition to the Spirit of Defpotifm
fhould be conducted with the moft fcrupulous
Regard to the exifting Laws, and to the
Prefervation of public Peace and good Order.*

THE frailty of human nature is one
of the commoneft of common-places. The
wifeft and beft of men are defirous of palliating
their errors, by claiming a fhare, as MEN, in
human infirmity. One of the infirmities moft
acknowledged and lamented is, a tendency to
rufh from one extreme to another; a pronenefs
to fall into a *vice*, in the defire of efcaping an
error. Thus the deteftation of defpotifm, and
the love of liberty, both of them rational and
laudable, have led many to factious and violent
conduct, which neither the occafion juftified,
nor prudence would *precipitately* adopt, even
if the occafion might appear to juftify them.

From faction and violence in the caufe of
liberty, which difgrace the caufe itfelf, and give
advantage to the favorers of arbitrary power,
I *moft anxioufly diffuade* all who love mankind
and their country. Faction and violence are
defpotic in the extreme. They bring all evils
of tyranny, without any confolation, but that
they are ufually tranfient; whereas tyranny is
durable. They deftroy themfelves, or are
deftroyed by force in the hands of a fuperior

power. In either cafe, much is *loft* to the caufe of liberty ; becaufe the perfons who have been betrayed by their paffions into exceffes, were probably *fincere* ; and if they had been alfo *difcreet* and moderate, would have been effectual as well as zealous promoters of the public good. It is certain, that very honeft men are very apt to be betrayed into violence by their warmth of temper. They mean good, and do ill. They become the inftruments of difpaffionate knaves ; and are often led into extravagances by the very party againft whom they act, in order that they may be expofed, and become obnoxious to cenfure.

Wifdom is gentle, deliberate, cautious. Nothing violent is durable. I hope the lovers of liberty will fhew the fincerity of their attach-ment by the wifdom of their conduct. Tumul-tuary proceedings always exhibit fome appear-ance of infanity. A blow ftruck with blind violence may inflict a wound or a bruife, but it may fall in the wrong place ; it may even injure the hand that gives it, by its own ill-directed force.

Man being a reafonable creature, will always fubmit to reafon, if you give time for his paffions to cool, and wait for the *mollia tem-pora fandi*, the proper opprtunities of addref-fing him. A FEW, in the great mafs of man-kind, may be corrupted by views of intereft, by expectations of preferment, by bribes, and by titles. But there are not rewards enough of this kind to corrupt the whole body of any people. The great body of the people will follow that which appears to them right, and juft, and true. Let it be clearly laid before them, and left for their calm confideration. If it fhould fo happen, which is very unlikely, that they fhould not adopt it, after underftanding it, and duly weighing its importance, then they muft be left to the error of their ways. *Si populus vult decipi, decipiatur.* If the people will be deluded, they muft be fo. Force cannot eradicate error, though it may deftroy life. Riot, tumult, turbulence may do great mifchief, but they carry no conviction.

Inflammatory language at popular meetings is to be avoided; and, indeed, multitudes of the *loweft* of the people are not to be wantonly convened. Without in the leaft impeaching their rights, it muft be allowed that their paffions are too violent, when heated by collifion with each other, and their judgments too weak, when not previoufly informed by reading and education, to act wifely when met in a large body, without authorifed guides, and without ftrict regulation. A man who is a fincere patriot, and not a *mere demagogue* for finifter purpofes, will be cautious of affembling crowds of the loweft of the people. Lord George Gordon's unfortunate conduct has left a lafting leffon. He, I firmly believe, intended none of that mifchief which enfued; but who can fay to the waves of a troubled fea, "thus far fhall ye go, and no farther?" I know, and have already commented on, the advantage taken from thofe riots by the friends of high-prerogative doc-rines, for difparaging the *people* at large, not-withftanding the people certainly had no concern in them.

Though decidedly a friend to the reform of the Houfe of Commons, I cannot agree with the Duke of Richmond in the propriety of universal fuffrage. I think his idea perfectly Utopian. Sir Thomas More never wrote any thing more visionary in his celebrated fiction; Sir Robert Filmer nothing more adverfe to *real* liberty. Univerfal fuffrage, I fear, would caufe universal confufion; and the friends of mankind would be inclined to fly for temporary refuge even to the throne of a DESPOT. Perfons in a ftate of *fervitude* could never be expected to give a *free* vote; and vagabonds and paupers would ufe their *liberty for a cloke of malicioufnefs*. I wifh the right of fuffrage to be extended *as far as it poffibly can*, without endangering public order and tranquillity; but *extreme* ignorance and *extreme* penury cannot with prudence be trufted with a power which both requires *knowledge* and commands *property*.

But whatever politicians may determine upon this point, I think it certain, that debates upon it connot be held in very large affemblies, into which, not only the loweft but the vileft of mankind are allowed admiffion, and all the privileges of counfellors, *de fumma rerum*, on matters of the higheft importance, without extreme danger of violating law, and difturbing, that order which is neceffary to comfort, and fecurity.

I wifh, therefore, that all preliminary confultation on this point, and all points like this, may be conducted by *writing*, by appeals to reafon in the *clofet*, and that a confiderable time may be allowed to cool all intemperate heats; and give *folidity* to the materials of the intended repair. At county meetings or affociations, I would have the civil power in full force; but never the military. The ftaff of the conftable fhould be more coercive than the fabre of the dragoon; for the conftitution admits the one as its own, but certainly looks at the other with horror. Every tumult, productive of mifchief, gives the friends of arbitrary power an opportunity for introducing the military, of arguing againft all *popular* interference in that very government which the *people* fupport by their induftry, and which, according to the law of God, nature, and reafon, they have a right to control by their fupreme authority. There may be cafes of the laft neceffity, which I fhudder to think of, in which nothing but the power of the people, acting by force, can maintain or recover their ufurped rights. Such muft occur but feldom. May our country never experience them!

There can be no good reafon affigned why government fhould not be, like every thing elfe, continually advancing to all the perfection of which it is capable. Indeed, as the happinefs of mankind depends more upon well-regulated and well-adminiſtered government, than on any thing ſubordinate in life or in arts, there is every reaſon for beſtowing all the time which every paſſing generation can beſtow, in bringing government to its utmoſt point of attainable perfection. It is the buſineſs and the duty of thoſe who now live, as they value their own happineſs and the happineſs of their poſterity, to labor in the reform of abuſes, and the farther improvement of every improveable advantage. Would any man be liſtened to with patience who ſhould ſay, that any uſeful art or manufacture ought not to be improved by ingenious projectors, becauſe it does *tolerably* in its preſent ſtate, ſatisfies thoſe who are ignorant of the excellence of which it is ſuſceptible, and cannot be altered, even for the better, without cauſing ſome *trouble*, for a *time*, among thoſe who have been accuſtomed to the preſent imperfect and erroneous methods of conducting it? No; encouragements are held out for improvement in all arts and ſciences, conducive to the comfort and accommodation of human life. What, then, in the *firſt* art, the art of diffuſing happineſs throughout nations, ſhall he who attempts improvement be ſtigmatized as an innovator, proſecuted as a ſeditious intermeddler, and perſecuted with the reſentment of thoſe who find their advantage in the continuance of error, and the diffuſion of abuſe and corruption? However courtiers may patronize ſilly eſtabliſhments, which claim a preſcriptive right to folly, inutility, and even mifchievous confequences, the common fenfe of mankind will revolt againft them, join in demanding reform, and in faying of old cuftoms, when become nuifances by alteration of circumftances, that inftead of being *fanctified* by long duration, they are now more *honored in the breach than the obfervance.*

But let the reformation be gentle, though firm; wife, though bold; lenient to perfons erring, though fevere againft error. Let her not alarm the friend of LIBERTY by fudden violence, but invite all to the caufe of truth and juftice, by fhewing that *fhe* is herfelf guarded, not only by truth and juftice, but by MERCY. Let us fhew ourfelves, in feeking political reformation, what we profefs to be, a nation of Chriftians, if not philofophers; and let not a groan be heard amid the acclamations of triumphant liberty, nor one drop of blood fadden the glorious victory of philofophy, and Chriftianity over PRIDE.

SECTION XXXIX.

The Chriſtian Religion favorable to Civil Liberty, and likewiſe to EQUALITY *rightly underſtood.*

YOU ſeldom meet with infidelity in a cottage. You find evil and miſery there, as in palaces; but you do not find infidelity. The poor love the name and religion of Jeſus Chriſt. And they have reaſon to love them, if they only conſidered the obligations they are under to them for *worldly* comfort, for liberty, for inſtruction, for a due conſideration in civil ſociety.

The rights of man, to mention which is almoſt criminal in the eyes of deſpotical ſycophants, are plainly and irreſiſtibly eſtabliſhed in the goſpel. There is no doubt but that all his creatures are dear to the Creator and Redeemer; but yet, from motives of mercy and compaſſion, there is an evident predilection for the POOR, manifeſted in our Saviour's preaching and miniſtry. Theſe are very ſtriking words: " The blind receive their ſight, and the lame walk; the lepers are cleanſed, and the deaf hear; the dead are raiſed up, and the POOR HAVE THE GOSPEL PREACHED TO THEM." The inſtruction, the conſolation, the enlightening of the POOR, are placed with the greateſt of his miracles, the recuſcitation of extinguiſhed life. Who, indeed, did trouble themſelves to care for the *poor*, till JESUS CHRIST ſet the glorious example? It was a *miraculous* thing, in the eye of the *world*, that a *divine* teacher ſhould addreſs himſelf particularly to thoſe who could not reward him with a worldly recompence! But he came to deſtroy that INE-. QUALITY among mankind, which enabled the rich and great to treat the poor as beaſts of burden. He himſelf choſe the condition of poverty, to ſhew the rich and proud of how little eſtimation are the trifles they doat upon, in the eye of him who made them, and who can deſtroy them at his pleaſure.

Let us hear HIM open his divine commiſſion. The words are very comfortable, eſpecially after reading the hiſtories of the tyrants who have bruiſed mankind with their rods of iron. We find them in the fourth chapter of St. Luke.

" *And there was delivered unto him the book of the prophet Eſaias; and when he had opened the book, he found the place wherein it was written:*

" THE SPIRIT OF THE LORD IS UPON ME, BECAUSE HE HATH APPOINTED ME TO PREACH THE GOSPEL TO THE POOR; HE HATH SENT ME TO HEAL THE BROKEN-HEARTED, TO PREACH DELIVERANCE TO THE CAPTIVES, AND RECOVERY OF SIGHT TO THE BLIND; TO SET AT LIBERTY THEM THAT ARE BRUISED;

"To preach the acceptable year of the Lord.

"And he clofed the book, and he gave it again to the minifter, and fat down, and the eyes of all them that were in the fynagogue were faftened on him.

"And he began to fay unto them, This day is the fcripture fulfilled in your ears.

"And all bare him witnefs, and wondered at the gracious words which proceeded out of his mouth: and they faid, Is NOT THIS JOSEPH's SON ?"

—And foon after, "All they in the fynagogue were filled with wrath, and rofe up, and thruft him out of the city, and led him unto the brow of the hill, (whereon their city was built), that they might caft him down head-long."

Thus their *ariftocratical* prejudices prevailed over the firft ftrong feelings of gratitude and grace. The fpirit of ariftocracy difplayed itfelf here its in its genuine colors; in pride, cruelty, and violence. Many of the fcribes (the lawyers) and pharifees were probably in the fynagogue, and their influence foon prevailed on the people to fhew their impotent malice againft their beft friend and benefactor. In all ages, fomething of the fame kind is obfervable. The proud fupporters of tyranny, in which they hope to partake, have always ufed falfe alarms, falfe plots, cunningly-contrived nicknames and watchwords, to fet the unthinking people

E e

againſt thoſe who were promoting their greateſt good.

When Chriſt began to preach, we read, in the ſeventh chapter of St. Luke, that the multitude and the publicans heard him; but the ſcribes and the phariſees *rejected* the counſel of God towards them. They, like all perſons of ſimilar temper and rank, flouriſhing by abuſes, could not bear *innovation*.

The moſt powerful argument they uſed againſt him was this queſtion :——HAVE ANY OF THE RULERS AND THE PHARISEES BELIEVED IN HIM? In modern times the queſtion would have been, Have any perſons of faſhion and diſtinction given countenance to him? Does my lord—or my lady—or Sir Harry go to hear him preach?—Or is he ſomebody whom nobody knows?—Such is the language of the ſpirit of deſpotiſm, in all times and countries.

THREE HUNDRED YEARS elapſed, in conſequence of theſe prejudices, before the goſpel was recognized and received at COURT. And I am ſorry to ſay that the COURT ſoon corrupted its ſimplicity. The pride of life, always prevalent among thoſe who aſſume to themſelves good things enough to ſupport and comfort thouſands of individuals equally deſerving, could never brook the doctrines of Chriſt, which favored liberty and equality. It therefore ſeduced the Chriſtians to a participation of power and grandeur; and the poor, with their rights, were often forgotten, in the moft fplendid periods of ecclefiaftical profperity. Many nominal Chriftians have been, and are, as ariftocratical as Herod and the chief priefts and pharifees of Judea.

But the authority of Jefus Chrift himfelf muft have more weight with Chriftians, than all the pomp and parade of the moft abfolute defpots in Europe, at the head of the fineft troops in the univerfe. He taught us, when we pray, to fay, *Our Father.* This alone is fufficient to eftablifh, on an immoveable bafis, the equality of human beings. All are bound to call upon and confider God as their Father, if they are Chriftians ; and, as there are no rights of primogeniture in Heaven, all are equal brothers and fifters, coheirs, if they do not forfeit their hopes, of a bleffed immortality. But thefe are doctrines which the great and proud cannot admit. This world is theirs, and they cannot bear that the beggar, the fervant, the flave, fhould be their equal. We can hardly fuppofe, in imagination, the Emprefs of Ruffia, the King of Pruffia, the Emperor of Germany, or any *grandee* with a riband, a garter, or a ftar, kneeling down, and from his *heart* acknowledging, in his *prayer*, a poor private in a marching regiment, a poor wretch in a workhoufe, or the fervant that rides behind his carriage, a *brother.* So void of reafon and religion is a poor helplefs mortal, when dreft in a little brief authority by the folly of thofe who fubmit to be trampled under foot by their equal; a man born of a woman, like themfelves, and doomed like themfelves after ftrutting on the ftage a few years, to the grave. Our Saviour, with a wifdom far above all the refinement of philofophy, frequently inculcated the vanity of riches and power, and the real pre-eminence of virtue.

And what fay the *apoftles*? Do they favor thofe who ufurp an unnatural and unreafonable power over their fellow-mortals, for the fake of gratifying their own felfifh vanity and avarice? Let us hear them.

St. Paul, in the firft chapter of the Firft Epiftle to the Corinthians, fays, "You fee your calling, brethren, how that not many wife men after the flefh, (worldly-wife men,) not many *mighty*, not many *noble* are called."

In the fecond chapter of ihe Epiftle of St. James, we read,

"Has not God chofen the poor of this world to be heirs of his kingdom?" To which is added,

"The RICH MEN blafpheme that worthy name by which ye are called."

Thefe paffages afford a very ftrong argument of the truth and divinity of the Chriftian religion, for they contain the very doctrines which were foretold feveral hundred years before the appearance of Chriftianity. ISAIAH, in his twenty-ninth chapter, fpeaking of the gofpel, and its doctrines and effects, exprefsly fays,

" The *meek* shall increase their joy in the Lord; and the POOR AMONG MEN SHALL REJOICE IN THE HOLY ONE OF ISRAEL."

The inference I would draw from all that has preceded, is, that the middle ranks and the poor, that is, the great majority of mankind, should place a due value on the gospel, not only for its religious, but also its civil and political advantages. It is the GRAND CHARTER OF THEIR FREEDOM, their independence, their equality. All the subtilty of lawyers, all the sophistry of ministerial orators, all the power of all the despots and aristocrats in the world, cannot annihilate RIGHTS, given, indeed by *Nature*, but plainly confirmed by the *Gospel*. The words already cited, are too clear and explicit to admit of misconstruction. JESUS CHRIST came to put an end to unjust inequality in this world, while he revealed the prospect of another, where the *wicked cease from troubling, and the weary are at rest*. O ye people, give not the tyrants such an advantage as to part with your gospel. Preserve it, watch over it, as the pearl of great price. It is your security for present and future felicity. Other Herods, other Neros may arise, who will rejoice to see you voluntarily renounce a system which militates against their diabolical rule; rejoice to see you give up that which all the persecution of the ancient Herods and Neros in vain attempted to abolish by shedding blood.

I think it may be depended on as indisputable, that men who endeavor to suppress all works in favor of truth*, liberty, and the happinefs of the middle and poor claffes of the people, would, if they had lived about one thoufand feven hundred and ninety-five years ago, have joined with the *high priefts* and rulers to *crucify* Jesus Christ. They would have profecuted and perfecuted him for fedition and high treafon. They would have defpifed and rejected the friend of Lazarus; and taken the part of Dives, even in hell. The fpirit of pride is of the devil, and thofe who are actuated by that fpirit, in all their conduct, would have fallen down and worfhipped him, if he would have put them on the pinnacle of the temple, and promifed them the kingdoms of the world, and the glory of them.

* *" That make a man an offender for a* WORD."
Isaiah, xxix. 21.

SECTION XL.

The Pride which produces the Spirit of Des-
potism conspicuous even on the Tombstone.
It might be treated with total Neglect, if it
did not tend to the Oppression of the Poor,
and to Bloodshed and Plunder.

DEATH is the great teacher and
censor of human vanity; but even death cannot
repress the pride of aristocracy, or the insolence
of riches, endeavoring to make wealth and
grandeur triumph over the law of nature, and
outshine others even from the coffin and the
grave. If we look into the churches and
church-yards, we see the most insignificant of
mankind honored with the most magnificent
monuments of marble, the proudest trophies,
sculptured urns, a flattering inscription, and a
gilded lie. The walls of the sanctuary are
hung with banners, escutcheons, helmets, and
spurs, which display the emptiness of that pre-
eminence which they are intended to emblazon.
The poor body, which all this paint and finery
attends, lies mouldering in the vault; and give
it but a tongue to speak, would exclaim, at
the gaudy sight, " Vanity of vanities ! Mock
not my humiliated condition with the contemptible pageantry that misguided my feet
from the path of reason and happiness, during
my mortal existence." The only means of

being honorably diftinguifhed, is to promote most effectually the general happinefs of human nature, and to feek private good in public beneficence.

The fpirit of defpotifm is remarkably vifible in the *maufoleum*. There are families who feem to think that their precious bones would be contaminated, even if depofited in the confecrated cemeteries of the church, where plebeians fleep, and therefore they erect proud temples in their private domains, where their fathers may rot in ftate, unapproached by the vulgar. If they were illuftrious inventors of arts and benefactors to mankind, the diftinction might be a juft compliment to their memory, and a ufeful incentive to emulation. But the perfons thus magnificently interred are ufually the moft infignificant of the human race; whofe very names would not be known a year after their deceafe if they were not deeply engraven on the marble.

Many an *alderman*, notorious for the meaneft avarice, as little diftinguifhed for beneficence as abilities, is decorated with the moft fumptuous memorials which the *ftone-cutter* can raife for money; while *Milton* the glory of the nation, a man elevated above the rank of common humanity, had no monumental marble. But all that the herald's office can effect, all that can be done by painting, gilding, and marble, cannot ennoble the greateft favorite of a court, the moft fuccefsful adventurer in the Eaft Indies, or the moft opulent contractor and

money-lender, like a Paradife Loft. The
nabobs find their influence cannot fecure the
efteem of a few contemporaries, though it may
command their votes, much lefs of whole
nations, and of late pofterity. Money, the
only god which worldlings worfhip, lofes its
omnipotence after the death of its poffeffor; and
even the inheritor often defpifes the man who
acquired it. The undertaker, the efcutcheon
painter, and the fculptor, are however employed
to keep up the falfe pageantry of infignificant
opulence; and a hearfe, covered over with
coats of arms, is ufed for the purpofe of impref-
fing the vulgar with a veneration for rank and
riches, while, in the minds of men of fenfe, it
excites ridicule, and converts a funeral into a
farce.

Indeed the empty parade of pride, and the
felf-importance of defpotifm itfelf, might fur-
nifh a laughable entertainment, if it were not
productive of mifchief, mifery, and bloodfhed.
To fupport the vanity, exclufive privileges, and
high pretenfions of thofe who have little perfonal merit or fervices to recommend them to
fociety, it is neceffary to have recourfe to military force and corruption. A fyftem of terror
and coercion can alone keep down the people,
and compel a tame acquiefcence under ufurped
power, abufed for the purpofes of oppreffion.

Standing armies are therefore the glory and
delight of all who are actuated by the fpirit of
defpotifm. They would have no great objection to military government and martial law,

while power is in their own hands, or in the hands of their patrons. The implicit submiſſion of an army, the doctrine, which the military ſyſtem favors, that men in ſubaltern ſtations are to act as they are bidden, and never to deliberate on the propriety of the command, is perfectly congenial with the ſpirit of deſpotiſm. The glitter, the pomp, the parade and oſtentation of war are alſo highly pleaſing to minds that prefer ſplendor and pageantry to ſolid and ſubſtantial comfort. The happineſs, which muſt ever depend on the tranquility of the people, is little regarded, when ſet in competition with the gratification of perſonal vanity. Plumes, lace, ſhining arms, and other habiliments of war, ſet off the *perſon* to great advantage; and as to the wretches who are ſlain or wounded, plunged into captivity and diſeaſe, in order to ſupport this finery, are they not *paid* for it? Beſides, they are, for the moſt part, in the loweſt claſs, and thoſe whom *nobody* knows.

Such is the love of ſtanding armies, in ſome countries, that attempts are made to render even the national militia little different from a ſtanding army. This circumſtance alone is a ſymptom of the ſpirit of deſpotiſm. A militia of *mercenary* ſubſtitutes, under officers entirely devoted to a miniſter, muſt add greatly to a ſtanding army, from which, in fact, it would differ only in name. Should the *people* be entirely *diſarmed*, and ſcarcely a muſket and bayonet in the country but under the manage-

ment of a minifter, through the agency of fervile lords lieutenant and venal magiftrates, what
defence would remain, in extremeties, either
for the king or the people ?

The love of pomp and finery, though ridiculous in itfelf, may thus become injurious to
liberty, and therefore to happinefs, by increafing the *military order* in the time of *peace*, and
when minifterial arts have contributed to render
that order devoted to purpofes of felfifh aggrandizement or borough influence. Minds, capable of being captivated with the filly parade
of war, are of too foft a texture to grafp the
manly principles of true patriotifm. They
will ufually prefer the favor of a court, which
has many *fhining* ornaments to beftow, to the
efteem of the people. A heart deeply infected
with the fpirit of defpotifm, defpifes the people
too much to be in the leaft folicitous to obtain
popular applaufe. Praife is but breath ; and
often, like the wind, veers about inconftantly ;
and certainly will defert a man, who has deferted
the virtuous and benevolent conduct which firft
excited it. But ribands, ftars, garters, places,
penfions, ufually laft for life ; and titles defcend
to the lateft pofterity. Honor, once gained by
royal fmiles, is a part of the family goods and
chattels, and goes down, from generation to
generation, without requiring to the day of
doom, any painful exertion, any meritorious
fervices, but leaving its happy poffeffors to the
free enjoyment of idlenefs and luxury. No
wonder, therefore, that where the felfifh fpirit

of defpotifm prevails, a bauble beftowed by a court fhall outweigh a whole people's plaudits. A coat of arms makes a figure on the efcutcheon and the tombftone; but not a fcrap of gilded and painted filk—not even a *bloody hand*, can be beftowed by the moft cordial efteem of the low multitude.

Heraldry *itfelf*, though a childifh, is a harmlefs vanity; but, but, as conducing very much to the fpirit of defpotifm, it becomes not only ridiculous, but mifchievous. It makes a diftinction, on which men plume themfelves, without merit and without fervices. Satiffied with fuch a diftinction, they will be lefs inclined to acquire merit and to render fervices. They can inherit a coat of arms; or they can buy one; or, which is more compendious ftill, they can borrow or invent one. It is enough that they are feparated from the *canaille*. The coach, the hall, the church, is crouded with their *atchievements*; there is no occafion for arduous exertion. They are now raifed above the vulgar. The work is done. Their name is up; they may flumber in the repofe of ufelefs infignificance, or move in the reftleffnefs of mifchievous activity. The coat of arms is at once a fhield for folly, and a banner in the triumph of pride.

But both pride and folly fhould be permitted for me to enjoy their baubles unmolefted, if they did not lead to CRUELTY. But pride and folly are the caufes of war; therefore I hate them from my foul. They *glory* in deftruction;

and among the moſt frequent ornaments, even of our churches, (the very houſes of peace,) are hung up on high *trophies* of war. Dead men (themſelves ſubdued by the univerſal conqueror) are repreſented, by their ſurviving friends, as rejoicing, even in their graves, in the implements of man-ſlaughter. Helmets, ſwords, and blood-ſtained flags hang over the grave, together with the eſcutcheons and marble monuments, emblematical of human ferocity; of thoſe actions and paſſions which Chriſtianity repudiates; for as well might oil and vinegar coaleſce, as War and Chriſtianity.

Spirit of Deſpotiſm! I would laugh at all thy extravagances, thy ſolemn mummery, thy baby baubles, thy airs of inſolence, thy finery and frippery, thy impotent inſults over virtue, genius, and all perſonal merit, thy ſtrutting, ſelf-pleaſing mien and language! I would conſider them all with the eye of a Democritus, as affording a conſtant farce, an inexhauſtible fund of merriment, did they not lead to the malevolent paſſions, which, in their effects, forge chains for men born free, plunder the poor of their property, and ſhed the blood of innocence.

F f

SECTION XLI.

CONCLUSION.

To meliorate the condition of human nature, can be the only rational end of government. It cannot be defigned to favor one defcription of men, a MINORITY of men, at the expence of all others ; who, having received life from him who alone can give it, received at the fame time a right to enjoy it in liberty and fecurity. This was the charter of God and nature ; which no mortal, however elevated by conqueft or inheritance, can annul or violate without impiety. All government which makes not the advancement of human happinefs, and the comfort of the individuals who are fubject to its control, the *prime* purpofe of its operations, partakes of defpotifm : and I have always thought that, in governments which boaft of a free conftitution, the views, even of ftatefmen and politicians who efpoufed the caufe of liberty, have been too circumfcribed. They have been attached to names and families. They feem not to have opened either their eyes or hearts to objects truly great, and affections fincerely catholic and philanthropic. I hate to hear public men, who certainly can have no right to their pre-eminence but for the public good, profeffing themfelves of the Rockingham Party, the Shelburne Party, the Portland Party, and appearing to forget, in their zeal for a few diftinguifhed houfes, the great mafs of the People, the PARTY of human nature. The majority of men are poor and obfcure. To them all party attachments to names and families, little known as public benefactors, muft appear at once abfurd and injurious. They are the perfons who ftand in moft need of protection and affiftance from the powerful. The rich, under all governments, have a thoufand means of procuring either comfort or defence. It is the mafs, the poor and middling ranks, unknown to, and unknowing courts or kings, who require all the alleviation which men enlightened by knowledge, furnifhed with opulence, elevated by rank, can afford to leffen the natural evils of life, aggravated by the moral and artificial. Government poffeffes the power of alleviating, and fometimes of removing, that moral and phyfical evil which embitters exiftence. How deplorable, when government becomes fo perverted, as to increafe the evil it was defigned to cure. Yet this has been, and is now the cafe on a great part of the globe; infomuch that the learned and judicious Dr. Prideaux, whofe integrity is as well known as his ability, ufed to fay, " That it was a doubt with him, whether the benefit which the world receives from government, was fufficient to make amends for the calamities which it fuffers from the follies, miftakes, and mal-adminiftration of thofe who manage it."

When it is confidered how little the moft boafted governments have been able or inclined to prevent the greateft calamity of the world, the frequent recurrence of WAR, it is natural to conclude, that there has been fome radical defect or error in all government, hitherto inftituted on the face of the earth. *Violence* may be ufed where there is *no* government. Governments pretend to direct human affairs by *reafon;* but war is a dereliction of reafon, a renunciation of all that refines and improves human nature, and an appeal to brute force. Man defcends from the heights to which philofophers and legiflators had raifed him in fociety; takes the fword, and furpaffes the beafts of the foreft in ferocity. Yet, fo far from thinking himfelf culpable, he deems his deftructive employment the moft honorable of all human occupations, becaufe governments have politically contrived to throw a gloffy mantle, covered with tinfel and fpangles, over the horrors of bloodfhed and devaftation. If governments, with all their riches and power, all their vaunted arts and fciences, all the myfterious policy of cabinets, all the wifdom and eloquence of deliberating fenates, are *unable* to preferve the *bleffing of peace,* uninterrupted, during the fhort fpace of twenty years together, they muft be dreadfully faulty, either in their conftitution or their adminiftration. In what confifts the fault? I think in the felfifh fpirit of defpotifm, purfuing the fordid or vain-glorious purpofes of the governors, with little regard to the real, fubftantial happinefs of the governed. Defpotifm, in fome mode or degree, has tranf-formed the fhepherds of the flock into wolves; has appropriated the fleeces, fhed the blood of the innoxious animals, tore down the fences of the fheepfold, and laid wafte the pafture.

Where is the government that has diftribu-ted property fo equitably, as that none to whom exiftence has been given fhould want the *neceffaries* of exiftence ; and where helplefs age and infirmity, as well as helplefs infancy, fhould find a pillow to repofe on, and plenty to nourifh it, without fupplicating a MAN, *equal*, by nature, for the cold fcanty relief of eleemo-fynary charity ? The truth is, power gradually *engroffes* property ; and the felfifh fpirit of def-potifm is ever ftriving to appropriate all the good, of every kind, which the earth is able to produce.

The truth is, *national glory*, the trappings of a court, the parade of armies, the finery of external appearance, have been the filly objects of *ftate* folicitude ; while MAN was left to bewail, in the receffes of want and obfcu-rity, that his mother had brought him into a world of woe, without means of comfort or fupport, with little other profpect than to labor without ceafing, to fight thofe who never injured him, and to die prematurely, un-known, and unlamented. All his wretched-nefs has been aggravated by the *infults* of unfeeling pride ; the *neglect* of ariftocratic gran-deur, which, under the fpirit of defpotifm,

mocked by the falfe pageantry of life, thofe
who were doomed to feel its real mifery.
The vain pomp and glory of the world, held
out the finger of fcorn to that wretchednefs
which itfelf contributed to create, and would
not relieve.

Three fcore years and ten, and thofe often
full of labor and forrow, conftitute the fpace
allotted to the life of man in a venerable
volume, full of beauty as well as inftruction,
and worthy of great attention independently of
the high authority attributed to it by the religion eftablifhed by the laws of this country.
Few and evil are our days, even when they
proceed to their natural extent, and are attended
with the common portion of health and profperity. Yet, as if a *fuperfluity* of years and
happinefs were lavifhed on men, the chief bufinefs of the greateft part of governments on the
whole earth has been to abbreviate life, to poifon and embitter its fweeteft pleafures, and
add new pungency to its anguifh. Yet fee
the falfe *glitter* of happinefs, the pomp and
parade which fuch governments affume; obferve
the gravity and infolence of fuperiority which
their minifters, their ftatefmen, and their warriors, affume, and you would imagine them a
commiffioned regency, lord lieutenants fent by
Heaven to rule this lower world, and to rectify
all diforders which had efcaped the vigilance of
the Deity. The time has been when they have
actually claimed the title of God's vicegerents,
and have been literally worfhipped as gods by

the fervile crew of courtiers; men gradually bowed down by defpotifm from the erect port of native dignity, and driven by fear to crouch under the moft degrading of all fuperftition, the political idolatry of a bafe fellow-creature.

After all the language of court adulation, the praifes of poets and orators, the ftatues and monuments erected to their fame, the malignant confequences of their actions prove them to have been no other than confpirators againft the improvement and happinefs of the human race. What were their means of conducting their governments, of exercifing this office of Heaven's vicegerents? Crafty, difhoneft arts, oppreffion, extortion, and above all FIRE and SWORD. They dared to ape the thunder and lightning of Heaven, and, affifted by the machinations of the Grand Adverfary of man, rendered their imitative contrivances for deftruction more terrible and deadly than the original. Their imperial robe derived its deep crimfon color from human blood; and the gold and diamonds of their diadems were accumulated treafures wrung from the famifhed bowels of the *poor*, born only to toil for others, to be robbed, to be wounded, to be trodden under foot and forgotten in an early grave. How few, in comparifon, have reached the age of three fcore and ten, and yet, in the midft of youth and health, their days have been full of labor and forrow. Heaven's vicegerents, feldom beftowed a thought upon them, except when it was neceffary either to inveigle or to force them to take the fword and march to flaughter. Where God caufed the fun to fhine gaily, and fcattered plenty over the land, his vicegerents diffufed famine and folitude. The valley which laughed with fcorn, they watered with the tear of artificial hunger and diftrefs; the plain that was bright with verdure, and gay with flowrets, they dyed red with gore. They operated on the world as the blaft of an eaft wind, as a peftilence, as a deluge, as a conflagration. And have they yet ceafed from the earth? Caft your eyes over the plains of Ruffia, Poland, a great part of Europe, the wilds of Africa, and the gardens of ASIA, European defpotifm has united with oriental, to unparadife the provinces of India.

Thus, if God, in his wifdom, has thought fit to allot us a *few evils* for the purpofe of difcipline, the GREAT ONES of the world have endeavored to make the *whole* of life an evil to the defpifed and neglected MILLION. The world is now old, and may profit by the leffons of Experience. SHE has decifively declared, that defpotifm is the grand fource of human misfortune, the Pandora's box out of which every curfe has iffued, and fcarcely left even Hope behind. Defpotifm, in its extreme, is fatal to human happinefs, and, in all its degrees and modifications, injurious. The fpirit of it ought therefore to be fuppreffed on the firft and flighteft appearance. It fhould be the endeavor of every good man, *pro virili*, as far as his beft abilities will extend, to extirpate all

arbitrary government from the globe. It
fhould be fwept from the earth, or trampled
under foot, from China to Peru. But no
power is capable of crufhing the Hydra, lefs
than the Herculean arm of a whole PEOPLE.

I lay it down as an incontrovertible axiom,
that all who are born into the world have a
right to be happy in it as the unavoidable evils
of nature, and their own difordered paffions,
will allow. The grand object of all good government, of all government that is not an
ufurpation, muft be to promote this happinefs,
to affift every individual in its attainment and
fecurity. A government chiefly anxious about
the emoluments of office, chiefly employed in
augmenting its own power and aggrandizing
its obfequious inftruments, while it neglects
the comfort and fafety of individuals in middle
or low life, is defpotic and a nuifance. It is
founded on folly as well as wickednefs, and,
like the freaks of infanity, deals mifchief and
mifery around, without being able to afcertain
or limit its extent and duration. If it fhould
not be punifhed as criminal, let it be coerced
as dangerous. Let the ftraight waiftcoat be
applied; but let MEN, judging fellow men,
always fpare the axe.

For what rational purpofe could we enter
into life? To vex, torment, and flay each
other with the fword? To be and to make
miferable? No, by the fweet mercy of Heaven!
I firmly believe, that the great King of Kings,
intended every fon and daughter of Adam to

be as happy as the eternal laws of Nature, under his control, permit them to be in this fub-lunary ftate. Execrated and exploded be all thofe politics, with Machiavel, or the Evil Being, their author, which introduce fyftems of government and manners among the great, inconfiftent with the happinefs of the majority. Muft real tragedies be forever acting on the ftage of human life? Muft men go on forever to be tormentors and executioners of men? Is the world never to profit by the experience of ages? Muft not even *attempts* be made to improve the happinefs of life, to improve government, though all arts and fciences are encouraged in their progrefs to perfection? Muft the grand art, the fublimeft fcience, that of meliorating the condition of human nature, be ftationary? No; forbid it reafon, virtue, benevolence, religion! Let the world be made more and more comfortable, to all who are allowed the glorious privilege of feeing the fun and breathing the liberal air. Our forefathers were duped by priefts and defpots, and, through the timidity of fuperftition and the blindnefs of ignorance, fubmitted to be made artificially miferable. Let us explode that folly which we *fee;* and let every mortal under the cope of heaven enjoy exiftence, as long as nature will allow the feaft to continue, without any reftraints on liberty but fuch as the majority of uncorrupted guefts unite in agreeing to be falutary, and therefore conducive to the general feftivity. Men are too *ferious* in purfuing toys, money, titles, ftars, ribands, triumphs, any thing that gives a momentary diſtinction, and gratifies an unmanly pride. They have embraced a cloud for a goddeſs. Let them diſpel the miſt, raiſed by falſe policy and cruel deſpotiſm. Let them at laſt diſtinguiſh real good, from its deluſive appearance. Let them value duly, and purſue diligently, ſolid comfort, health, cheerfulneſs, contentment, univerſal benevolence, and learn to reliſh the ſweets of nature and ſimplicity. They will then ſee happineſs in ſomething beſides the poſſeſſion of *gold;* beſides thoſe *external* marks of ſuperiority which raiſe them to notice, and diſtinguiſh them from their equals without a difference. Strife and wars will ceaſe, when men perceive that their higheſt happineſs is moſt eaſily attainable in a ſtate of contented tranquillity; their guide, nature, and their guard, innocence.

The principal objects of all rational government, ſuch as is intended to promote human happineſs, are two; to preſerve *peace,* and to diffuſe *plenty.* Such government will ſeldom tax the neceſſaries of life. It will avoid WARS; and, by ſuch humane and wiſe policy, render taxes on *neceſſaries* totally ſuperfluous. Taxes on *neceſſaries* are uſually cauſed by war. The poor, however, are not eaſily excited to inſurrection. It is a baſe calumny which accuſes them. They are naturally quieſcent; inclined to ſubmiſſion by their habits, and willing to reverence all their ſuperiors who behave

to them juftly and kindly. They deferve to
be ufed well. They deferve confidence. But
oppreffion and perfecution may teach them to
lift their gigantic arm, and then vain will be
refiftance. Let not wars then be wantonly
undertaken, which befides their injuftice and
inhumanity, tend more than any thing elfe, by
increafing taxes, to compel infurrection. The
poor man hears great praifes beftowed on the
government he lives under, and perpetual
panegyrics on the conftitution. He knows
little of general politics. He judges from the
effects he FEELS. He knows that malt,* leather, candles, foap, falt, and windows, without which he cannot exift in comfort, are fo
heavily taxed as fometimes to exclude him
from obtaining the fcanty portion he would
require. In return for the defalcations from
malt, leather, candles, foap, falt, and windows; he fees penfions, places, rich contractors, difgraceful, ruinous, and bloody wars.
Yet he rifes up early, and goeth forth to his
work and his labor, with cheerfulnefs. Is he
not a worthy, refpectable member of fociety,
and deferving of every indulgence ? Ought he
to be infulted by approbrious appellations, confidered as of no political confequence, as poffeffing no rights, and little removed from the

---

* I heard a great borough-monger of eleven or twelve
thoufand a-year affert, while he held a glafs of Madeira in
his hand to wafh down a plentiful dinner, that *malt* could
not be reckoned among the *neceffaries* of the poor laborer,
becaufe he might drink *water*, which is very *wholefome.*

cattle? Suppofe millions of fuch men in a country, ought not their wifhes to be confulted. and a regard for their comfort and fecurity to ftop the fword, while emerging from its fcabbard at the command of a MINISTER?

Great reforms ufually come from the people. They are flow to anger, and fubmit in patience. But grievances may become intolerable; and then their energy difplays itfelf like a torrent, that has long lain ftill and placid within the dam, which oppofed its courfe to a certain point, but could refift no longer.

If ever any people fhould be roufed to take their own affairs into their own hands, I hope they will refute the calumnies of the proud, by acting with juftice and mercy. All human creatures are weak and fallible; kings and minifters have exhibited remarkable inftances of this common imbecility. Great allowances fhould therefore be made for their errors and even *crimes*, which, probably, originated in error. I wifh to fee the Britifh government made as perfect as humam ingenuity and virtue can render it; but I would effect reform in it, without injuring the perfon or deftroying the life of the moft obnoxious individual. I would pardon much to human infirmity. Not one drop of blood fhould be fhed, nor a fingle mite of property violated. No injuftice whatever fhould difgrace the wifdom of the people. Compenfations fhould be made by the public to all individuals, of all parties and perfuafions, when compelled to relinquifh poffeffions or privileges lawfully in-

G g

herited, or honeftly acquired. The moft liberal, expanded generofity fhould vindicate the honor of human nature, too long infulted. Minifters and grandees, who form the ariftocracy, either of opulence or nobility, however tyrannical and infolent in the day of their profperity, fhould live out the little fpace allotted to man, in a ftate of eafe and affluence adapted to their habits and education. I would fhew them how truly noble and glorious it is to forgive. And they could not be formidable againft an united people. For how weak, how tranfitory is man? Death, *natural*, unprecipitated death, will foon tame the haughtieft fpirit that ever fwelled the fancied importance of a crown; and the infirmities attending the approach of death, the gradual decays of age, will ufually teach a leffon of unfeigned humility.

The people, at prefent, appear to be funk in a political lethargy. But let not minifters confide too much in the fymptoms. A calm precedes a ftorm. Long continued abufes, heavy burdens, and fevere grievances, without a dream of hope, may awaken the lion. Then, I think, thofe who have fhewn an inclination to fet up a power unknown to conftitutional freedom, and to render government hoftile to the people, may juftly fear.

And who, it may be afked, are they? I am happy in the opportunity of declaring it my opinion, that the KING is not among them. They are men to whom neither the King nor the people are dear. They are, in a word,

the *oligarchy of borough-mongers*, whofe power
is founded on an ufurpation ; and whofe affumed
SOVEREIGNTY is no lefs inconfiftent with the
real freedom of a king than of a people. A
moft refpectable fociety, not long ago, afferted
in a petition to the Houfe of Commons, and
offered to prove it at the bar, that *one hundred and fifty-four men* nominate and appoint a
majority of the Houfe. Has it not been
fufpected, that a WAR might have been made
and fupported, to prevent the annihilation of
this oligarchy ; by turning the attention of the
people from a reform of parliament, and endeavoring to give a deadly ftab to liberty. If
the fufpicion be well founded, this very circumftance is the ftrongeft argument for reform
which has ever been produced. Oceans of
blood, and *treafure* enough to relieve all the
poor in the nation for many years, lavifhed to
eftablifh a defpotifm, inimical to the King, the
people, and to human nature ! We have now
reached the fource of the evil, a fource not fo
concealed as the fountain of the Nile. It is the
corruption of boroughs, and the interference
of minifters, peers, placemen, penfioners, and
expectants, in parliamentary elections, which
caufes the *fpirit of defpotifm* to increafe; for
nature, reafon, and felf-intereft too, if they
were not counteracted by corrupt influence,
would revolt at it. The egg would be inftantly
crufhed, if it were not conftantly guarded and
foftered in the warm, well-fortified neft of

borough-influence, directing all measures and disposing of all patronage.

But they are all *honorable* men, who are concerned in this influence. They may not be morally worse or better than others in their situation. Their situation renders them politically iniquitous. The world is governed by men, and men by their passions, and their supposed interest. But it is the business of laws to restrain them. The people are bound to watch the conduct of all whose conduct is influential on their welfare. Unlimited confidence should be given to no man, when the happiness of millions is concerned in the consequences of his actions or counsels.

" The common people," says a sensible author, " generally think that *great* men have *great* minds, and scorn *base* actions; which judgment is so false, that the basest and worst of all actions have been done by *great men*. They have often disturbed, deceived and pillaged the world; and he who is capable of the *highest* mischief is capable of the MEANEST. He who plunders a country of a million of money would, in suitable circumstances, steal a silver spoon; and a conqueror, who stands and pillages a kingdom, would, in an humbler situation, rifle a portmanteau." I should not, therefore, choose to expose my watch or purse in a crowd, to those men who have plundered Poland, if, instead of possessing a crown of jewels, and the pocket of submissive nations, they had been in the circumstances of a *Barrington.* Nor, though men should be called *honorable,* will it be safe to trust our liberties to their honor, without some collateral security; especially when we see them interfering with and controlling elections, contrary to express laws, and contrary not only to the dictates of *honor,* but of common honesty. They *usurp* a power for the gratification of pride and avarice, which they cannot hold but to the injury of the lawful and right owners. How differs this in a moral view, from robbery? It differs, in a political view indeed, inasmuch as it is infinitely more injurious to society.

The opposers of reform, the invaders of the people's rights, are no less blind and shortsighted than meanly selfish. Let them pour their venom on the people, and dispute popular claims to natural right, as much as they please; the people must at last triumph, and liberty will in time flourish all over Europe. Court parasites, and selfish grandees, will do right to use a little foresight; to consider what *revolutions* may be, by viewing what have been; and not to exasperate mankind too much, lest the irritation should produce, what God avert, sanguinary vengeance.

I take my leave on this occasion, recommending, from the bottom of my heart, to men in power, measures of CONCILIATION. Let them come among us with *healing* in their wings. Let them concede with cheerfulness, whatever cannot be denied without injustice.

Let them fhew themfelves real friends to liberty and man. The Englifh nation is remarkable for generofity and good-nature. All their mif-. takes will be forgiven. *There will be no leading into captivity, and no complaining in fur ftreets.* Mercy and truth fhall meet together; and *righteoufnefs and peace* kifs each other. In a word; *let parliament be reformed.* This mea-fure will remove all grievances, and fatisfy all demands. It will at once give permanency to the throne, and happinefs to to the people. Kings will be republicans, in the true fenfe of that term; and the fpirit of defpotifm become the fpirit of philanthropy.

THE END